Migration and Cultural Contact Germany and Australia

Edited by Andrea Bandhauer and Maria Veber

SYDNEY UNIVERSITY PRESS

Published 2009 by SYDNEY UNIVERSITY PRESS
University of Sydney Library
www.sup.usyd.edu.au

National Library of Australia Cataloguing-in-Publication entry

Title: Migration and cultural contact : Germany and Australia /
          editors, Andrea Bandhauer, Maria Veber.
ISBN: 9781920898632 (pbk.)
Notes: Bibliography.
Subjects: Germans--Australia--History.
          Australians--Germany--History.
          Australia--Foreign relations--Germany
          Germany--Foreign relations--Australia.
          Germany--Emigration and immigration.
          Australia--Emigration and immigration.
Other Authors/Contributors:
          Bandhauer, Andrea.
          Veber, Maria.
Dewey Number:
          305.8430994

Cover image: 'From the Heart of the Forest to the Edge of the Road, Terania Creek NSW 1982' (IT125). *Ingeborg Tyssen: Photographs*, ed. John Williams, Canterbury, NSW: T&G John Williams.

Cover design by Miguel Yamin, the University Publishing Service

Contents

Acknowledgements

We would like to acknowledge the School of Languages and Cultures at the University of Sydney for its generous support, beginning with its assistance in the organisation of the symposium "Germans in Australia", which was convened at the University of Sydney in 2006. The support of the school facilitated the participation of internationally renowned scholars at the symposium and the seeding grant awarded by the Faculty of Arts at the University of Sydney enabled archival research to be carried out at the Strehlow Research Centre in Alice Springs.

We would like to thank Scott Mitchell, Graeme Shaughnessy and Penny Joy of the Strehlow Research Centre for allowing us free access to the Strehlow archive and for their invaluable help. We also thank Michael Cawthorn and the Strehlow Research Centre Board for making available images of the Strehlows and of the Hermannsburg Mission. We are very grateful to John F. Williams who allowed us to use a photograph by his late wife, the well-known Australian photographer Ingeborg Tyssen (1945–2002). We finally thank Ava Schacherl-Lam for her care in editing the manuscript, Giles Tanner for his valuable suggestions and Agata Mrva-Montoya and Susan Murray-Smith at Sydney University Press for their forbearance and enthusiasm in their dealings with us.

Editors' Note

The spelling of Aboriginal terms used in this text follows the orthography developed by the Institute for Aboriginal Development. We allow variants to remain in quotations from primary and secondary sources.

Contributors

Andrea Bandhauer

Andrea Bandhauer is Senior Lecturer in Germanic Studies at the University of Sydney. She teaches German Literature as well as International & Comparative Literature and has published in the areas of migration and postcolonial studies, literary and textual theory, gender, performativity, and contemporary Austrian literature. Her recent publications include articles and book chapters on cultural studies (Germanistik as Kulturwissenschaft) and the Turkish/German writer Emine Sevgi Özdamar and the contemporary Austrian authors Margret Kreidl and Elfriede Jelinek. She is also co-editor and contributor to *New Directions in German Studies: A Context of Interdisciplinarity* (2005).

Gerhard Fischer

Gerhard Fischer is Head of German Studies at the University of New South Wales in Sydney. His research areas include theatre and literature of the 20th century, about which he has published numerous articles and books, e.g. *The Mudrooroo/Müller Project* (1993); *GRIPS. Geschichte eines populären Theaters, 1966–2000* (2002), as well as the collection *The Play within the Play* (2007), edited together with Bernhard Greiner. He has also published on migration history, with special focus on the topic "Identität und Multikulturalität", and on Australia during World War I (*Enemy Aliens*, 1989). As convenor of the Sydney German Studies symposia, he has published volumes on German literature of the 20th century, e.g. on Walter Benjamin, Hans Magnus Enzensberger, Heiner Müller, Erich Kästner, and on literature written since the German unification in 1990 – *Schreiben nach der Wende. Ein Jahrzehnt deutscher Literatur, 1989–1999* (2001; 2nd ed. 2008). The volume "W.G. Sebald: Schreiben ex patria/Expatriate Writing" is currently in press (2009). Fischer is a member of the Australian Academy of the Humanities.

Birte Giesler

Birte Giesler is a Lecturer in Germanic Studies at the University of Sydney. In 2004, she was granted the Feodor Lynen Fellowship of the Humboldt Foundation and has been a Lecturer in Germanic Studies at the University of Sydney since 2005. She has published two books and numerous articles in the area of 18th- and 19th-century women writers (Friederike Helene Unger and Hedwig Dohm), the German Bildungs-roman, intertextuality, the motif of the artificial human, contemporary drama and cultural memory in contemporary German novels.

Ortrud Gutjahr

Ortrud Gutjahr is both the Chair of Neuere Deutsche Literatur und Interkulturelle Literaturwissenschaft [Contemporary German Lit-erature and Intercultural Literature Studies] and the Director of the Arbeitsstelle Interkulturelle Literatur- und Medienwissenschaft [In-stitute of Intercultural Literature and Media Studies] at the University of Hamburg. She is on the international board of the Internationale Vereinigung für Germanistik [International Association for German Studies], on the academic council of the Gesellschaft für Interkulturelle Germanistik [Society for Intercultural German Studies] and contrib-utes to the numerous journals such as the *Recherches Germaniques, Germanica, LIMBUS: Australian Yearbook for Germanic Literary and Cultural Studies* and *Acta Germanica*. She is the editor of the series *The-ater und Universität im Gespräch,* and *Interkulturelle Moderne,* as well as co-editor of the series *Jahrbuch für Literatur und Psychoanalyse.* Her books include *Einführung in den Bildungsroman* (2007). She is editor of the volumes *Heinrich von Kleist* (2008) and *Intrakulturelle Fremdheit: Inszenierung Deutsch-Deutsch Differenzen in Literatur, Film und Theater nach der Wende* (2009) and co-editor of *TABU: Interkulturalität und Gender* (2008) and *Maskeraden des (Post-)Kolonialismus: Verschattete Repräsentationen 'der Anderen' in der deutschsprachigen Literatur und im Film* (2009).

Anna Kenny

Anna Kenny is an anthropologist based in Alice Springs, Central Australia. She has conducted field research with Indigenous people since 1991 and her research engagement has involved analysing Indigenous issues in the media, native title land claims and the protection of sacred Indigenous sites threatened by mining proposals. She is particularly interested in the sociocultural history and ethnology of inland Australia. She has written about Indigenous cultures, multicultural society and the intellectual history of Central Australia. She is currently working on a book and film on Carl Strehlow, based on her PhD.

Kathrine M. Reynolds

Kathrine Reynolds is an Australian scholar working on colonial and migration history in Australia. An Honorary Associate in the Department of History at the University of Sydney, she is the author of *The Frauenstein Letters: Aspects of Nineteenth Century Emigration from the Duchy of Nassau to Australia* (2009) and is currently working on a new book exploring the German migration to Australia of the 1880s.

Fredericka van der Lubbe

Fredericka van der Lubbe gained a PhD in German Linguistics from the University of Sydney in 1999. Currently she works at the University of Technology, Sydney as a Lecturer in European Studies and German Studies. Her research interests include Anglo-German relations in the 17th and 18th centuries, German language standardisation and language management. She is the author of *Martin Aedler and the "High Dutch Minerva": The First German Grammar for the English* (2007).

Maria Veber

Maria Veber is a member of the academic teaching staff in the Germanic Studies department at the University of Sydney. Her research interests include literary and textual theory, gender, performativity, migration studies, and 19th-century German literature. Her recent publications include articles and book chapters on cultural studies (Germanistik als Kulturwissenschaft), cultural contact and migration, and she co-edited and contributed to the volume *New Directions in German Studies: A Context of Interdisciplinarity* (2005).

Walter Veit

Walter Veit became Adjunct Associate Professor at the Department of German Studies at Monash University after he retired in 2000. Before retirement, he taught German literature and philosophy, Comparative Literature, European Studies, was Visiting Professor at the universities of Cologne, Berlin and Kiel, and at present supervises a number of PhD candidates. He was president of the Australian and South Pacific Association of Comparative Literature Studies (ASPACLS), vice-president of the Contemporary European Studies Association of Australia (CESAA) and a member of the Executive of the International Comparative Literature Association (ICLA). His research and publications comprise the areas of literary theory, comparative and intercultural studies, the history of ideas, Australian-German intellectual relations and travel literature.

John F. Williams

John Williams is a historian and photographer. He has written five books, the most recent being *Modernity, the Media and the Military: The Creation of National Mythologies on the Western Front* (2009). Retrospective exhibitions of his photography have been staged at the Art Gallery of NSW; the National Gallery of Victoria and the Museum of Sydney. He is currently researching racism in late-19th-century Australian and German colonies in Paraguay and constructing photographic panoramas of sites of memory, myth and suffering as they relate to the 20th century's world wars.

Judith Wilson

Judith Wilson is a lecturer in German Studies at the University of Adelaide. Her present research is focused on intercultural and postcolonial approaches to German Studies and German-Australian connections in the 19th century. She is currently investigating the role of Australia as an imaginary space in the works of 19th-century German women writers and, in the context of this research, has published on the semi-fictional biography of the naturalist collector, Amalie Dietrich, as well as on novels by Amalia Schoppe and Therese Forster Huber.

Some Ideas about Forms of Cultural Contact Resulting from German-Australian Migration

Andrea Bandhauer and Maria Veber

This book is situated within a tradition of scholarship on cultural contact between Germany and Australia. Our aim in editing this volume has been to offer a series of insights into ongoing interdisciplinary research by scholars involved in areas such as German literary and cultural studies, history and ethnology.

The volume has grown out of the symposium "Germans in Australia" held in the Department of Germanic Studies at the University of Sydney in March 2006. The symposium's aim was to re-activate and review an extensive tradition of scholarship on Germans in Australia, as well as to comprise a collection of studies on German migration and cultural contact that discuss migrant movements to Australia, reciprocal cultural exchange and influence as well as contact between German missionaries and Indigenous Australia.

In this volume, particular attention is given not only to ways in which each country has made an impact on the culture, intellectual thought and aesthetics of the other, but also the way in which the stream of cultural exchange progressed between Germany and Australia. It contains the analysis of historical accounts of German migration to Australia and its impact on German communities both in Germany and Australia, as well as on Australian society as a whole. It also explores the impact of this migration movement on readings of cultural exchanges that flowed from contact between Australian and German cultures, interpretations of European cultural theory and ethnographic discourses based on readings of Australian Indigenous society and ritual, investigations of the appropriation of Indigenous songs by representatives of

German and European modernist literature and aesthetics, and critical analyses of imaginations, fictional and otherwise, of the Australian
continent.

The chapter headings structuring our book reflect the variety of
forms of cultural contact explored by the respective contributors. In
Gutjahr's and Veit's core contributions under the first section heading, "Cultural Disseminations of Missionary Ethnography", the contact
between the Central Australian Arrernte tribe and Carl Strehlow, the
German Lutheran missionary-turned-ethnographer, takes centre stage.
Strehlow, who had acquired an impressive knowledge of the Arrernte
and Luritja languages[1] in order to convert these Indigenous peoples
to Christianity, exceeded his missionary brief by writing down and
translating their songs into the German language, and having them
published in Frankfurt, Germany (1907–20). The dissemination of
Carl Strehlow's seven volumes *Die Aranda- und Loritja-Stämme in
Zentral-Australien* (*The Aranda and Loritja Tribes in Central Australia*)
through their publication in Germany is an example of how direct contact between individuals from different cultures turned into a form of
cultural contact in which Australian Indigenous knowledge became a
cultural product that was launched into and appropriated by European
discourses. In their elaboration of the unexpected impacts of Strehlow's
activities in Hermannsburg, Gutjahr's and Veit's contributions exemplify
the broader notion of cultural contact that informs this book. Cultural
contact here does not necessarily assume direct contact by individuals, nor do the various impacts of the "exchange" necessarily imply a
corporeal presence of the other in the respective countries. Indeed, in
this case the textual processing of Arrernte knowledge and spirituality, which also occurred at the expense of any acknowledgement of the
reality of their living conditions as a result of their double colonisation
by both the British and the German Lutherans, exemplifies not only the
violence that is inherent when contact occurs in "the space of colonial
encounters" (Pratt 1993: 6), but also that violation is part of any act of
cultural appropriation that follows upon contact.

Gutjahr's and Veit's contributions show very clearly that the textual
processing of Arrernte culture in Germany, and indeed other European

---

1 See Mulvaney, Morphy & Petch 2001: 118–19; Austin-Broos 2009: 19.

countries, fed into the European interest in so-called primitive cultures on the one hand, and primitivism as a cultural phenomenon on the other. Gutjahr discusses how, at the turn of the 20th century, these primitive forms of culture functioned as models for the earliest stages of the development of European culture. Veit in turn examines the interest in primitivism on the part of various individual artists and art movements. Here, primitivism represented the birth of a new artistic practice and indeed a new aesthetic that – so it was hoped – could function to regenerate not only European art practice but also the broader European culture and, by extension, the European self. Both contributions make clear the Eurocentric perspective of these appropriations of the Indigenous Other. As van Alphen shows with reference to Freud's *Das Unheimliche* (1919) [*The Uncanny*], such interpretations and appropriations represent European encounters with the Other that are always principally an encounter with the European Self, and that result in a projection of that Self onto the Other (van Alphen 1991: 11). The appropriations of so-called primitive cultures occurred with the idea that these peoples provided a glimpse into an originary form of the human self, or into a previous stage of human development, or even functioned as the enabling mechanism that allowed one to gain a deeper understanding of the "man of culture" of that era – to look behind the cultural veneer in order to understand the history of humanity.

Gutjahr contextualises Strehlow's work within the philological, ethnographic and psychoanalytic scholarship in Europe at the end of the 19th and early 20th centuries. Writing from a philological perspective, she shows how Strehlow's linguistic knowledge and understanding – as his editor, Leonhardi, emphasises in the foreword to Strehlow's work, Strehlow could communicate with the Arrernte in "their mother tongue" (Leonhardi 1907: 1) – enabled and delivered an unprecedented insight into what Strehlow conceived as Arrernte and Luritja "myths, legends and fairy tales".[2]

The centrality of language in Strehlow's contact with the Arrernte and Luritja meant that from the outset he differed from the British

---

2 See Nicholls' insightful contribution "Anglo-German mythologies: the Australian Aborigines and modern theories of myth in the work of Baldwin Spencer and Carl Strehlow" (Nicholls 2007).

colonisers, for he sought to gain something through personal contact with the Arrernte and Luritja that was of value to him: their language. This was initially envisaged to be employed as a communicative tool to prove to the Aborigines that Christianity was in actual fact not a foreign concept but indeed a universal truth. Yet this linguistic exchange with those he sought to familiarise with Christian concepts developed into a powerful interaction that – as Kenny discusses in her contribution on Strehlow's mission – even led, to a degree, to Strehlow's revision of his vocation from that of a converter to a collector and ethnographer, thus preserver, of Indigenous tradition. However, as Veit states, the appropriation of Indigenous narratives always means that they are taken out of their context and "acquire an unfamiliar meaning on both sides" (see Veit's contribution to this volume). This phenomenon becomes especially evident in Gutjahr's delineation of how European discourses of the human incorporated the ethnographer's interpretation of Indigenous myth in order to project the civilised European Self onto, and search for the origin of the European Self in, "die Wilden" [the primitives]. Gutjahr thus demonstrates that most of what was derived from the rituals and ceremonies of the so-called primitives had in the 19th and at the beginning of the 20th centuries become a self-referential and self-perpetuating hermeneutic endeavour. Freud's attempt to universalise the human psyche by transcending continents from the comfort of his home in Vienna is one of the clearest examples of this.[3]

Strehlow's translation work with respect to the Arrernte and Luritja narratives not only provided a new insight into the organisation, spirituality and "Welterfahrung" [experience of the world] of these people; they also provided writers, in this case the Dada artists, with new linguistic material, which they used to invent a new poetic aesthetic that subverted mainstream literary conventions and perceptions. As Veit shows, Tristan Tzara, through his own French translations of the Arrernte and Luritja songs via Strehlow's transcriptions and translations,

---

3 The anthropologist Austin-Broos describes the Arrernte as the icon of Europe's primitive and states that the Western-Arrernte, Strehlow's main source of reference, "have been frozen in the European gaze, circa 1900. Their culture then has become *the* culture of a people lodged in mythical time. A century and more after the invasion, the task of anthropology is to dislodge them from that time and address their experiences" (Austin-Broos 2009: 21).

4

fantasised about the resurrection of an originary poetic language and rhythm that would render a new manifestation of art possible.

The contributions in the second section of the book titled "Living the Mission: Religious Disseminations" focus on the life and work of Carl Strehlow at the Hermannsburg Mission in Central Australia. Kenny explores the way in which Carl Strehlow tried to establish a Lutheran world in Ntaria, the Arrernte land to which he had been posted. She examines his mission practice in the context of his training at the Neu-endettelsau Mission Seminary and traces his intellectual roots back to a number of Lutheran teachers and scholars who provided the different intellectual strands that informed Strehlow's practice. The theologian Warneck is particularly notable in this context, as he emphasised – in the tradition of Luther – the importance of learning local languages in order to most effectively convert people to Lutheran Christianity. Kenny demonstrates how Strehlow, in the remote context of the Finke River Mission, was able to replicate a Lutheran community based on patriarchal notions of the Lutheran family.

Further insight into this Lutheran "holy family" is provided by Bandhauer's and Veber's contribution, which examines this concept not only with regard to the patriarchal structure that was imposed on the Arrernte in the framework of Strehlow's missionary work in their community, but also with respect to its replication and application within the confines of Strehlow's own family. Bandhauer's and Veber's attention to the creation and allocation of gender-specific roles and the part played by this in the configuration of the patriarchal structure commences with a reading of the letters of courtship exchanged by the young Carl and his fiancée Frieda at the beginning of their relationship, while Carl was first in Bethesda then Hermannsburg, and Frieda still in Germany.

While Kenny's focus is Strehlow's public role as the head of the mission, Bandhauer's and Veber's concern is the private sphere of the family beginning with the courtship relationship between Strehlow and his fiancée, then wife, Frieda Keysser. This private sphere is the central focus of their correspondence as Frieda prepares to migrate to the foreign territory of Central Australia. The narratives that Carl provides of everyday life at the mission and those that Frieda relates about her preparations for migration and marriage illustrate the extent to which both were prepared to go in order to impose pre-given structures of Lutheran life and religious practice in their new environment. Frieda's subordinate and supporting role as Carl's companion in his missionary project simultaneously indicates her authority in the household of the mission station. Their correspondence with each other, as well as with superiors and acquaintances in the course of their life at the Hermannsburg Mission, provides insights into the couple's experience and makes comprehensible their standing in Australian history as "an icon of intercultural experience", as Austin-Broos calls it (Austin-Broos 2009: 21).

The third section engages with narratives of national and cultural identity. The four contributions in this section review a number of accepted historical accounts of migration and exploration as well as the critical discourse around these narratives. Their diverse analyses yield new and unexpected insights into aspects of cultural contact arising from German participation in different episodes of Australia's history.

Fischer's informative survey of scholarship concerning "the German presence in Australia" offers an overarching context for his argument that the accepted discourse regarding the success of Australia as a settler society in terms of the tripartite "assimilation-integration-multiculturalism" model must be called into question when considering the German migrant experience since World War I. Fischer draws attention to the apparent paradox that whilst the last two decades have seen a substantial increase in the number of persons identifying as German-Australians compared to that in the immediate aftermath of both World Wars I and II, there has simultaneously been a serious decline of German as a community language compared to other European languages such as Italian, French and Dutch. He seeks to explain his observations through the hypothesis that the changing perception of Germans by Anglo-Celtic Australians shaped and continues to shape the experience and self-perception of German migrants in Australia. This perceived connection to their country of origin and its historical heritage never ceases to have some bearing on the lives of Australian residents from a German background, even if they themselves wish to identify mainly or absolutely with Australian society. Drawing on social, historical, linguistic and other research about German communities in Australia to formulate his argument, Fischer discusses the sociopolitical impact of

World Wars I and II, as well as that of events that do not even involve the migrant country, such as the fall of the Berlin Wall. How German-Australians fared with regard to policies designed and implemented by the Australian government is, according to Fischer, always also a reflection of what occurs in Germany.

Likewise on the subject of Anglo-Celtic perceptions and changing attitudes towards Germans in Australia and Germany during wartime is Williams' contribution to this volume. Williams demonstrates that what is often perceived as anti-German sentiment in Australia undoubtedly has its roots in Australia's World War I experience. His even-handed treatment of anecdotes and experiences of German-Australian World War I veterans and their families related as oral history, in letters, film and newspaper articles, provides examples of both positive and negative attitudes on the part of Anglo-Celtic Australians and Australian government policies, particularly those of the Australian Imperial Forces (AIF), towards German-Australians. Until World War I, a primarily positive attitude towards German-Australians and Germany as a nation predominated, with Australia and Germany having enjoyed a healthy trade relationship that in the eyes of the British even threatened to displace Britain's favoured trading-partner status with Germany. Although the experience of World War I caused a hiatus in relations between the two countries, Williams' examination of primary sources of the time demonstrates that German-Australian relationships within Australia were much more complex. Letters from German-Australians who had enlisted in the AIF and were accepted to fight alongside the British against their country of origin or ancestral heritage testify to the complexity of Australian perceptions of their German compatriots. Australians who were part of the German migrant community found themselves in a liminal space, a space where what Geertz calls "systems of meaning" (Geertz 1973: 12) meet and clash, in which self-perceptions on the one hand, and the ascriptions that the majority projected onto the German migrant community on the other, needed to be negotiated on a daily basis. Fischer's and Williams' analyses of particular narratives and counter-narratives of cultural contact thus portray the problematic nature of generalisations, showing that these are always influenced by specific imaginations of nationality and ethnicity.

Also investigating the topic of migration but parting from the discussion of German-Australian migrant life in the 20th and 21st centuries is Reynold's sociohistorical study dealing with a relatively large-scale German immigration wave from the Duchy of Nassau to Australia in the 19th century. Reynolds, like Williams, also uses personal letters as a primary resource, in this case the correspondence between those who migrated from Nassau to Australia and those who stayed behind in Nassau. Reynolds enquires why such a comparatively large proportion of that population chose to migrate at that particular juncture, and in comparing and contrasting the material in these letters with state records, she shows that the reasons given for migration by the Nassau immigrants in their personal correspondence often differ from that stated in the official data. With reference to the psychological theory of the "migration-prone personality" elaborated by Cropley and others (1986), Reynolds suggests that the impulse to migrate could be as rooted in the individual's psychology as it may be externally motivated.

Another survey of letters which reveals discrepancies between narratives of a particular event is van der Lubbe's examination of letters exchanged between the head of the British Admiralty, the Earl of Sandwich, and the father and son team, Johann and Georg Forster. Her contribution is based on exhaustive archival research that casts light on the struggle for determination and ownership of the Cook narrative both in terms of what was written, and also in terms of what van der Lubbe calls "the race for the press". Writing the narrative of Cook's second voyage was an important step in the composition of a foundational myth about the discovery of Australia. Who had been approved to write it, who had the rights to it and who was then authorised to publish and translate it, all emerge as highly controversial and contentious issues. The Forsters, who were originally commissioned to write the story, found themselves increasingly sidelined by the interests of the British Admiralty, for both official and private reasons.

The urge to control Cook's story is a salient example showing how seemingly undisputable "factual" reports can be materially tainted by the personal interests of those who assert ownership. This demonstrates how narratives that are endowed with the status of official histories, and that allegedly represent the interests of the nation, are in fact dependent on and effectively determined by an authorised narrative perspective. Thus, the British Admiralty sought to dismantle Forster's original account, an account they had previously agreed to support, and subordinate it to the overriding perspective of Cook's diaries. This point can be developed further using an insight of the historian White, who writes that "plot is not a structural component of fictional or mythical stories alone; it is crucial to the historical representations of events as well" (White 1987: 51). In these terms, legitimation and authority are immanent to narrative form and are established within and through the act of narration itself.

The fourth and final section of the volume presents discussions of two utopian representations of Australia in German-language fiction. The time lapse of two centuries between the fictional works considered in this segment of the book facilitates a comparison between an 18th-century example of the literary formula of idealising the non-European wilderness on the one hand, and a contemporary deconstruction of this idealisation on the other.

Wilson interprets the novel *Abentheuer auf einer Reise nach Neu-Holland* (1793) [*Adventures on a Journey to New Holland*]. In this novel by Therese Huber, who had never set foot on Australian soil and who drew her information partly from accounts written by the above-mentioned Georg Forster, the convict colony of Australia, and more specifically Norfolk Island, is presented as a counterpoint to perceived undesired and dangerous developments in Europe, such as those in postrevolutionary France. Europeans who had suffered injustice and violation in France and in Britain are miraculously united on Norfolk Island. Its empty spaces become the projection screen for fantasies of refuge and the opportunity for self-regeneration and new beginnings. Through her analysis of the thematic complex 'revolution-guilt-regeneration' that shapes the trajectory of the plot, Wilson shows how the island, which historically was the prison for the most hardened convicts, in this literary imagining becomes the site for a new society. This new society draws heavily on the idealised middle-class family as the source of "an ideal model of governance", as much because of the moral values it espouses, as for the humanising influence it exerts on the public sphere.

While the novel Wilson discusses is a sentimental utopian projection typical of its time, Urs Widmer's 1993 novella, *Liebesbrief für Mary* [*Love Letter for Mary*], is an ironic deconstruction of stereotypical images of Australia as a contemporary utopia in the German-speaking world. Giesler shows that Australia, and especially the Outback, functions as an ideal and as a site of desire and longing, in which two authors search for a woman they both loved and lost to the continent. Widmer parodies the European fixation on the vast and pristine spaces of the Australian Outback by locating this utopia as a non-existent place in a non-existent desert in the – whilst existent – very barren Outback. Drawing on a cocktail of stereotypical perceptions of Australian Aboriginal myths on the one hand, and of Australia as the dumping site for nuclear waste – a disaster zone indeed – on the other, Widmer's novel, according to Giesler, can be read as a text where the idea of the foreign and exotic as a new possibility of authentic origin is at least deconstructed, if not altogether decomposed.

This last section presents examples of readings of literary texts, which are situated within an anthropological context of literary scholarship. Literary anthropology assumes that the human is not only constituted by language, but also by literature. Travel accounts – including non-fictional ones – letters, historical narratives, as well as translations and appropriations of the myths of perceived original and primitive cultures share with literature their capability and need to fictionalise and imagine (see Assmann, Gaier & Trommsdorff 2005). Where intercultural contact is concerned, this need often originates from a strong urge to assert one's own identity, culture and nationality as well as – as Wolfgang Iser puts it with regard to the fictive and the imaginary – "to extend oneself" (Iser 1993: xi) by appropriating and thus fictionalising the Other.

This volume, we hope, shows how scholars of literary criticism, history and ethnography can, through textual and linguistic analysis, both uncover these fictionalisations, and, as well, reveal the meanings of these fictionalisations for the respective author's experience of cultural contact.

Bibliography

Alphen E van (1991). The Other Within. In R Corby & JTh Leerssen (Eds), *Alterity, Identity, Image: Selves and Others in Society and Scholarship.* Amsterdam, Atlanta: Rodopi.

Assmann G, Gaier U & Trammsdorff G (2005). *Zwischen Literatur und Anthropologie: Diskurse, Medien, Performanzen.* Tübingen: Gunter Narr.

Austin-Broos D (2009). *Arrernte Present, Arrernte Past: Invasion, Violence, and Imagination in Indigenous Central Australia.* Chicago/London: University of Chicago Press.

Cropley A, Becker K, Lüthke K & Lüthke F (1986). Forming the Decision to Emigrate to Australia: Some Recent German Experience. *Australian Journal of Politics and History,* 32: 52–62.

Geertz C (1973). *The Interpretation of Cultures.* New York: Basic Books.

Iser W (1993). *The Fictive and the Imaginary: Charting Literary Anthropology.* Baltimore: Johns Hopkins.

Leonhardi MF von (1907). Vorwort. In *Mythen, Sagen und Märchen des Aranda-Stammes in Zentral-Australien.* Gesammelt von Carl Strehlow, Missionar in Hermannsburg, Süd-Australien, bearbeitet von Moritz Freiherrn von Leonhardi. Frankfurt a. M.: Baer, 1–3.

Mulvaney J, Morphy H & Petch A (Eds) (2001). *My Dear Spencer: The Letters of F.J. Gillen to Baldwin Spencer.* Melbourne: Hyland House.

Nicholls A (2007). Anglo-German Mythologies: The Australian Aborigines and Modern Theories of Myth in the work of Baldwin Spencer and Carl Strehlow. *History of the Human Sciences,* 20(1): 83–114.

Pratt ML (1993). *Imperial Eyes: Travel Writing and Transculturation.* New York/London: Routledge.

White H (1987). *The Content of the Form: Narrative Discourse and Historical Representation.* Baltimore: The Johns Hopkins University Press.

I
Cultural Disseminations
of Missionary Ethnography

1
Missionary Scholarship and Cultural Theory: Carl Strehlow's Aboriginal Studies in the Context of European Knowledge Discourses on Taboo and Totemism[1]

Ortrud Gutjahr

At the end of the 19th and beginning of the 20th centuries in Europe, the Indigenous people of Australia became the focal point of scientific interest with respect to the question of the beginnings and fundamental conditions of culture. Ethnologists, cultural anthropologists, sociologists and religious studies scholars were united in their conviction that there was no better place to observe the establishment of social norms and religious foundations in early forms of socialisation than in Aboriginal cultures, since customs and practices that had developed untouched by the achievements of advanced civilisations and outside the reach of Western modernisation processes were preserved intact here. Even though there was a navigational route between Europe and Australia, the continent "Down Under" was for most scholars an unattainable research destination. And this was due less to geographical distance than the difficulties of an outsider gaining access to the largely secret rites of the Indigenous peoples. Most significantly, the goal of achieving an understanding of Aboriginal peoples was difficult to reach, given that the tribal languages were for the most part not transcribed.[2] For this

---

1 Original article "Forschungsmission und Kulturtheorie. Zur Stellung von Carl Strehlows Studien über die Aborigines im Kontext der europäischen Wissensdiskurse über Tabu und Totemismus." By Ortrud Gutjahr in German; translated into English by Maria Veber. All subsequent translations also by Maria Veber and from here on marked as MV.
2 It was said that 200 to 300 languages were spoken in Australia before the arrival

reason, it was indispensable to have local intermediaries who were in close contact with a particular tribe, and who were ideally also linguistically competent. Only such people could transmit and make available to Western discourses knowledge about the forms of social organisation in tribal societies that were still living in close contact with nature. The missionary Carl Friedrich Strehlow (1871–1922), who spent the larger part of his professional life among Aboriginal people in Central Australia, can be classed as a pre-eminent example of such a linguistically adept mediator between Australia and Europe.

Strehlow's Ethnographic Mission

Strehlow, who was born in northern Germany,[3] entered the mission seminary in the Franconian town of Neuendettelsau in 1888. In 1892, contrary to his expectations, he was sent to Australia.[4] He first worked together with the missionary J.G. Reuther at the Bethesda Mission in Killalpaninna, close to Cooper's Creek. Together they translated the New Testament into the Diyari language. In October 1894 Strehlow was placed in charge of the Hermannsburg Mission close to Alice Springs.[5] Even if, in order to appropriately anchor the Christian message, part of the missionary mandate was to engage with the customs and mores, and above all, the religious beliefs of the Indigenous population, the activities of the linguistically talented Strehlow moved far beyond the prescribed sphere. In his missionary capacity, he learned the languages of the Luritja and Arrernte people with whom he was in close contact, and began to take down in writing their narratives about their tales,

---

of Europeans. Most of these have now died out, and of those that still exist, only about 10 per cent are still acquired by children as their mother tongue (see Dixon 2002).

3 Carl Strehlow was born on 23 December 1871 in Fredersdorf/Uckermark and passed away in 1922 in Australia (see Strehlow 1969).

4 Strehlow was informed only shortly before his departure that he would not, as he had hoped, be travelling to North America as a priest, but instead to Australia as a missionary (see Wendt 2001: 179).

5 The missionary married Frieda Keysser in 1895 in Adelaide. Keysser migrated from Germany to fulfil her calling as a missionary's wife, and the couple had six children. More biographical details on Strehlow and the significance of his wife for the mission work can be found in the article by Andrea Bandhauer and Maria Veber in this publication.

myths and customs. He published these records for a German reader-ship in a continuous series from 1907 to 1920 in the newly established *Veröffentlichungen aus dem städtischen Völker-Museum Frankfurt am Main* [*Publications of the City Ethnographic Museum Frankfurt am Main*]. The contributions, edited by Moritz Freiherr von Leonhardi, appeared under the title *Die Aranda- und Loritja-Stämme in Zentral-Australien* [*The Aranda and Loritja Tribes in Central Australia*]. With this collection of stories from the Indigenous population of Australia, Strehlow made an important contribution to the newly established Frankfurt Ethnographic Museum (1904), whose collection of objects and texts was closely connected with the scientific research of the day.

That Strehlow, as indicated by the subtitle of his publication, *Mythen, Sagen und Märchen des Aranda-Stammes* [*Myths, Sagas and Fairy Tales of the Aranda Tribe*], was only in a position to take down this material because he understood the language of the tribe's members, is particularly emphasised in Leonhardi's Editor's Foreword: "This lin-guistic knowledge enables him to engage with the Indigenous people in their mother tongue – an advantage which cannot be rated too highly; given that the task at hand is to comprehend, reconstruct and fix in writing the difficult and in part quite complex reasoning of these origi-nal peoples" (Leonhardi 1907b: 1). Linguistic expertise was accentuated in this way in order to bring Strehlow's contribution into sharp relief against the recently published studies *The Native Tribes of Central Aus-tralia* (1899) and *The Northern Tribes of Central Australia* (1904). The authors of these two foundational studies, the anthropologist Baldwin Spencer (1860–1929), professor of biology at the University of Mel-bourne, and Francis James Gillen (1855–1912), employed by the South Australian Telegraph Department and stationed at Alice Springs, had met in 1894 during the Horn Expedition and together they undertook several anthropological expeditions to the Aborigines. During a three-month long gathering of many tribes in Alice Springs they were the first Europeans to study ceremonies and dances performed on this occa-sion.[6] If the Aborigines had until then been regarded as the lowest rung on the human evolutionary ladder, Gillen and Spencer demonstrated in

---

6 It was Spencer who coined the term Dreamtime for the prehistorical time of the Aborigines.

their extensively documented but also very accessibly described study, that the various tribes of Central Australia possessed a highly complex structure of cultural rites and customs. Although Leonhardi praises the vividness of Gillen's and Spencer's presentation of the rites that the two researchers had themselves experienced and also photographed, he also notes that they possessed limited linguistic competence:

> That Gillen, even though he lived with the Aranda for de-
> cades, still uses pidgin English interspersed with some Aranda
> words when talking to the Indigenous people, I know from
> Strehlow, who knows him personally and has observed his
> communication with the blacks; from Spencer, who was only
> fleetingly in the area, a thorough knowledge of the language
> can hardly be expected (Leonhardi 1907a: V, transl. MV).

Leonhardi here attempts to strengthen the claims of Strehlow's linguistic competence and the validity of his work in the face of Spencer's and Gillen's insights, which had been gained through participatory observation and were presented so vividly.

Through his "aural witness" the missionary, whose clergyman status prevented him from being eyewitness to the rites, connected into the philological process of the transference of the spoken to the written word as it had been authoritatively stamped by Jacob and Wilhelm Grimm at the beginning of the 19th century in Germany. Strehlow, too, had informants relate orally transmitted stories to him, in order to put these into writing and in so doing create a cultural memory archive. If the Grimm brothers' concern was to extrapolate the *Volksgeist*, or spirit of the people, from fairy tales and sagas, then Strehlow presented an extensive collection of primary material which could reveal the Arrernte's understanding of themselves and the world.

The material conveyed to the missionary was a tale of origin about the genesis of the world, referring to totem ancestors who possessed the qualities of a specific animal, and whose territory is sacred to their descendants. According to this narrative, one of the ancestors had promulgated an exogamic marriage system which another ancestor had "re-impressed upon them" after a phase of quite unrestrained behaviour that included all the possible permutations of incestuous relationship (Strehlow 1907–20: 8, transl. MV). Strehlow attempted to clarify the connection to the dead and the establishment of tradition within each tribe through his representation of the totemic cults. Gillen and Spencer had already focused heavily on the totemic system in order to shed light on the forms of social organisation of the individual tribes. According to this system the social and religious life of the individual is determined by the membership of a particular clan whose totem – a holy animal, the killing and eating of which is forbidden – functions as a guarantee of community. "[Y]et the totemic system of the Arunta shows us the one essential feature common to all totemic systems, and that is the intimate association between the individual and the material object, the name of which he bears" (Spencer & Gillen 1968: 127).

This quotation demonstrates that Spencer and Gillen formulated a quite promising message for the German missionary. Of all tribes, the two researchers had singled out the one under his stewardship, that is, his "community", because it was possible to deduce a foundational structure of totemism from their totemic belief system. In the chapter entitled "Die totemistischen Vorstellungen der Aranda und Loritja" [The Totemic Beliefs of the Aranda and Loritja], Strehlow attempts to deduce further essential features of totemism from the sagas of the Arrernte. As he demonstrates, the orally transmitted stories convey the idea that the ancestors lived on earth as animals, assumed animal form temporarily, or at the very least were in close relationship with a natural object. For this reason the totem animals are taboo. They cannot be killed, or if they are killed, then only with scrupulous care and in a prescribed manner. Upon death, the original ancestors' spirits withdrew into underground caves, while their bodies transformed themselves into natural objects such as rocks, trees, bushes or fish-filled water holes. The Arrernte posit a transgenerative link between these original totem ancestors and their descendants: the totem ancestors are thought of not only as emanations of nature which are present in their descendants, but also as the forces that beget future generations, since the seeds of as yet unborn children are stored in the natural objects.

As Strehlow explains, the Arrernte commonly view sexual intercourse only as a pleasurable activity. Its reproductive function is either not known, or only known to the older members of the tribe, who withhold this knowledge from the younger people.[7] According to their totemistic belief, a child comes into being when a woman passes by the transformed body of a totemic ancestor, which may for example be a bush. At this point a seed that had been stored there enters her hips and she might feel nausea or perhaps a severe pain. The child who is then born belongs on the one hand to the totem that the mother encountered when she became aware of her pregnancy, and on the other to the mother's totem. Each member of the tribe bears responsibility for the propagation of their totems. In order to do this, rituals are necessary to come into contact with the totem ancestors, the keepers of the seeds for new life.

Strehlow's linguistically simple and fact-orientated collection of material clearly demonstrates that his engagement with the totemism of the Arrernte is not simply founded in the desire to find entry points for his Christian beliefs out of missionary zeal. In a continuation of Spencer's and Gillen's studies, his ethnographic mission also inevitably contributed to the project carried out by various scientific disciplines in Europe of decrypting totemism as a fundamental form of social community building that was still closely allied with nature. The intensive research and discussions on taboos and their conventions from the 18th century onwards led to totemism becoming an object of fascination in the ethnographic literature around 1900, as Europeans thought that the *missing link* between the primitive state and cultural development was to be found there.

The Question of the Origin of Culture[8]

The beginning of the search for original forms of culture and a pre-civilisation lifestyle of humanity in Europe is directly linked with the attempt to reconstruct the development of the history of humanity via the ways in which overseas ethnic groups defined the "horizon of expectations" of their lives, that is, the ways in which they defined the boundaries of what could be expected against what was allowable, as well as what was possible. Jean-Jacques Rousseau (1712–78) above all

---

7 This description became the subject of heated controversy immediately after publication, as Leonhardi explains in his Foreword.
8 This section follows Gutjahr 2008.

was definitive for this aspect of anthropological discourse in 18th century Europe. His *Discours sur l'origine et les fondements de l'inégalité parmi les hommes* (1755) [*Discourse on the Origin and Basis of Inequality Among Men*] formulated the criticism that while up to then the pre-civilisation natural state of man might have been the theme of philosophical considerations, it had all too seldom been the object of observation. Since the original primitive man of prehistory (*l'homme naturel*) was no longer to be found on earth, Rousseau sought to define him by calibrating the qualities of present day civilised man (*l'homme civil*) against the qualities of the pre-civilised man (*l'homme sauvage*) described by travellers on voyages of discovery. Rousseau criticised the fact that in spite of many descriptions from distant parts of the world, only the European was well known, while "the true features that differentiate nations … have almost always escaped [our] notice" (Rousseau 1994: 107). Against the backdrop of Rousseau's cultural anthropological model and his appeal that greater investment be made in describing unknown peoples than had previously been the case, the observation of previously unknown peoples in foreign parts of the world was intensified on following voyages of discovery. The French scientist Louis Antoine de Bougainville (1729–1811), who identified the prototype of the Noble Savage in Tahiti's inhabitants, was the first captain to attempt a voyage around the world (1766–69) directed from an anthropological point of view. But the first to focus on the customs, traditions and religious practices was the English Captain James Cook (1728–79) in his observations of the South Sea Islanders.

Cook explored New Zealand and mapped the east coast of Australia – then still referred to as New Holland – on his first circumnavigation of the globe (1768–71) in service of the British Crown (see Aughton 2002). On his second trip around the world (1772–75) he advanced to the South Pole and refuted the idea of the existence of a southern continent known as *Terra Australis*. By the time he embarked on his third expedition in July 1776 in the ships *Discovery* and *Resolution*, Cook already possessed significant fundamental ethnological and anthropological knowledge about population groups in the southern hemisphere, and was also familiar with the style of quasi-ethnographic description through the account of his previous journey (see Cook 1961) and that of

Georg Forster (1754–94). As well as describing the geography, flora and fauna, people's appearance, and the dress and dwellings in the places visited on the third expedition, Cook also described the customs and traditions of the Indigenous population in his travel journal, including a behaviour pattern known as *tapu* or *tabu*, which posed a conundrum for him. The Tongan Archipelago in the South Seas (the Friendly Islands), Tahiti (the Society Archipelago) and Hawaii (the Sandwich Islands) in particular became for Cook the areas in which he observed taboo customs, of which he kept records from April 1777. With respect to the term taboo, Cook followed Forster. In his account of Cook's second voyage, the latter asserted with reference to the name of the principal island of the Friendship Islands, known as "Tongatabbu", that "Tabbu is just simply an auxiliary added to the name of several islands in the South Seas" (Forster 2007: 467, transl. MV). Cook then stated in the record of his third voyage that the taboo rules regulating cohabitation on "Tonga'taboo"[9] were so authoritative that they even determined the name of the island: "[N]ay it is probable, that the additional word taboo to the name of the island which is simply Tonga has been added from this very custom as expressing its singularity" (Cook 1967: 948). In the description of a mourning ceremony a custom that remained opaque to the European eye is also described as a "taboo":

> There is another custom amongst them call'd Taboo whose precise meaning we do not well understand. The word itself implys no more than that a thing is not to be touch'd, and therefore every thing that is under such restriction for certain reasons is said to be Taboo'd. It seems to be a custom of great force and extent and in some measure may be reckon'd of the sacred or religious cast, relating to things hallow'd and forbidden (Cook 1967: 947).

Cook was convinced that taboo customs were connected to the veneration of holy entities, things and procedures, and attested to the respect in which people of greater authority were held. As he was able to observe, the violation of these behavioural rules attracted serious

---

9 "Tonga'taboo … the most considerable of these islands and the seat of government" (Cook, 1967: 918).

sanctions. For this reason he explained the word taboo as "the common expression when any thing is not to be touched, unless the transgressor will risqué some very severe punishment as appears from the great apprehension they have of approaching any thing prohibitet by it [sic]" (Cook 1967: 948).

Cook observed diverse customs regulated by taboos and noted, for example, that clan chiefs whom he had invited to dine on his ship were prevented from accepting certain foods as a result of taboo rules, or he saw that a woman who had washed a dead king was herself temporarily subject to a taboo. In addition, he noticed in the course of dropping anchor at numerous islands that there were similar taboos, but that their effect, termed *mana*, was different (see Freud 1974e: 312; Mana & Tabu 1972; Kraft 2004: 15). From these observations it obviously became clear to Cook that taboos represented a foundational behavioural codex underpinned by religion, even though this codex ultimately remained a phenomenon of "mysterious signification" (Cook 1967: 982).

The Ethnographic Gaze and Cultural Research

Cook's account of his voyage led to taboos becoming understood as a description for phenomena that were held to be holy, inviolable, untouchable and forbidden. This triggered the quest for the origins of these religious laws and prohibitive sanctions, and in the course of the 19th century repeated attempts were made to define the term more precisely. The English doctor and researcher Edward Shortland (1812–93), who had lived with the Maoris in New Zealand for the larger part of his life, and who had studied their customs and traditional practices, attempted to define the etymological meaning of the word in his work *Traditions and Superstitions of the New Zealanders* (1854). He interpreted the syllable *ta* as "to mark/designate" and *pu* as "extraordinary" or "strong" (see Betz 1981: 141). But since subsequent research was conducted pre-eminently by English and German missionaries, who noted the different manifestations and modes of action of taboos, the preferred understanding of the term was in connection with holy rites and superstitions.

However, the ethnographic work of the English missionary William Ellis (1794–1872) was definitive for the further development of research on taboos. Between 1816–24 he was sent to different South Sea Islands, where he focused on customs and rituals. Against the backdrop of Enlightenment thought and self-determination, he interpreted these as arbitrary, backward and irrational. His study, published under the title of *Polynesian Researches* (1829), proposed that taboos were to be understood as regulative mechanisms in the service of social control, and became an important resource for further anthropological studies because of its precisely detailed descriptions. The term taboo became part of the technical terminology of ethnography, where it was deployed to describe religious concepts of magic and the social structures of prohibitionary sanctions of the "primitive people" of the Pacific.[10] The *Brockhaus* encyclopaedia article from 1886 thus still notes the following in the article "Tabu":

> On most of the South Sea islands, taboo (Tapu) designates in part the rules regarding the sanctity and inviolability of divine objects, persons or places, in part the sanctity and inviolability of the same, and in part also the undertakings that are supported by the advantages conferred by this sanctity. Before the arrival of the Europeans, the islanders, specifically the inhabitants of the Society Archipelago and the Sandwich Islands, were enslaved by this terrible superstition of taboo, which imposed a good many privations and cost the lives of many thousands of innocent people. The king was taboo, divine and invulnerable, likewise everything he touched: for this reason he did not enter any house other than his own, as then nobody else would have been able to use it again. Even the cup he drank from would be destroyed immediately afterwards. But the priests would also pronounce a taboo on objects and places that nobody could then touch or access, and even on certain food from which one then had to abstain. This superstition has been increasingly disappearing since the European and American missionaries succeeded in opening the doors to Christianity (Brockhaus 1886: 439, transl. MV).

---

10 Seibel contends that the term taboo underwent a change in meaning in the context of the Victorian moral codex. However, the term was in fact not used to describe social structures in Europe (see Seibel 1990: 75–76).

Even at the end of the 19th century taboos were aligned with super-stition, which the missionary work functioned to overcome. Yet these missionary interventions threatened not only to put an end to the belief system of the original taboos, but also to their signification.

Taboo and Totemism in Knowledge Discourses around 1900

Charles Darwin's (1809–82) sensational and influential text *On the Origin of Species* (1859), which appeared in German only one year after its publication in English, established that modern civilised man was part of a long generational chain of animal and human ancestors. Since that time, the possibility of studying the early forms of one's own culture in the so-called primitive races was considered to be a practicable route to the origins of culture.[11] In this context totemism then also became a popular focus of ethnology, in the belief that not only had a core taboo system been discovered, but also the original form of religion.

Enabling this to occur at this juncture was, crucially, the division of the humanities in Europe at the end of the 19th century into new scientific branches and areas of study. Research into totemism and taboo gained impetus through new disciplines such as the sociology of religion, cultural anthropology, ethnic psychology and, not least, psy-choanalysis. From a scientific perspective the various approaches that were concerned with the significance and systematisation of taboo and totemism can be quite literally understood as expressions of Clifford Geertz's "thick descriptions", since they involved nothing less than "con-struing social expressions in their surface enigmatical" (Geertz 2000: 5). The publications on taboo and totemism appeared in quite rapid suc-cession, since the results of one study would be promptly taken up and further developed in new publications in other disciplines.

The consolidation of the science and the establishment of the new area of study specifically dealing with taboo research is credited to Wil-liam Robertson Smith (1846–94), author of the study *Lectures on the*

---

11 The philosopher and sociologist Herbert Spencer (1820–1903) applied the find-ings of evolutionary theory to societal development when establishing his theory of evolutionism. His socio-Darwinian approach is first set out in the 1851 work *Social Statics*.

Religion of the Semites (1889), which showed that sacrificial rites with a religious foundation form the origins of culture. The Scottish orientalist, who transposed evolutionary theory onto analyses in religious studies and founded the sociology of religions as a discipline, sought to find the elements common to pre-modern and modern experience. He viewed "the institution of totemism", which did not yet postulate an individualised god, as the precursor of religion:

> In the totem stage of society each kinship or stock of savages believes itself to be physically akin to some natural kind of animate or inanimate things, most generally to some kind of animal. Every animal of this kind is looked upon as a brother, is treated with the same respect as a human clansman, and is believed to aid his human relations by a variety of friendly services (Smith 1889: 117; Smith 1967: 87–88).

Smith views taboos as "rules of holiness" (Smith 1889: 142; Smith 1967: 110) as well as profane "precautions against the invasion of mysterious hostile powers" (Smith 1889: 143; Smith 1967: 111) and presents them as central elements of Judaism, Christianity and Islam, rather than as solely an expression of magical beliefs, as had previously been the case (see Douglas 1966). Smith studied these three central world religions with the goal of identifying similar archaic and atavistic elements of belief, and in this way transposed the ethnographic term taboo onto religious prescriptions.

The degree to which missionary reports functioned as the basis for taboo research around 1900, the frequency with which new research directions were created in response to the findings and the degree of interconnectedness of the individual directions, can be made clear using the example of James George Frazer (1854–1941). Frazer, whose training was in classical philology, changed course to the history of religion and ethnology, and in 1921 was appointed to the first chair in anthropology at Cambridge. After he had summarised the insights of ethnology and religious studies current at the time in an extensive article on the term "taboo" for the new edition of the *Encyclopaedia Britannica* edited by William Robertson Smith (Frazer 1888), Frazer published his two-volume work *The Golden Bough* (1890). He expanded this work, which appeared one year after Smith's *Lectures on the Religion of the Semites*, to 12 volumes during the period between 1911 and 1915.[12] Frazer had previously made "his unpublished collections on the superstition and religious observances of primitive nations" (Smith 1889: ix; Smith 1967: xii) available for Smith's work. Now he devoted a separate volume, entitled *Taboo and the Perils of the Soul*, to the different forms of taboo. This relied on the reports of the missionary Ellis, who asserted that taboos were part of a superstitious belief that needed to be overcome. Frazer described taboos as "forbidden actions" that, in close relationship with magic, represented a preliminary stage of religion. In his assessment of taboos as a magical belief system, Frazer's argument has an Enlightenment impetus:

> If the supposed evil necessarily followed a breach of taboo, the taboo would not be a taboo but a precept of morality or common sense. It is not a taboo to say, "Do not put your hands in the fire"; it is a rule of common sense, because the forbidden action entails a real, not an imaginary evil. In short, those negative precepts which we call taboo are just as vain and futile as those positive precepts which we call sorcery. The two things are merely opposite sides or poles of one great disastrous fallacy, a mistaken conception of the association of ideas. Of that fallacy, sorcery is the positive, and taboo the negative pole (Frazer 1922: 19–20).

Like other scholars, Frazer also proceeds from the belief that superstition and taboo are linked, but in his attempt to use this link to ascertain the origins of human social formations, he effects a paradigm shift in taboo scholarship. Up until that point, and on the basis of Cook's observations and missionaries' reports, the taboos of inhabitants of the South Sea archipelagos had been the principal focus of research. Now the Indigenous peoples of Australia moved into centre stage as the ethnic group which, as the description *Aborigines* (the Original Ones) indicates, was considered to hold the promise of shedding light on early forms of social formation. Frazer commences from the premise that

---

12 It first appeared under the title *Attis, Osiris: Studies in the History of Oriental Religion*, 2 Vols., London 1890. The repeatedly expanded work first appeared in the period 1907–12 under the title *The Golden Bough* (taken from a William Turner painting), with the subtitle *A Study in Magic and Religion*.

taboo regulations result from an insufficient understanding of causality, and that the Australian Aborigines aspired to avoid damage to themselves by following these prescriptions. Although Frazer states at the end of his comprehensive study that he has now completed a "long voyage of discovery" (Frazer 1922: 714), he nevertheless belongs to the not insignificant number of "armchair ethnologists" who never carried out their own research. He thus relies on the research of Spencer and Gillen, who Strehlow was soon after also to use as a reference.

Paradigm Shift: From Taboo to Totem

After the Scottish ethnologist John Ferguson MacLennan (1827–81) had, in encyclopaedia articles on "Totemism",[13] first focused attention on this social reference system, Frazer, in his work *Totemism and Exogamy* (1887) sought to use totemism to deduce the rules of exogamy that proscribed sexual contact between members of a clan. Early reports had been used to establish that while young men were taboo in the initiation phase, women in contrast were taboo during menstruation and after giving birth, and now particular attention was directed to the incest taboo. The philosopher and psychologist Wilhelm Wundt (1832–1920), who made a significant contribution to the development of psychology as a discipline and founded the first Institute for Experimental Psychology in Leipzig, stood in the foreground of this work with his focus on the connection between taboo and marriage laws in his ten-volume work *Völkerpsychologie* (1900–20) [*Ethnic Psychology*] and his writings *Probleme der Völkerpsychologie* (1911) [*Problems of Ethnic Psychology*] and *Elemente der Völkerpsychologie* (1912) [*Elements of Ethnic Psychology*]. Wundt viewed the task of an ethnic psychology that touched closely on ethnology, history and sociology to be "the investigation of those psychic processes that provide the foundation for the general development of human communities and the emergence of communally produced intellectual products of universal validity" (Wundt 1904: 1–2), whereby his main concern was the prehistory and intellectual particularity of individual peoples. He believed his investigation of language, myth, religion and traditions would enable him to reach back into the cultural structures of primeval times, and was confident that one could not draw

---

13 The articles appeared in the journal *Fortnightly Review* (1869–70).

a definite boundary between nature and culture, as the so-called state of nature always already corresponded to an at least primitive state of culture. Nevertheless, Wundt distinguished between primitive races, in which animal and instinctive behaviour predominated, and civilised people, to whom a rational order based on law and morality was intrinsic. Wundt stopped observing Polynesian taboo customs[14] because "neither the social culture nor the mythology of the Polynesians was so primitive that we may from the outset expect to find there a system of prohibitions such as the laws of taboo" (Wundt 1906b: 302). He assumed that in Polynesia taboos were graded according to rank and distinction, while in Australia the laws of taboo were essentially applicable to all members of the individual tribes.

Wundt, like others, was of the opinion that the conditions of the earliest cultural forms were most likely to be found with the Indigenous inhabitants of Australia, relying on Spencer and Gillen among others, as well as the interpretations of Smith and Frazer, since he himself also lacked experience in field research. He thus conjectured that the earliest social norms developed in an original conjunction of totemism, taboo and exogamy. On this basis the beginnings of culture were best observed in a context where "within a primitive culture taboo customs dovetail with other elements of mythological thinking" (Wundt 1906b: 302). His reading of totemistic sacrificial rites in Australia concludes that awe of the ancestral totem animal, which is at the same time revered as a demon protector, forces abstention from its flesh as an expression of "piety towards the Old Ones" (Wundt 1906b: 335). Wundt refers specifically to Smith, who views the sacrifice not only as a human tribute to God, but also as a symbol of confraternity with God.

The degree to which research scholarship on taboo and totemism are interlinked around the turn from the 19th to the 20th centuries is

---

14 A comprehensive study that to a large extent gathered together previous findings on these taboo customs appeared in 1930. It had been prompted by the decision of the Faculty of Philosophy at the University of Leipzig in 1922 to hold an essay competition. The terms of reference were as follows: "Tapu. A summarising study of the distribution, the definition, the record of efficacy, the forms and the character of the concept of tapu (taboo) and its analogue forms ought to be provided" (Lehmann 1930: V). For a more recent account of Polynesian taboo customs, see Meiser 1995.

made very clear when one looks at the example of Émile Durkheim (1858–1917), the French sociologist, who came across Wundt's writings in 1885. Durkheim met the ethnic psychologist on a study trip to Germany and agreed with the latter's view that a commonly held moral codex was indispensable for the formation of a society.[15] In *Die elementaren Formen des religiösen Lebens* (*Les formes élémentaires de la vie religieuse*, 1912) [*The Elementary Forms of the Religious Life*], a foundational and pathbreaking work, he delineates the significance of religion for the communal life of societies, ascertaining that religious ceremonies and practices are central to the establishment of identity and social cohesion. Durkheim refers back to both Smith's *Lectures on the Religion of the Semites*, with their emphasis on totemism as the earliest possible form of religious expression, and also to the understanding in Frazer's *Encyclopaedia Britannica* article of taboos as "the institution in virtue of which certain things are withdrawn from common use" (Durkheim 1947: 300). Durkheim, like everyone else, endorses the unanimously shared opinion around 1900 "that Australia is the most favourable field for the study of totemism" (Durkheim 1947: 93) and, like other researchers before him, requires primary sources to support his armchair ethnology. He is the first to base his theories on Strehlow's collections of myths, sagas and legends, of which three fascicles had by that point appeared, as well as the field studies of Spencer and Gillen.[16] Durkheim, who first needs to introduce the missionary and his research, finds that "the observations of Strehlow, though completing, making more precise and sometimes even rectifying those of Spencer and Gillen, confirm them in all that is essential" (Durkheim 1947: 92). The French sociologist refers to the Australian-based missionary's work when he, for example, discusses the spelling of a name or description that differs from that given in Spencer's and Gillen's studies, and when he makes reference to myths of origin, analyses the clan structure of the tribes, delineates the differences between paternal and maternal to-

---

15 Durkheim presented Wundt's theses in 1887 in his article "La science positive de la morale en Allemagne".
16 Durkheim maintains that the fourth fascicle only appeared once his own book had been completed (see Durkheim 1947: 91).

tems, or describes the kind, form, origin or functioning of a totem.[17] Durkheim's procedure makes it clear that he evaluates the classification system that enables Strehlow to organise the mass of material as a significant proof of the complex foundational structure of totemism. In Durkheim's opinion, Strehlow showed that totemism "is in reality an absolutely general organization" (Durkheim 1947: 152). The principles of this order that was grounded in religion were explained in detail by Durkheim on the basis of the ethnographic collection assembled by Strehlow. One year after the appearance of the highly regarded work of the French sociologist, the Austrian psychoanalyst Sigmund Freud (1856–1939) presented a study which made reference to Durkheim's work, but sought a different kind of access to taboo and totemism.

Taboo and Totemism in Individual Development

In his extensive work *Totem und Tabu* (1913) Freud extrapolates from ethnographic findings in an attempt to formulate judgments about individual development. Using his psychoanalytic approach, he seeks to present observational findings about pre-modern societies outside Europe in a form that would best reveal their relevance for Western societies. In introductory and explanatory remarks he concedes that while deliberating on the fundamental conditions of culture he consulted numerous writings on the sociology of religion and cultural anthropology, such as those of Smith, Frazer, Wundt and Durkheim, which all appeared at the end of the 19th and beginning of the 20th centuries.[18] Freud's central concern was to explain man's capacity for cultural development and to demonstrate that stages of cultural development that have supposedly been surmounted still remain, albeit in hidden form, characteristic of people in modern societies. Like his predecessors, he was also an "armchair ethnologist", and studied the ethnographic writings that had caused a furore on account of their new hypotheses about the development of humanity. And Freud, like others before him, also used the studies of Aboriginal tribes because he conjectured that these provided a key to understanding the earliest stages of civilisation: "On

---

17 "Strehlow has collected 442 items in these two societies" (Durkheim 1947:104).
18 Freud relies particularly on Smith 1894; Lang 1905; Wundt 1904; Wundt 1906; Frazer 1910; Storfer 1911.

external as well as internal grounds I choose for this comparison those tribal groups that have been described by the ethnologists as the most backward, pathetic, primitive people, the original inhabitants of the newest continent, Australia, which has also preserved in its fauna so much that is archaic and that has been destroyed elsewhere" (Freud 1974e: 295).

Freud – who was at least indirectly familiar with Strehlow's early publications through his reception of Durkheim – emphasises in the introduction to his work on cultural theory that the concept of totem was considerably more in need of explanation than that of taboo, since the meaning of taboos was largely clarified and since these in particular were to be found in modern society. "In contrast, totemism is alien to the way we feel things today, in reality it was given up long ago and as a socio-religious form of organization it has been replaced by new forms, and has left insignificant traces in the religion, custom and practice in the life of contemporary civilized peoples" (Freud 1974e: 292). Freud first presents this form of religiously grounded practice of the Aborigines in detail, in order to make it more real to his readers:

> In the place of all the religious and social institutions that are lacking in the Australian's society we find the system of *Totemism*. The Australian tribes are broken up into smaller confraternities or clans, each of which names itself after its *totem*. Now, what is a totem? As a rule it is an animal, edible, harmless or dangerous, feared, less frequently a plant or a natural force (rain, water), that has a particular relationship to the entire clan. The totem is in the first instance the progenitor of the clan, but it is then also the clan's protective spirit and helper, the one who sends the clan oracles, and despite the fact that it is otherwise dangerous, it knows and spares its children. In return the totem members are under the holy obligation, according to which infractions incur automatic punishment, not to kill (destroy) their totem and to abstain from its meat (or the pleasures that it otherwise offers) (Freud 1974e: 296).

Starting from these totemistic foundational structures and Darwin's hypothesis that in prehistoric times humans lived as a primeval horde, Freud develops a narrative of origin with which he attempts to elucidate the epochal shift from the natural state to culture, which in his view must have occurred as a cumulative cultural evolution over a long period and across many generations.[19] Since the origin of cultural development lies in an historical time that cannot be recalled and can "nowhere [become] the object of observation" (Freud 1974e: 425), it can only be inferred speculatively (see Fernandez-Schmid 1988). From a series of opinions about the history of humanity that he grafted from highly regarded writings in ethnography and the history of religion, but also to some degree drew from his own studies in the development of the individual, Freud thus construed a sequence of events that was as hypothetical as it was coherent: according to this so postulated narrative of origin, humanity lived as a primeval horde under the dominion of an all-powerful father, who, in order to maintain his position of supremacy and sexual dominance, banished or killed his sons, until a new group succeeded in turning the tables and murdering the autocratically ruling father. However, since this murder took place without any reference to any moral commandments, it could only be linked with the concept of guilt through its repetition in remembrance rituals. Freud accordingly hypothesises that the murdered father was communally eaten. This act expresses the ambivalence towards the revered but also hated father who stood in the way of the brothers' claims to power and their sexual needs. However, after the hatred of the father had been expressed, penitence set in, and so the two fundamental regulators of social organisation were established: the taboo against killing and the incest taboo.

According to Freud these two taboos became necessary in the interests of survival: a reciprocal sparing of the other, and sexual abstinence with respect to the father's women were deemed necessary, and the law of exogamy was enforced in order to maintain the strength of the fraternal horde.[20] So it was only the killing and incest taboos that allowed

---

19 As Freud expounds in his lengthy appendix to *Massenpsychologie und Ich-analyse* [*Group Psychology and the Analysis of the Ego*], he wanted his narrative about the development of culture understood as a pictographic representation by means of which humanity's increase in experience, which in actuality occurred across a long generational chain, could be told succinctly (see Freud 1974d).

20 Cassirer accused Freud of having augmented his construal of origin with a sexual mythology (see Cassirer 1949: 41–42).

the establishment of "the first form of a social organization based on the renunciation of individual drives (*Triebverzicht*)" and a kind of "social contract" (Freud 1974b: 530): "This replacement of the power of the individual by that of the community is the decisive cultural step" (Freud 1974a: 225). The power that accrues to the group is thus based in taboo regulations that enable the inclination towards violence to be suppressed and sexual energy to be diverted for the protection of all. Freud here defines the beginning of culture as the shift from the unrestrained expression of instinctual drives to a form of social organisation that could only come into existence at the price of regulating the drives. Beside these pragmatic motives that sprang from the immediate struggle for survival and led to the establishment of the foundational taboos, it is crucial that the essential authority for the development of culture, that is, conscience, could only be established through the murder of the father. For Freud, both the implementation of taboos and the cementing of their effectiveness are unthinkable without the individual conscience as an internal censorship mechanism.

In order for the initial foundations of a community cemented by cultural cohesion to be passed on trans-generationally and further developed, the internalisation of regulatory mechanisms was necessary. In Freud's narrative the physical ingestion of the father thus stands for the psychic introjection of his law. From writings on the totemic customs of pre-modern societies he concludes that the ritualistic funerary eating of the dead man (Totenmahlzeit) in the first commemoration ceremony for the murdered father was followed in the later development of culture by the totem meal (Totemmahlzeit), in which a revered and dangerous animal was consumed. In *Totem und Tabu* Freud expounds in detail on the barriers against incest erected in the Aboriginal Australian clans and finds

> that exogamy linked with the totem accomplishes more, that is, it aims at achieving more, than the prevention of incest with the mother and sisters. For the male it also excludes the possibility of sexual union with all the women of his tribe, that is, with a number of female persons who are not related to him by blood, by treating all these women as though they were blood-relations (Freud 1974e: 299).

In presenting Aboriginal culture as an exemplary case, Freud's interest lies in establishing an explanatory model for the cultural development of humanity as a whole. He thus explains further that the community that he views as "the original form of humanity" as it were, lives in a state of tension with respect to the taboo, as it wants to contravene the taboo but at the same time maintains its sense of duty-bound conscience by upholding the taboo: "the taboo is an imperative of conscience, its infraction results in the emergence of a terrible feeling of guilt that is as natural as its provenance is unknown" (Freud 1974e: 358). In spite of this, for Freud the incest and killing taboos are "psychologically not equivalent" (Freud 1974e: 427). Although the proscription against incest enables the establishment of "the first form of a social organization based on the repression of drives" (Freud 1974b: 530), this is established on pragmatic grounds, since otherwise the new social form would be weakened in the struggle of the brothers over women. In contrast, the "sparing of the totem animal", which Freud understands to be the symbolic father, is based "solely in emotional motives" (Freud 1974e: 427). The ritual becomes a funeral and memorial ceremony for the father and serves both the creation of meaning and the social and moral sanctioning of the prohibition of killing. As in his narrative of origin, Freud here also determines the killing taboo to be a central regulatory mechanism for totemism, one that must arrogate unbroken validity up to the present day. Freud thus diagnosed the fragility of a civilisation based on violence, one in which culture remains a thin veneer: "[O]ur unconscious murders even for trivialities" (Freud 1974f: 57).

If Freud's study *Totem und Tabu* already programmatically names both of the fields of study taken from ethnological research, so the subtitle *Einige Übereinstimmungen im Seelenleben der Wilden und der Neurotiker* [*Resemblances Between the Psychic Lives of Savages and Neurotics*] identifies Freud's methodological approach, namely the use of the behaviour of psychologically disturbed people to shed light on the genesis and the ambivalent structure of taboos. Here, individuals with an obsessional neurosis, who have created their own taboos and follow them as stringently as primitives (Freud 1974e: 318), are a salient example of the similarity between contemporary modes of individual behaviour and those in pre-modern societies as described in ethnological writings. With respect to the question of the origin of culture, totemism became so attractive for Freud because the basic laws forbade the killing of the totem animal and required members of the same totem clan to abstain from sexual intercourse with one another. It was here that Freud could find a confirmation of his foundational hypothesis, namely that the killing and incest taboos are fundamental regulative mechanisms that are linked – as he showed in his narrative of cultural development – with what were originally the strongest drives.

Freud also construes Christian religion according to the terms of his narrative of origin. He believes that humanity's original sin was without doubt a sin against "God the Father" and that "this sin was an act of murder" (Freud 1974e: 437). He proceeds from the assumption that Christian doctrine is humankind's "most naked avowal of the guilty deed of primeval times" because the only son is sacrificed and this sacrifice is also linked with "the absolute renunciation of women" (Freud 1974e: 437). Freud integrates the Christian narrative of redemption into a concept of culture by emphasising the establishment of guilt according to his interpretation of cult sacrifice. In the previous century William Robertson Smith, who Freud draws on a number of times in *Totem und Tabu*, had already contended that sacrifice cements a community because hatred is directed towards a third party and so enables the maintenance of peace (see Smith 1894). Freud extends this view in his interpretation of sacrifice as a healing ritual for a community that has become incapable of acting because of catastrophes or guilt-inducing actions.[21] The conceptualisation of ritual sacrifice as an act that strengthens a community is an articulation of a psychological explanation, namely, that all those who took part in the holy killing experienced a release of instinctually driven arousal and excitement, and bear collective guilt for this act. In a sense they become a community of the guilty.[22]

---

21 With reference to Freud's example of the "Fort-Da" game, Heinsohn views the sacrificial ritual as a game that re-enacts, as it were, the great flood and apocalypse (see Heinsohn 1997: 81–82).
22 Burkert viewed the killing of the victims as the transformation of an aggression that could no longer be vented in big-game hunting. Burkert hypothesised that the loss of the hunting tradition led to a genetically anchored permanent disposition towards aggression (see Burkert 1972; Burkert 1984; Burkert 1990).

Freud's reading of totemism, however, allows him to extract an explanation not only for the founding of the Christian religion, but indeed also for that of culture. Freud defines as culture "all that, in which human life has elevated itself out of its animal conditions and in which it distinguishes itself from the life of animals" (Freud 1974c: 139–40). Just as repressed material resurfaces in neurosis, so – in his opinion – does that which was collectively repressed articulate itself in cultural practices, particularly in rituals. From here it is a natural next step for Freud to read the totemistic practice of Australian Aborigines as a symbolic staging of an original experience and as the return of the repressed. In the course of his engagement with taboo and totemism, Freud thus develops a theory of culture in which culture is demarcated against a nature thought of as invariable, one that in any given situation only ever assumes a veneer of culture, that is, the drives (see Gutjahr 2006; Schmid Noerr 1993).

In what is in essence a foundational definition, Freud concludes in *Das Unbehagen in der Kultur* (1929–30) [*Civilisation and its Discontents*] that the word "civilisation" describes the entirety of achievements and institutions in which our life departs from that of our animal ancestors and which serve two purposes: "the protection of humanity against nature and the regulation of the relationships of humans amongst themselves" (Freud 1974a: 220). In contrast to a nature viewed as original and pre-occurring, civilisation is however not understood in principle as nature's Other, but in terms of evolutionary theory as its specific further development within the human species. Culture begins with that momentous developmental step with which humans gain the capacity to master their feelings and keep themselves in check in order to be able to create compulsory rules and forms of organisation that improve and protect the quality of life within a community. From a culturally critical perspective, Freud declares that processes determined by drives are not overcome by cultural development, but are only cloaked in different guises through the operation of culture, and he proceeds from the assumption that the man of culture has not prevailed over the primitive man controlled by his drives, but that he carries the latter hidden within. Freud reads the asynchronicity of cultures in terms of an evolutionary model that enables one to draw conclusions about earlier developmental steps of one's own (European) culture on the basis of the cultural practice of pre-modern societies (see Waibl 1980).

Without doubt, Freud's decidedly self-enlightened approach represents a milestone in the study of taboo and totemism that then served as a point of reference for cultural anthropology and particularly for the newly established discipline of ethnopsychoanalysis. So for example, the Hungarian psychoanalyst Géza Róheim (1881–1953) tried to verify the hypotheses formulated by Freud in *Totem und Tabu* by undertaking his own field studies of Australian Aborigines (see Róheim 1925; Róheim 1945). Róheim interpreted many Aboriginal legends as "myths of transition", by means of which developmental stages of the human life cycle and most particularly the dramas of puberty could be socially integrated and invested with cultural meaning. Freud's attempt at a psychoanalytically oriented cultural theory that explained phenomena of Western civilisation with reference to ethnographic observations was reformulated as a theory of the individual by Róheim, who then sought to explain the behaviour of the Aboriginal people themselves. In his study *The Eternal Ones of the Dream: A Psychoanalytic Interpretation of Australian Myth and Ritual*, Róheim proceeds from the assumption that because of totemism the "Australian" culture is "fundamentally homogeneous with local variations" (Róheim 1971: iv). He emphasises that "every native is a representative of an ancestor who figures in the mythical narrative" (Róheim 1971: 1).

For Freud it was precisely the presentation of totemism in the large number of ethnographic reports that appeared in the period around 1900 that provided him with the "missing link" for his psychoanalytic theory. Freud makes clear that religious perceptions and the resultant behaviour patterns of people who – from a European perspective – lived far beyond Western civilisation at the other end [Down Under] of the world are profoundly anchored in their own psychosocial development. Like many scientists of his time, Freud could only develop his theory because he was able to draw on insights that had reached Europe through "ethnographic missions" such as that of Carl Strehlow, which productively advanced European knowledge discourses. However, with his perception that the peoples of Western cultures also passed through a totemistic phase in their childhoods, Freud – who never set foot on

Australian soil – brought engagement with Australian Aborigines far further into Europe than any ethnographer had done so to that point.

Bibliography

Aughton P (2002). *Endeavour: The Story of Captain Cook's First Great Epic Voyage.* London: Cassell.

Spencer B & Gillen FJ (1968 [1899]). *The Native Tribes of Central Australia.* New York: Dover.

Betz W (1981). Tabu – Wörter und Wandel. *Meyers enzyklopädisches Lexikon.* 25 Vol., Vol. 23. Mannheim: Meyer, 141–44.

Brockhaus (1886). *Brockhaus Conversations Lexikon.* 16 Vol., 13th edition, Vol. 15. Leipzig: Brockhaus.

Burkert W (1972). *Homo necans: Interpretationen altgriechischer Opferriten und Mythen.* Berlin & New York: de Gruyter.

Burkert W (1984). *Anthropologie des religiösen Opfers: Die Sakralisierung der Gewalt.* München: Carl-Friedrich-von-Siemens-Stiftung.

Burkert W (Ed) (1990). *Wilder Ursprung: Opferritual und Mythos bei den Griechen.* Berlin: Wagenbach.

Cassirer E (1949). *Vom Mythus des Staates.* Zurich: Artemis.

Cook J (1961). *The Journals of Captain James Cook on his Voyages of Discovery.* John Cawte Beaglehole (Ed). Vol. 2: The Voyage of the Resolution and Adventure 1772–75. Cambridge: Haklyut Society at the University Press.

Cook J (1967). *The Journals of Captain James Cook on his Voyages of Discovery.* John Cawte Beaglehole (Ed). Vol. 3: The Voyage of the Resolution and Discovery 1776–80. Cambridge: Haklyut Society at the University Press.

Dixon RMW (2002). *Australian Languages: Their Nature and Development.* Cambridge: Cambridge University Press.

Douglas M (1966). *Purity and Danger: An Analysis of Concepts of Pollution and Taboo.* London: Routledge.

Durkheim É (1947). *The Elementary Forms of the Religious Life [Les Formes Élémentaires de la Vie Religieuse* (1912)]. Glencoe/Illinois: Free Press.

Ellis W (1831). *Polynesian Researches.* 4 Vol., 2nd edition. London: Fisher, Son & Jackson.

Fernandez-Schmid SB (1988). *Der Mensch als kulturelles Wesen in Freuds Psychoanalyse.* Zurich: Universität Zürich.

Forster G (2007 [1777]). *Reise um die Welt.* Illustriert von eigener Hand, mit einem biographischen Essay von Klaus Harpprecht und einem Nachwort von Frank Vorpahl. Frankfurt a. M.: Eichborn.

Frazer JG (1888). Tabu. *Encyclopaedia Britannica*, Vol. XXIII. Edinburgh: Black.

Frazer JG (1910). *Totemism and Exogamy.* 4 Vol. London: Macmillan.

Frazer JG (1922). *The Golden Bough: A Study in Magic and Religion* (Abridged Edition). New York: Macmillan.

Freud S (1974a). *Das Unbehagen in der Kultur.* Mitscherlich A, Richards A & Strachey J (Eds), *Studienausgabe.* Vol. IX: Fragen der Gesellschaft. Ursprünge der Religion, Frankfurt a. M.: S. Fischer, 191–270.

Freud S (1974b). *Der Mann Moses und die monotheistische Religion.* Mitscherlich A, Richards A & Strachey J (Eds), *Studienausgabe.* Vol. IX: Fragen der Gesellschaft. Ursprünge der Religion, Frankfurt a. M.: S. Fischer, 455–581.

Freud S (1974c). *Die Zukunft einer Illusion.* Mitscherlich A, Richards A & Strachey J (Eds), *Studienausgabe.* Vol. IX: Fragen der Gesellschaft. Ursprünge der Religion, Frankfurt a. M.: S. Fischer, 135–89.

Freud S (1974d). *Massenpsychologie und Ich-Analyse.* Mitscherlich A, Richards A & Strachey J (Eds), *Studienausgabe.* Vol. IX: Fragen der Gesellschaft. Ursprünge der Religion, Frankfurt a. M.: S. Fischer, 61–134.

Freud S (1974e). *Totem und Tabu.* Mitscherlich A, Richards A & Strachey J (Eds), *Studienausgabe.* Vol. IX: Fragen der Gesellschaft. Ursprünge der Religion, Frankfurt a. M.: S. Fischer, 287–444.

Freud S (1974f). *Zeitgemäßes über Krieg und Tod*. Mitscherlich A, Richards A & Strachey J (Eds), *Studienausgabe*. Vol. IX: Fragen der Gesellschaft. Ursprünge der Religion, Frankfurt a. M.: S. Fischer, 33–60.

Geertz C (2000 [1973]). Thick Description: Toward an Interpretive Theory of Culture. In *The Interpretation of Cultures: Selected Essays*. New York: Basic Books, 3–30.

Gutjahr O (2006). Kulturbegriff. Lohmann M & Pfeiffer J (Eds), *Freud-Handbuch*. Stuttgart: Metzler, 239–45.

Gutjahr O (2008). Tabus als Grundbedingungen von Kultur: Sigmund Freuds 'Totem und Tabu' und die Wende in der Tabuforschung. In Benthien C & Gutjahr O (Eds), *Tabu: Interkulturalität und Gender*. Paderborn: Fink, 19–50.

Heinsohn G (1997). *Die Erschaffung der Götter: Das Opfer als Ursprung der Religion*. Reinbek bei Hamburg: Rowohlt.

Kraft H (2004). *Tabu: Magie und soziale Wirklichkeit*. Düsseldorf & Zurich: Walter.

Lang A (1905). *The Secret of the Totem*. London: Longmans.

Lehmann R (1930). *Die polynesischen Tabusitten: Eine ethno-soziologische und religionswissenschaftliche Untersuchung*. Leipzig: Voigtländer.

von Leonhardi MF (1907a). Vorrede. *Die totemistischen Kulte der Aranda- und Loritja-Stämme in Zentralaustralien*. I. Abteilung: Allgemeine Einleitung und die totemistischen Kulte des Aranda Stammes, dargestellt von Carl Strehlow, Missionar in Hermannsburg, Süd-Australien, bearbeitet von Moritz Freiherrn von Leonhardi. Frankfurt a. M.: Baer, v–xviii.

von Leonhardi MF (1907b). Vorwort. *Mythen, Sagen und Märchen des Aranda-Stammes in Zentral-Australien*. Gesammelt von Carl Strehlow, Missionar in Hermannsburg, Süd-Australien, bearbeitet von Moritz Freiherrn von Leonhardi. Frankfurt a. M.: Baer, 1–3.

Mana und Tabu (1972). *Mana und Tabu: Kulturphänomene aus der Südsee*. Ausstellung des Amtes für Kultur der Hansestadt Lübeck aus den Beständen der Museen für Kunst und Kulturgeschichte, Völkerkundesammlung, Museum am Dom: 11. Juni bis 30. Juli. Lübeck: Senat der Hansestadt Lübeck.

Meiser U (1995). *Sie leben mit den Ahnen: Krankheit, Adoption und Tabukonflikt in der polynesisch-tonganischen Kultur.* Frankfurt a. M.: Brandes und Apsel.

Róheim G (1925). *Australian Totemism: A Psycho-Analytic Study in Anthropology.* London: Allen & Unwin.

Róheim G (1971 [1945]). *The Eternal Ones of the Dream: A Psychoanalytic Interpretation of Australian Myth and Ritual.* New York: International University Press.

Rousseau J-J (1994 [1755]). *Discourse on the Origin of Inequality.* Trans. Franklin Philip, ed. Patrick Coleman. Oxford and New York: Oxford University Press.

Schmid Noerr G (1993). Zur Kritik des Freudschen Kulturbegriffs. *Psyche* 47: 325–43.

Seibel K (1990). *Zum Begriff des Tabus: Eine soziologische Perspektive.* Frankfurt a. M.: Universität Frankfurt a. M.

Smith WR (1889 [1894]). *Lectures on the Religion of the Semites. First Series: The Fundamental Institutions.* 2nd Edition. Edinburgh: Adam and Charles Black.

Smith WR (1967). *Die Religion der Semiten.* Mit einem Vorwort v. mil Kautzsch u. einem Anhang. Wissenschaftliche Buchgesellschaft: Darmstadt.

Storfer AJ (1911). *Zur Sonderstellung des Vatermordes: Eine rechtsgeschichtliche und völkerpsychologische Studie.* Leipzig and Wien: Deuticke.

Strehlow TGH (1969). *The Journey to Horseshoe Bend.* London: Angus & Robertson.

Strehlow C (1907–1920). *Die Aranda- und Loritja-Stämme in Zentral-Australien.* Bearbeitet v. Moritz Freiherr von Leonhardi. Vol. 1. Frankfurt a. M.: Baer.

Waibl E (1980). *Gesellschaft und Kultur bei Hobbes und Freud.* Wien: Löcker.

Wendt R (2001). *Sammeln, vernetzen, auswerten: Missionare und ihr Beitrag zum Wandel europäischer Weltsicht.* Tübingen: Narr.

Wundt W (1904). *Völkerpsychologie: Eine Untersuchung der Entwicklungsgesetze von Sprache, Mythus und Sitte.* Vol. 1: Die Sprache, 2nd ed. Leipzig: Engelmann.

Wundt W (1906). *Völkerpsychologie: Eine Untersuchung der Entwicklungsgesetze von Sprache, Mythus und Sitte.* Vol. 2: Mythos und Religion, 2nd ed. Leipzig: Engelmann.

2
Dada Among the Missionaries: Sources of Tristan Tzara's "Poèmes Nègres"[1]

Walter F. Veit

The title of this essay promises to deal with three interrelated matters. I propose to do so in the following order:

First, I shall offer a few crucial biographical dates of Carl Strehlow, one of the German Lutheran missionaries from Neuendettelsau (Bavaria) who worked among the Arrernte and Luritja Aborigines in Hermannsburg, Central Australia.

Second, I shall give an outline of the early phase of the Dada movement in Zurich and its High Priest, Tristan Tzara, who performed, in French, songs of Indigenous peoples of Africa, Australia and Oceania, which he had translated from ethnological publications mainly by French and German missionaries.

Third, I shall juxtapose four Australian Aboriginal cult songs – as collected and translated by Carl Strehlow – with Tristan Tzara's translation into French and mine into English, followed by a consideration, *pars pro toto*, of different strategies in interpreting these songs.

The material and the context of this research are rather vast, complex and contentious. I shall restrict myself to the essential literary aspects. Other aspects will have to be reserved for future work.

Carl Strehlow (1871–1922)

Who is Carl Strehlow? According to the short biography in the *Australian Dictionary of Biography* (Veit 1990: 121–22),[2] Carl Theodor

---

1 As part of our research project, this essay is dedicated to Irmline Veit-Brause. All translations by W. Veit unless otherwise indicated.
2 See also P.A. Scherer, in: *The Australian Dictionary of Evangelical Biography*.

Friedrich Strehlow was born on 23 December 1871, the seventh child of the schoolteacher Carl Strehlow and his wife Friederike, née Schneider, in Fredersdorf, a village north of Berlin in the Uckermark. He was educated at his father's Free Lutheran School. On 1 August 1888, he started his studies at the Lutheran Mission Seminary in Neuendettelsau, in the vicinity of Nuremberg in southern Germany. Although preparing to become a pastor of the Lutheran Church of America, at the end of his studies on 31 August 1891, he agreed to become a missionary for the Hermannsburg Mission (Lüdemann 2000: 459) to work among the Indigenous peoples of Australia.

On 3 July 1892, Strehlow was solemnly ordained as preacher and missionary of the Evangelical Lutheran Church of South Australia with a first posting to the Diyari Mission at Bethesda/Killalpaninna, which was directed by Pastor Reuther.[3] Under his guidance, Strehlow started to study the language of the local Diyari tribe, showing exceptional aptitude. Shortly afterwards, Strehlow and Reuther began the translation of the New Testament into Diyari (Reuther & C. Strehlow 1897). The translation was published in 1897 after Strehlow had started working at Hermannsburg on 12 October 1894 for the Finke River Mission.[4]

In order to find out whether he was prepared for the arduous assignment, it is helpful to consider the seminary curriculum: among all the theology courses, there is no course in ethnography despite the fact that ethnology was of rising popularity in universities (Veit 2004a: 136–50).[5] Although the seminal work for the anthropology of northern and Central Australia by Baldwin Spencer and Francis Gillen began to appear

---

Sydney: Evangelical History Association, 1991, 357; U. van der Heyden, in: Gerald H. Anderson (Ed), *Biographical Dictionary of Christian Missions*. Grand Rapids: Eerdmans Publishing Company, 1999, 646; also J. van Gent, in: Chr. F. Feest, & K.H. Kohl (Eds) *Hauptwerke der Ethnologie*. Stuttgart: Kröner 2001, 459–65; Petermann, 2004, 807f; T.G.H. Strehlow 1969.
3 For more detailed information on the influence of Reuther and Strehlow's linguistic work among the Diyari, see article by Maurice Schild 2004.
4 For a short history of Hermannsburg, Northern Territory, see Leske 1977 and Harms 2000.
5 An expanded version has been published as *"Arbeiter im Weinberg" oder "Der ungebildete Missionar" Aspekte der nicht-theologischen Bildung der Missionare.* (Berliner Beiträge zur Missionsgeschichte 8) Berlin: Wichern Verlag, 2005.

in print from 1897 onward, it seems not to have been available immediately to Carl Strehlow. In fact, as we come to understand the details only now, the stimulus for serious anthropological research, beyond occasional observations during missionary work to be published in church journals, came to Carl Strehlow via letters from the German "armchair anthropologist" Moritz von Leonhardi, in which he asked questions regarding Arrernte society, beliefs and customs. Moritz von Leonhardi became his mentor in the new science (Kenny 2005: 54–70).

In 1910/12, we find Carl with Friederike and their six children in Germany[6] giving lectures on his Aboriginal research at the Völker Museum in Frankfurt.

Stimulated and mentored by Moritz von Leonhardi, Carl Strehlow had started to collect myths and legends from old Arrernte and Luritja men living in and around Hermannsburg. On 23 June 1908, Strehlow had dispatched the first fascicle of 104 pages of his *Myths, Legends and Fairy Tales of the Aranda and Loritja Tribes of Central Australia,* (edited by von Leonhardi and published in Frankfurt by the Ethnological Museum) to Pastor Ludwig Kaibel, at the time inspector of missions in Adelaide and Strehlow's superior. Strehlow had not indicated that it was the first part of an ongoing project that, when completed in 1920, was to become a seven-part comprehensive work on the Arrernte and Luritja tribes in Central Australia (C. Strehlow 1907–20).[7] Right from the start, it encountered opposition from professional anthropologists such as Walter Baldwin Spencer, who saw their research objects contaminated by Christian teachings (Veit 2005: 38).

Carl Strehlow's development from missionary to ethnologist can be seen as paradigmatic for many European missionaries in all parts of the world since the early 19th century. During the 28 years of service at Hermannsburg, he became – in keeping with the typical approach

---

6 The *Deutsches Geschlechterbuch* provides the following information: "1.*24.3.1897 Friedrich Johannes Gottfried, + 4.8.1947 at Woschega as Russian prisoner of war; 2.*8.2.1899 Martha Maria Auguste, + ?; 3. *12.10.1900 Rudolf Karl Theodor, + ?; 4.*15.6.1902 Karl Paul Hermann, + ?; 5. *15.5.1905 Hermann Ernst Wilhelm, + since1945 missing in action; 6. *6.6.1908 Theodor George Henry, + 1978 Adelaide."
7 On the collaboration between Carl Strehlow and Moritz von Leonhardi, see H. Völker 2001 and Kenny 2005.

taken by German missionaries – first a student of the Diyari, Arrernte and Luritja languages in order to preach the Gospel to Aborigines in their own language. He developed from being a Lutheran preacher into an authority on the life of the Aborigines of Central Australia, into one of the great philologists (Kneebone 2001: 145–72) of Australian native languages and into one of the most impressive ethnologists at the turn of the century in the tradition of continental Europe.

The Dada Revolution

In scholarly consideration of the philological and cultural significance of the relationship between a literary movement and the ethnographic work of a German missionary at the beginning of the 20th century, ethical and political questions have arisen about the relationship between the European explorers and collectors, and the Explored and Collected. Whole areas of critical studies have emerged, from which I only refer to the Orientalism debate initiated by Edward Said. Such explicit debates did not exist at the turn of the 19th to the 20th centuries, when ethnographic collection[8] played a vital role in the work of numerous artists: Picasso (though he denied it) (*The Age*, 13 March 2006: 7); the group of German artists known as *Die Brücke* (Moeller 2006), that included Emil Nolde (Moeller 2002), who joined a German ethnographic expedition to Papua as an artist; and the sculptors and painters Erich Heckel, Karl-Ludwig Kirchner, Max Pechstein, Karl Schmidt-Rottluff and Otto Müller. Similarly, the protagonists of the Dada movement saw no moral or intellectual impediment to their appropriation of ethnographic material.

However, the cognitive aspect of scholarly and missionary interest in Indigenous culture is worth considering. In the context of appropriating Indigenous art, the question as to the perception of Indigenous peoples by the explorer has vexed anthropologists and philosophers alike. How could one best work as a scientist or artist and at the same time escape the accusation of intellectual imperialism, let alone cultural colonialism? That which applies to Indigenous art generally, so avidly collected at the time, applies to Australian Aboriginal songs too: they

8 On the importance of museums, galleries and art collectors for Dadaists and surrealists see Tythacott 2003.

are taken out of their social and cultural context by the ethnographer who places them into a context that is exotic to them. They acquire an unfamiliar meaning on both sides. The philosopher recognises the dialectic problems in the hermeneutic situation of understanding/ misunderstanding of the other (Veit 1997: 163–74). When European ethnographers research non-European, alien, "exotic" worlds, a primal misunderstanding is inevitable. The presence of the Europeans is often imposed and therefore resented. Furthermore, the ethnographer's own system of beliefs and values is – and must be – radically challenged, to the extent that the observer's own culture may itself become subject to critique. James Clifford distinguishes two possible approaches: an older process of investigation in which the investigator subordinates the Observed to his own cognitive and evaluative system; and a newer approach in which the observer consciously tries to retain the distinctiveness of the Observed, to recognise as equal the worldview of the Other, and to preserve the Other as Other. I am not confident that the epistemological problem is solved in Clifford's way. But I agree with Clifford that when appropriating alien cultures, it is enlightening to observe the effects of the contrast between the cognitive intentions of anthropology on the one hand, and of Surrealism or of the Dada movement on the other:

> anthropological humanism begins with the different and renders it – through naming, classifying, describing, interpreting – comprehensible. It familiarises. An ethnographic surrealist practice, by contrast, attacks the familiar, provoking the irruption of otherness – the unexpected (Clifford 1988: 145).

It is precisely such "innovative dialogue between the European artist's work and his inspiration by the art of Indigenous peoples" that is the underlying interest of this essay. And for all I can see, in the present study of the songs of Central Australian Aborigines, the role of the mediator, Carl Strehlow, is just as crucial as is the role of the poet Tristan Tzara (Samuel Rosenstock), who used Indigenous art from many parts of the world for his own work. Although Tristan Tzara asked neither the Indigenous owners nor the copyright holders of Strehlow's collection of Aboriginal poetry for their agreement, he cannot be accused – as Picasso was accused – of "stealing" because he acknowledged its provenance, even if it has become rather laborious to identify these sources today. When his work was later printed, they were introduced as translations. Obviously, Tzara adapted his translations of the German or French translations of the Indigenous chants to his own purposes. What does "adaptation" mean? What form does it take? What is its purpose?

The "recycling" of art in all its genres has had many uses, parody is one of them. By parody I mean the re-use of literary forms and images which, in the case of the Dada revolt, had an overt critical intent. Furthermore, the parodist acknowledges the authority inherent in the authenticity, originality and simplicity of the original, and the new form and depth of meaning so much sought after in European intellectual life before and after World War I. Like Picasso, who greatly influenced Marcel Janco, the Dadaist painter and sculptor, and Tzara's compatriot and co-founder of the Zurich movement, Janco illustrated Dada publications with his versions of African sculpture. Having survived the barbarity of the war in neutral Switzerland, the chaotic, anti-war Dada moved to Paris in 1918/19 (Dachy 2005: 268ff; Dachy 2006: 78ff). Here the real was soon to be supplanted by the surreal. While Richard Huelsenbeck continued Dada in Berlin (Huelsenbeck & Tzara 1985: 36ff; Huelsenbeck 1987: 22ff; Dachy 2006b: 32ff), where it became distinctly political, André Breton broke ties with Tzara and established Surrealism in Paris at the end of the Great War in a deliberate attempt to channel the chaotic and anarchic energies of Dada into a disciplined program of creating a primordial world. Tzara continued with his "anti-poesy" (Béhar & Carassou 1990: 180–85) as the original Dada in Paris before and after World War II, surviving the German occupation in hiding in the south of France. But both their poetics, which were grounded in a Messianic anticipation of the new in the wake of cataclysmic events expected to lead to a universal rejuvenation, were already foreshadowed by most artists and writers of the preceding and continuing German Expressionism movement, while Hugo Ball developed his critique of the *fin de siècle Zeitgeist* (Ball 1919; Ball 1993; Ball 1992 [1946]; Ball 1974; Ball 1984). Their journals, with such telling titles as *Der Sturm* and *Die Aktion*, both starting in 1910, offer enough evidence for their radical stance. The apocalypse came with the outbreak of World War I which killed many of them, and dispersed the surviving protagonists and the movement over the globe. Dadaism became a global project (Dachy 1994; Dachy 2006b; Schuhmann 1991; Verkauf et al. 1958; Dachy 2002). Its influence on a belated avant-garde in Australia has recently been documented and placed into the larger context of modernism (Stephen et al. 2006).

Returning to the beginnings of Dada during the first year of World War I, Ball and Huelsenbeck, along with a number of other German intellectuals (Huelsenbeck 1987: 21) from very different social, professional and intellectual backgrounds, gathered in Zurich. Ball and Hulsenbeck had espoused Expressionism and organised soirées in Berlin lecturing on politics in Spain and Russia. At one such evening, on 12 May 1915, in which Expressionist writers in Berlin read their own poetry, Huelsenbeck contributed a declamation of "negro poems and Ball read[s] out pre-Dada nonsense poems".[9] However, their opposition to the war made their stay in Berlin precarious. Both moved as political refugees to Switzerland, where they were joined by Tristan Tzara who had arrived in Zurich during the autumn of 1915.

On 5 February 1916, Ball and Tzara opened the famous Cabaret Voltaire in the *Holländische Meierei*, Spiegelgasse, with two evenings devoted to French and Russian Modernist writings (Ball 1992: 19). When Richard Huelsenbeck arrived in Zurich on 26 February, he joined Ball, also reading from his own works. During the soirée on 30 March 1916, the *Poème simultan* and the *Chant nègre I & II* were performed for the first time accompanied by "big and small exotic drums" (Huelsenbeck 1964: 146). However, we do not know which *chants nègres* were performed at that time, just as we do not know what "Negro" poems Huelsenbeck performed during the earlier "Expressionist" meetings in Berlin. The earliest documentary evidence of the Zurich performances emerged publicly only after the early demise of the Cabaret Voltaire in an advertisement of the "I. DADA-ABEND" [First Dada Soirée] on 14 July 1916 (Schrott 1992: 49) which, according to Suzanne Perrottet and Hans Arp, performing members of the group (Schrott 1992:

---

9 See: "Dada: A Chronology." In Sheppard, 1981, 160–188; also: "Chronologie I." In Schrott 1992, 10–11; Sanouillet, 1990 (orig. Zurich: Arche, 1985), incl. chronology.

51)[10], turned out to be rather chaotic (Schrott 1992: 40; Sheppard 1981: 167). The advertisement states: "Chant nègre I (after their own motifs performed by Huelsenbeck, Janco, Tzara)" and "Chant nègre II (after motifs from the Sudan sung by Huelsenbeck and Janco)". During the opening party of the Gallery Dada, "primitive poetry" was read, but there is no further detailed information. The "Second Dada Soirée" on 14 April 1917 was devoted to the group of artists of the Berlin art school publishing in the journal *Der Sturm*. It included works by Max Ernst, Lionel Feininger, Wassily Kandinsky, Oskar Kokoschka, Alfred Kubin and Georg Muche, and was followed by the third soirée on 28 April 1917. Only the "Fourth Dada Evening", "Alte und Neue Kunst", on 12 May 1917, offered a tripartite program. During the second part, according to the program handout, Tzara read "Vers Nègres (tribus [tribes]: Aranda, Ewe, Bassoutos, traduits de [translated by] T. Tzara)" and in the third part he read again "Vers Nègres, (tribus Kinga, Loritja, Ba-Ronga; traduits de T. Tzara)". A further German language handout for the same evening and its repeat performance on 19 May, announces: "NEGER-GEDICHTE übersetzt und gelesen von [NEGRO POEMS translated and read by] Tzara / Aranda, Ewe, Bassoutos, Kinga, Loritja, Baronga / [also read by] Hennings, Janco, Batt, etc. Aegidius Albertinus, Narren-hatz, Gesang der Frösche [Song of the Frogs]." The repeat performance was urged by "the appetite [of the public] for the mixture of instinctive combination and wild bush drums" (Schrott 1992: 105).

But it is only in the first and second issues of the magazine *DADA RECEUIL LITTÉRAIRE ET ARTISTIQUE [Dada Anthology of Literature and Art]*, published in July and December 1917 after the establishment of the Gallery Dada on 17 March 1917, that we find some complete texts printed with scant identification, such as "CHANSON DU CACADOU de la tribu Aranda extrait du volume de poèmes nègres traduits par Tr. Tzara (en préparation)" [COCKATOO'S SONG of the Aranda tribe, an extract from the volume of Negro poems translated by Tristan Tzara (work in progress)] in the first issue, indicating Tzara's plan to publish a

---

10 Incidentally, while the word *Dada* already appears for the first time in a letter by Ball to Tzara dated 29 February 1916, the group accepts it as the title for a planned magazine in late April; it appears in print in the first issue of the magazine *Cabaret Voltaire*, which was dated 15 May but only went on sale on 24 May.

volume of similar poetry (Sanouillet 1976: 16), and in the second issue "2 POÈMES NÈGRES, tribu Loritja" [2 NEGRO POEMS, Loritja tribe] (Sanouillet 1976: 41–42). Neither the later Zurich issues No. 3 (December 1918) and Nos. 4–5 (*Anthologie Dada*, 15 May 1919), nor No. 6 (*Bulletin Dada*, February 1920) and No. 8 (*Dadaphone*, March 1920), published in Paris after Tzara and Dada had moved there, present further texts of Indigenous poetry. Unfortunately, the planned publication of the entire collection of Tzara's *Poèmes Nègres* mentioned in his letter to Doucet did not eventuate. Moreover, no single poems beyond those published in Dada almanacs and programs for the Dada soirées were printed in contemporary publications. It seems that at the time, Tzara's *Poèmes Nègres* simply vanished from sight.

In 1971, they appeared in Henri Béhar's edition of the *Oeuvres Complètes* [*Complete Works*] based on manuscripts in the Archive Tristan Tzara. Those that appeared in the Dada programs and almanacs were reprinted in 1976 in Michel Sanouillet's *DADA*. They were also translated into German and published in 1992 together with relevant documents and artwork by Raoul Schrott in his *DADA 15/25*. In 2002, Pierre Joris published his English translation in his collection *4×1*. And in 2006, Marc Dachy reissued Béhar's edition with some corrections in his *Découverte des arts primitives* (Tzara 2006).

Which sources did Tzara use for his creations? We can only speculate as to who or what gave Tzara the idea to go to the library of Zurich Technical University and read the most recent anthropological research publications – monographs published before 1915 – by French and German missionaries working in Africa and Oceania, such as Henri-Alexandre Junod, Eugène Casalis, Bruno Gutmann, and Carl Strehlow among many others, or the French diplomat-turned-writer Jean Paulhan. Tzara also read research papers in anthropological journals, particularly in the Viennese journal *Anthropos*, founded by Wilhelm Schmidt (S.V.D.) in 1906 and still published today. He found further material in works by French and German anthropologists residing in Paris, Hamburg or Berlin and using material from missionary fieldwork to write their books, in particular Carl Meinhof, the pastor and founder of African studies in Germany. Tzara must have perused quite a number of publications, most – but by no means all – of which Henri Béhar has been able to identify in a general way in his "Notes" to Volume One of his edition, crediting Browning (Browning 1979: 96–98) with the identification of the Arrernte-Strehlow texts. However, because it seems that Béhar himself did not have access to the manuscripts, it is important to go back to these manuscripts in order to examine Tristan Tzara's presumably difficult handwriting.[11] Therefore I do not propose to present a comprehensive list and scrutiny of all his sources. I shall turn only to the sources provided by Carl Strehlow, who from afar and without his knowledge, contributed to Modernist poetry through his anthropological studies among the Arrernte and Luritja people at Hermannsburg.

What is the idea and ideology of early Dada? Walter Benjamin is one of the few contemporary observers who saw Dada/Surrealism as the avant-garde[12] of something new that was difficult to comprehend in terms of traditional notions of rationality:

> the passionate phonetic and graphic metamorphic games that have pervaded avant-garde literature – whether it be called Futurism, Dadaism or Surrealism – in its entirety for 15 years now are magical experiments with words, not artistic gimmickry (Benjamin 1966: 207, transl. WV).[13]

In contrast, more recent critics of Tristan Tzara's early work, in particular of the *Poèmes Nègres*, have often been rather ambivalent, if not indeed dismissive. Gordon F. Browning, for example, having had access to the autographs in the Doucet Archives, offers the following critical assessment:

> In the communal atmosphere of the Galerie Dada, Tzara echoed his colleagues' enthusiasm for the development of a new art and their esthetics of purification and impersonality.

---

11 In a personal letter, Henri Béhar points out that the recent edition of the poems by Marc Dachy contains new readings because he has had access to the manuscripts.

12 For a comprehensive survey of avant-garde as notion and movement in literature see Weisgerber, 1984.

13 Originally published in *Die Literarische Welt 1* (8th & 15th Feb. 1929): "magische Wortexperimente, nicht artistische Spielereien sind die passionierten phonetischen und graphischen Verwandlungsspiele, die nun schon 15 Jahre sich durch die gesamte Literatur der Avantgarde ziehen, sie möge Futurismus, Dadaismus oder Surrealismus heißen."

He did not, however, contribute a corresponding "new poetry" to the Galerie Dada soirées. Instead, he read primitive
poetry. *Art nègre* was presumably a compromise designed to
embody his companions' standards for abstract art: imper-
sonality, communal creation, new materials – but without
going back to sentiment, logic, representation, or even intelligibility. This compromise was acceptable, as we can see by
Janco's comments on *poésie nègre*: "Cette poésie ... en effet
nous semblait le commencement de la poésie abstraite qu'on
ne traduisait plus" [This poetry ... in effect seems to us to
be the beginning of abstract poetry that isn't translated any-
more] (Browning 1979: 96).

It seems to me that Marcel Janco's comments make it clear that
something new had been achieved, something so primordial that it
cannot be translated into historic languages. Although quoting what
Tzara had said about his interest in Indigenous art, one can only assume
that Browning refused to take the new art seriously because it seemed
to disregard logic, intelligibility and even representation as the classical
values of literature, Tzara's "rags of a renaissance copy":

Dada proclaimed Negro art and literature, not only because
the artistic and literary expressions of the peoples of Africa
and Oceania had been considered primordial on the scale
of human evolution, but also because Dada tried to identify
its own manner of expression with the communicative men-
tality of the primitives in dance and spontaneous invention
(Janco IV: 8, transl. WV).

Thus the process of creating these poems as described by Browning
on investigation of the autographs – which, as mentioned before, seem
to be in bad handwriting given the many reading errors that still persist
in the *Oeuvres Complètes* and even in Dachy's edition – reveals to him a
very determined personal approach:

Tzara translated many primitive poems, but published only
a few. The selection he made among his rough drafts indicates a choice between the meaningless sound on the one
hand, and the logical, syntactical discourse on the other.
The original pencil drafts done in the library include stories

from Madagascar, with their mythologies and naive anthro-pomorphism. The second draft reflects a selective process, where largely only tattooing songs, marriage songs, and ritu-al chants are copied over, with all the German words looked up. This process was further refined as only a selection from these poems was then typed into a third draft. The few final poems that Tzara published, though translated into French, emphasise rhythm over meaning, subordinating French syn-tax to the original word order, as can be seen in "Chanson du Cacadou" from *Dada 1*, July 1917 [the poem follows] Though no words or phrases are specifically offensive, we may see a tacit provocation in the fragmentation, repetition, and banality of the text, published in a "recueil littéraire et artistique." Although the text is borrowed, the poem with its ellipses, repetitions and verbs in the infinitive, remains an example of fragmentation short of nonsense, and of meaning short of narration and personal sentiment. But it lacks Tzara's personal imagery for this banalization, fragmentation, and disrupted meaning (Browning 1979: 97–98).

It is at this point that Browning tells the reader in a footnote that contrary to an assertion by Huelsenbeck that Tzara made these songs up, many can be traced to publications by European missionaries and explorers, for example: contributors to *Anthropos*, Carl Meinhof, *Die Dichtung der Afrikaner*; Carl Strehlow, *Die Aranda- und Loritja-Stämme in Zentral-Australien* (Browning 1979: 111, fn 16). But he does not seem to be aware that the "primitive" stories and mythologies from Madagascar which Tzara used are in fact mediated by the celebrated writer Jean Paulhan, who published his collection of Malagasy stories and songs under the title *Les hain-tenys*[14] in Paris in 1913. It only goes to show that the identification of the sources is difficult and, as matters stand, incomplete.

However, in order to prove his point, Browning compares the syntax of Tzara's "Chanson du cacadou" with the syntax of Strehlow's

14 French translations of Malagasy poetry: "Les hain-tenys sont des poèmes populaires en usage chez les Malgaches, et particulièrement chez les Merinas" [The 'hain-tenys' are poems popular amongst the Malagasy people, particularly amongst the Merinas].

German rendering of the Arrernte *ititja*-cult song. It appears that he did not recognise the reason why most lines do not follow the rules of German syntax. Tzara translates into French the string of words given in Strehlow's interlinear translation of the Arrernte or Luritja texts to which he then juxtaposes a normal syntactical and interpretative translation. We have to conclude that Tzara chose the interlinear version for his translation into French deliberately in order to participate – albeit at least twice removed – in the magic of the Aboriginal cult songs and thereby to attempt to overcome the perceived restriction and constrictions of the languages he knows and – when performing them in public – to get closest to the original sound and rhythm which he could not fathom in any other way. Tzara recognised in those interlinear versions all the possibilities and strategies of defamiliarisation or estrangement used by Dada and later avant-garde writers, including simultaneous and pure sound poems, in order to epiphanically reveal the new. We should not forget that these poems were performed in spectacular fashion, supported by the rhythmic beating of "Negertrommeln" [Negro drums] and accompanied by "Negertänze" [Negro dances]. Hugo Ball reports in his diary about the soirée on 30 March 1916 among other events:

> The *poème simultan* (after the example of Henri Barzun and Fernand Divoire) was followed by *Chant nègre I and II*, both for the first time. *Chant nègre I* (or *funèbre*) was already prepared and was executed like a Vehmic court in black cowls and big and small exotic drums. The melodies for *Chant nègre II* were provided by our esteemed host Mr Jan Ephraim who, some time ago, lived with African contacts for a prolonged period and did his best as enlivening primadonna for the performance (Ball 1992: 87).

Thus the translation and performance of Australian Aboriginal cult songs produce a new openness to meaning by destroying the meaning(s) we are used to. Tristan Tzara, Richard Huelsenbeck, Walter Serner and others have presented their – frequently diverging – philosophy of Dada, if we can call it that, in a number of statements called "manifestos" or "proclamations", of which a number were published later as *Seven Dada Manifestos* (1916–21) (Tzara 1963; Tzara 1981; Tzara 1984; Béhar 1975: 394, 705ff; Tzara 2006: 26–27). Particularly important for our purposes are Tzara's "Notes" because they deal with special aspects of his work. I wish to quote from his "Note sur l'art nègre", in itself a piece of (mild) Dada writing, originally published in September 1917 in the new French journal *SIC*, which offers some insight into the differences Tzara saw between European art and that of Africa and Oceania, and indicates Dada's desire to return to the supposed original naivety, creativity and spirituality of the latter:

> The new art is first of all: concentration, angle of the pyramids up to the summit, which is a cross; but first we have dissected purity, then the object; we approached its surface, we pierced it. We wanted a clarity which is direct. Art forms groups of areas, with their special professions, with their limits. The influences of alien nature, which are mixed, are the rags of a renaissance copy, which still hangs on the souls of our neighbours [Nächsten], because my brother has a soul with sharp branches, black in autumn.
>
> My other brother is naive and good and laughs. He is in Africa or somewhere in Oceania. He focuses his vision on the head, the body in the wood, which is hard like iron, patient, without bothering about the conventional relationship between the head and the rest of the body. His thought is: humans walk on two legs, new relationships are formed according to degrees of necessity: thus the expression of purity is born.
>
> Out of darkness we fetch the light. Simple, rich, luminous naivety, the different materials, scales of form. In a balanced hierarchy.
>
> EYE; button, open wide, round, sharp, in order to penetrate through my bones and my belief. Change my country into a prayer of joy and anxiety. Cottonwood eye, groove in my blood.
>
> Art, in the childhood of time, was a prayer. Wood and stone were truth. In humans I see the moon, plants, the dark, metal, stars, and fish. So that the cosmic elements remain symmetrical. Deform, cook. The hand is strong, big. The mouth contains the power of obscurity, invisible substance, virtue, fear, wisdom, fire.

Nobody has ever seen so clearly the white grinding [das
weiß mahlen] as I during this evening (Albert-Birot 1980;
Schrott 1992: 118).

Tristan Tzara's Arrernte and Luritja texts

I would like to turn now to the textual origins of the few songs of
Poèmes Nègres which Tristan Tzara acknowledged translating/translit-
erating from Arrernte and Luritja Totemic Songs (Béhar 1975: 443–44,
451–52). Béhar correctly identifies them as derived from Carl Strehlow's
collection of totemic songs of the Arrernte and Luritja tribes of Central Australia (C. Strehlow 1907–1920)[15] to be performed at sacred and
secret cult rituals. They are edited in accordance with the traditional
philological methodology that Carl Strehlow had encountered during
his studies of critical editions of the Bible and classical literary texts,
and which he then adapted to anthropological research: each song is
presented firstly, with a description of the eponymous ceremony of the
song, and secondly, with an introduction that offers an outline of the
song to aid understanding. Only then does Strehlow give us, presented
by the printer in two columns, first a transliteration of the songs in the
Arrernte or Luritja language, under each verse of which he prints his
German *interlinear* translation – Schrott follows him up to that point
(Schrott 1992: 128) – and, in the second column, a translation into standard German. According to Aboriginal lore, the original Arrernte and
Luritja language texts offered in Carl Strehlow's books are both secret
and sacred.[16]

   Respecting cultural sensitivities, I present the four poems only in
their various translations, which provide a sufficiently clear impression
of their content and linguistic transformations.

   The Luritja song *Le Kangourou* is the first of the 79 poems in Béhar's
edition, the *Chanson du cacadou*, the Rain Song *À l'ouest des nuages végé-*

---

15 The songs are found in Vol. I, Teil III: *Die totemistischen Kulte der Aranda- und
Loritja-Stämme*. I. Abteilung: Allgemeine Einleitung und Die Totemistischen
Kulte des Aranda-Stammes (1910) and II. Abteilung: Die Totemistischen Kulte des
Loritja-Stammes (1911), 1.5, 54–56.
16 The original Arrernte and Luritja chants in Carl Strehlow's transcription have
recently been published in Stephen, McNamara & Goad 2006, 31–36.

tant [*In the West the Clouds Stagnate*] and the *Chanson du serpent* follow later as nos. 19 to 21. There follows in Béhar as no. 22 a short prose piece with the title *Un héro est avalé à l'ouest* [*A hero is swallowed in the west*] [Dachy reads *Un heron* ...] – suggesting that it is also of Luritja origin although I have not been able to identify it in Strehlow's texts. Apart from that, the story of a man swallowed by a sea-monster does not really relate to the Central Australian desert landscape. Béhar, following the cryptic note in the manuscript "dans une legende melapolynésique" [In a Melapolynesian legend] affirms in the Notes its provenance as: "Conte d'origine océanique d'après indication manuscrite" [Oceanian tale of origin according to manuscript information], however without giving the precise provenance of the original. In fact, Joris (2002: 27) and Schrott (1992: 128) present it as of Luritja origin, with Schrott (1992: 128) arbitrarily superimposing it onto an African mask. I would argue that the text has not been derived from an Australian source and have therefore disregarded it here.

Among Tzara's *Poèmes nègres* only a three-part Maori poem entitled *Toto-Vaca* – there are two more with the same title – is presented in the original language. According to Tzara, the poem was his own invention, presumably intentionally following the example of Hugo Ball's, Richard Huelsenbeck's, and Kurt Schwitters' *Klanggedichte* [*sound poems*], of which Ball's *Gadji Beri Bimba* performed during the First Dada Soirée on 14 July 1916, or his later *Karawane* are two of the earliest examples. However, Tzara has been found out. Browning asserts that it is definitely a Maori poem which Tzara seems to have taken from an as yet unidentified German language collection and, furthermore, has tried to give a translation of in nos. 40 and 79 which still remains a mixture of Maori and French (Béhar 1975: 454–56, 717–22 n12, n14, n19; Joris 2002: 29–30). Although I have not been able to track down the relevant source, we have to assume that the original was accompanied by a German translation. Carl Strehlow was much more meticulous in his work. However, we have no indication that he ever appreciated the cult songs as poetry.

When reading and comparing Tzara's rendering of four Aboriginal totemic songs in his *Poèmes Nègres* with the originals, it becomes obvious that he did not use Carl Strehlow's readable, and at the same time explanatory, translation into German for his own translation. He used the German interlinear version, which met his perception of authentic primitivism and primordiality emerging from the destruction of normal orderliness.

The texts in the following presentation, juxtaposing Carl Strehlow's two translations into German with my translation into English and Tzara's poetic rendering in French, will give the reader a chance to see and evaluate the various arguments regarding Tzara's Dada poetry advanced by others and myself. Obviously, the comparison of Tristan Tzara's poetry with Carl Strehlow's ethnographic work is only part of the evidence, just four poems out of 79. More work is clearly necessary.[17]

In order to make comparison of the texts easier, my first column presents Tristan Tzara's translation, the second Carl Strehlow's interlinear translation, the third my translation of that interlinear version, and the fourth Carl Strehlow's standardised version with my translation into English.[18]

---

17 Recent publications in Modernism studies include: Béhar 2005; Forcer 2006; Tzara 2006; Metzger 2007; Stephen, McNamara & Goad 2006, 31–36, where Carl Strehlow's transcriptions of the original Arrernte and Luritja songs are published together with my translations into English.

18 [Carl Strehlow's] Introduction to the Kuntanka-songs. They depict how in primeval times two Kangaroo-Tukutita or Totem-Gods, one of whom was speared in the tail, migrated to Nankali [i.e. Raincloud], a place situated from here toward the south-west (1). During this migration they hopped over a plain covered with thick grass; they tripped over the utungu-grass (2). After that they hopped over good firm ground (3) and came to a waterhole; after quenching their thirst there, they squirted water at each other to cool down (4). They continued wandering in the pebble-covered creek (5), munching flowers with bent backs (6) and reached Kaltjiti [i.e. White Mountain] (7). But because they saw a big fire on it, they ran on quickly and lay down in the shade of a manjiri [i.e. a kind of Mulga tree] (7–9). From here they came to Rebilka [i.e. Sleeping Place], where they scratched out a place for sleeping, the scratched out soil flying off widely (10). During the night they heard "beating" sounds which were produced by men who beat the ground heavily with their sticks (11). After that these Mallu-Tukutita with red bodies wandered on in the moonshine and came to a great rock cave into which they went, loosened their hair and lay down to sleep (12–16). The next day they wandered on between punpu-bushes and came to Nankali, where they left tail impressions on the ground and threw themselves down propped on their elbows (17–19). This

61

I. Tristan Tzara, Oeuvres Complètes I, 443–4, Loritja *Le Kangourou*	Strehlow I, III.ii, pp. 2–5 Carl Strehlow's interlinear version Loritja *Der Känguruh-Kultus*.[18] (Mallu Kuntanka.)	English interlinear version (WV)	Carl Strehlow's normalised translation & English version (WV)
1 Il écarta[19] la queue mouvante dans la queue il l'écarta	1 Beweglich speerte, Schwanz speerte.	1 Agile speared, Tail speared.	1 Den beweglichen [Schwanz] speerte er, The agile [tail] he speared, In den Schwanz speerte [er ihn]. In the tail he speared [him].
2 l'herbe les fait trébu-cher l'herbe outoungou	2 Gras stolpern machte, Utungu-Gras.	2 Grass tripping made, Utungu-grass.	2 Das Gras machte sie stolpern, The grass made them trip, Das Utungu-Gras [machte sie stolpern]. The utunga-grass [made them trip].
3 ici nous {tous les}[3] deux sur la bonne plaine / ici nous deux sur la bonne terre	3 Hier unser beider eben auf gutem / Hier unser beider auf Boden auf gutem.	3 Here our both level on good / Here our both on ground on good.	3 Hier [sind] beide auf gutem, ebenen [Boden], Here [are] both of us on good, flat [ground], Hier [sind] wir beide auf gutem Boden. Here [are] we both on good ground.

cult is performed in Nankali.
19 Probably a misunderstanding of *speeren* (to spear) as *sperren* (to extend, spread).
20 Brackets [] indicate emendations by Carl Strehlow; {} emendations by Marc Dachy in Tzara, 2006, going back to the manuscripts. All translations of Strehlow's texts are mine.

4 bu se baisser s'age-nouiller / se mouiller

5 le gravier cliquette / dans le {C}reek

6 ils mangent des fleurs en claquant la langue / et courbent le dos

7 sur la montagne blan-che la montagne blanche / ils sautillent vite

8 peut-être c'est {f}ʒeu, peut- être c'est feu / qui s'élargit montant sur la colline.

4 Getrunken niederbük-kend knieen, / Sich nass machen.

5 Steingeröll klappernd / In dem Creek ist.

6 Blumen Mund schmat-zen / Rücken gekrümmt war.

7 Der weiße Berg, der weiße Berg / Hüpften schnell weiter.

8 Feuer vielleicht ist, Feuer vielleicht ist, / Auf steigt Berg ausbreitete.

4 [Having] drunk bend-ing down kneeling, / Themselves wet making.

5 Stone pebbles rattling / In the creek are.

6 Flowers mouth munch-ing / Back bent down was.

7 The white mountain, the white mountain / Hopped quickly on.

8 Fire perhaps is, fire perhaps is, / Upraising mountain spread.

4 Nachdem sie im Knien getrunken haben, / After they have been drinking kneeling down, / Bespritzen sie sich mit Wasser. / They splash themselves with water.

5 Das Steingeröll klappert / The pebbles rattle, / In dem Creek [indem die Känguruh dar-über laufen]. / In the creek [while the kangaroos run over it].

6 Schmatzend fressen sie Blumen, / Munching they eat the flowers, / Nachdem sie ihren Rücken krummgebo-gen hatten. / After they had bent their backs.

7 Am weißen Berg, am weißen Berg / At the white mountain, at the white mountain / Hüpfen sie schnell vorüber. / They quickly hopped along.

8 Wahrscheinlich ist es Feuer, wahrschein-lich ist es Feuer, / Probably it is the fire, probably it is the fire, / Das aufsteigend sich auf dem Berg aus-breitete. / Which rising spread on the mountain.

9 ce sont {des} ventres / sous un arbre moulga	9 Bäuche sind / Manjiri[21] unter.	9 Bellies are / Manjiri under.	9 Mit ihren Bäuchen liegen sie With their stomachs they lie Unter einem Mulgabaum. Under a Mulga tree.
10 là c'est leur couche, leur couche / ils ont gratté la terre et l'ont jetée loin	10 Schlafplatz ist, Schlafplatz ist, / Ge- scharrt habend weithin geworfen.	10 Sleeping place is, sleeping place is, / Scratched having far thrown.	10 Hier ist ihr Schlafplatz, hier ist ihr Schlafplatz, Here is their sleeping place, here is their sleeping place, Wo sie beim Scharren die Erde weithin geworfen haben. Where they when scraping have thrown the soil far away.
11 avec leurs bâtons en l'est / ils donnent des nouvelles	11 Mit Stöcken im Osten / Sagen [sie] sagen [sie].	11 With sticks in the east / [They] say, [they] say.	11 Mit ihren Stöcken im Osten [den Boden schlagend] With their sticks in the east [beating the ground], Geben sie [den Känguruhs] Nachricht. They give [the kangaroos] notice.

---

21 A species of Mulga tree (*Ac. aneura*) with shiny leaves.

12 Im Scheine des zunehmenden Mondes erkennen sie den Weg, In the light of the waxing moon they recognise the way, Im Mondschein gingen die [Kanguruh] Männer weiter. In the light of the moon the [kangaroo] men went on.	12 Other moon apparent become the path Moon / men went.	12 Anderer Mond offenbar werden Weg Mond / Männer gingen.	12 une autre lune devient évidemment chemin / lune les hommes s'en vont
13 Ihre Körper sind rot, Their bodies [corpses] are red, Ihre Leiber sind rot. Their bodies [and souls] are red.	13 Body red, Body [and soul] red.	13 Körper rot, Leib rot.	13 corps rouges rouges
14 Der große Felsblock The great rock bolder Ist sehr hart. Is very hard.	14 Rock block / Very hard is.	14 Felsen Block / Sehr hart ist.	14 roc de granit est dur
15 O ihr spitzrückigen, o ihr spitzrückigen [Känguruhs] O you sharp-spined, o you sharp-spined[kangaroos], Geht in die Felsenhöhle hinein! Go into the rock cave!	15 Back pointing up, back pointing up / into the rock cave go into!	15 Rücken hervorstehend, Rücken hervorstehend/ in die Felsenhöhle geht hinein!	15 les dos pointus, les dos pointus / entrez dans la caverne

16 leurs cheveux épars, longs / tombent, tombent	16 Langes Haar aufgelöst, / Fällt herab, fällt herab.	16 Long hair released, / Falls down, falls down.	16 Ihr langes, aufgelöstes Haar Their long, untied hair Fällt [auf den Boden] herab, fällt [auf den Boden] herab. Falls down [to the ground], Falls down [to the ground].
17 ils courent, ils courent / sous les arbres pounpou	17 Punpu [Baum] unter / Umherwandern, umherwandern.	17 Punpu [tree] under / wandering around, wandering around.	17 Unter den punpu-Bäumen Under the punpu trees Wandern sie umher, wandern sie umher. They wander about, they wander about.
18 où sont ces arbres gommiers / battre avec la queue battre avec la queue	18 Wo Gummibäume[22.] jene? / Mit dem Schwanz schlug, mit dem Schwanz schlug.	18 Where gumtrees those? / With the tail beat, with the tail beat.	18 Wo sind jene Gummibäume? Where are those gumtrees? [Bei welchen sie] mit dem Schwanz [den Boden] schlugen. [Where they] beat[the ground] with the tail, beat the ground with the tail.
19 contre les arbres gommiers à l'écorce épaisse / ils poussèrent les coudes {se ruèrent avec}	19 Gummibäume dicke Rinde / Ellbogen speerten.	19 Gumtrees thick bark / Elbows speared.	19 Bei den Gummibäumen mit dicker Rinde Near the gumtrees with the thick bark Stießen sie den Ellbogen [in den Boden]. They pushed the elbow [into the ground].

22 *Gummibäume*: in botanical terms, Australian gumtrees are Eucalypts; the German *Gummibaum* denotes the *Ficus elastica*.

II. Tristan Tzara, Oeuvres Complètes I, 451[23]	Strehlow I, III.i, pp. 96–98 [Aranda][24]	English interlinear translation	Carl Strehlow's translation & English translation (WV)
Aranda *Chanson du cacadou*	Carl Strehlow's interlinear version		
1 ici pointes de branches certainement / ici des grains mêlés à la balle[25] certainement	1 "Hier Zweigspitzen gewiss, / Hier mit Spreu vermischte Samen, gewiss."	1 "Here branch tips certainly, / Here with chaff mixed seeds certainly."	1 "Wahrhaftig, hier [liegen Mulga]-Zweigspitzen, / "Truly, here are [lying] tips of [Mulga] branches, / Wahrhaftig, hier [liegen] mit Spreu vermischte Samenhaufen." / Truly, here [are lying] heaps of seeds mixed with chaff."

23 H. Béhar 1975: 717, fn 8; Dada I, Zurich, July 1917, 16–17.
24 [Carl Strehlow's] Introduction to the tjurunga song. It portrays how in primeval times several Cormorant totemic ancestors, who are represented by the two actors, broke off many tips of Mulga-branches [*ititja – Acacia aneura*] with seed pods in Kularata and piled them up and threshed them out in excavated depressions in the ground (*ankula*), where there is today a round lake; how after that they piled up the Mulga seeds in an enormous heap, roasted them in hot ash and milled them on flat stones while continuously licking their fingers (1–8). At the place where during primeval times the great heap of Mulga seeds had been heaped up, there is now a round lake enclosed by sandhills (9). After the Mulga pods are described in the following verses (10–11), at the end the white Cockatoo with pink breast and head feathers (*Cacatua leadbeateri* [Vijors, 1831]) is asked to crush and chew as many Mulga pods as possible (12).
25 *balle*: probably misunderstanding or shortcut for German (*Spreu-*)*Haufen*, English (*chaf-*) *bale*.
26 Not in ms.

67

2 sur la place creusée les poser / des amas des amas {y}[26] poser	2 Auf ausgehöhlten Platz hinlegen, / Haufen Haufen hinlegen.	2 On excavated place put down, / Heaps heaps put down.	2 Auf der Tenne schütten sie [die Samen] auf, They pile [the seeds] on an excavated place, Einen Haufen nach dem anderen schütten sie auf. One heap after another they pile up.
3 beaucoup d'amas poser/ des amas des amas poser / {des amas poser}[27]	3 Viele Haufen hinlegen, / Haufen Haufen hinlegen.	3 Many heaps put down, / Heaps heaps put down.	3 Viele Haufen schütten sie auf, Many heaps they pile up, Einen Haufen nach dem anderen schütten sie auf. One heap after another they pile up.
4 de grands amas poser	4 Haufen Haufen hinlegen, Große Haufen hinlegen.	4 Heaps heaps put down, / Big heaps put down.	4 Einen Haufen nach dem anderen schütten sie auf, One heap after another they pile up, Große Haufen schütten sie auf. Big heaps they pile up.
5 profonds amas poser {de}[28] grands amas poser	5 Tiefe Haufen hinlegen, / Große Haufen hinlegen.	5 Deep heaps put down, / Big heaps put down.	5 Hohe Haufen schütten sie auf, High heaps they pile up, Große Haufen schütten sie auf. Big heaps they pile up.

27 In ms.
28 Not in ms.

6 {s}ur un amas verser des noyaux germés[29] des noyaux germés	6. Auf einen Haufen aufschütten, Ausgewachsene Körner, ausgewachsene Körner.	6 On one big heap up, Fully grown seeds, fully grown seeds.	6 Auf einen Haufen schütten sie [alles] zusammen, On one heap they pile up [everything] together, Die reifen Körner, die reifen Körner [schütten sie auf]. The ripe seeds, the ripe seeds [they pile up].
7 des noyaux germés couchés[30] brunir / des noyaux germés couchés brunir	7 Ausgewachsene Körner stehend bräunten, / Ausgewachsene Körner stehend bräunten.	7 Fully grown seeds standing roasting. / Fully grown seeds standing roasting.	7 Die reifen Körner haben sie im Stehen geröstet, The ripe seeds they have roasted standing up, Die reifen Körner haben sie im Stehen geröstet. The ripe seeds they have roasted standing up.
8 des noyaux germés veulent frotter[31] / des noyaux germés veulent lécher	8. "Ausgewachsene Körner wollen reiben, / Ausgewachsene Körner wollen lecken."	8 "Fully grown seeds wanting to grind, / Fully grown seeds wanting to lick."	8 "Die reifen Körner wollen wir [zu Brei] zerreiben, "The ripe seeds we want to mill [into mash], Den aus reifen Körnern [hergestellten Brei] wollen wir lecken." [The mash produced] of ripe seeds we want to lick."

---

29 germés – ausgewachsen: TT translates – germinated; Strehlow means: fully grown, ripe.

30 couchés: lying down, Strehlow has: stehend.

31 Mistranslation: frotter – ab-reiben, Strehlow has zer-reiben.

9 ronde celle³² sur les collines de sable / ronde celle sur le sable	9 Rundes jenes auf Sandhügeln, / Rundes jenes auf Sandhügeln.	9 A round [waterhole] that one on sandhills, / A round [waterhole] that one on sandhills.	9 Ein rundes [Wasserloch] ist [jetzt] dort zwischen Sandhügeln [gelegen], Ein rundes [Wasserloch] ist [jetzt] dort zwischen Sandhügeln [gelegen]. A round waterhole is [now situated] there between sandhills, A round waterhole is [now situated] there between sandhills.
10 des gousses {cosses}³³ sont là / avec des cicatrices fouettées {il y a beaucoup qui dorment là}³⁴	10 Schoten liegen / Mit Narben versehen viele liegen.	10 Seedpods are lying, / With cicatrices scratched many are lying.	10 [Mulga]-Schoten liegen [dort], [Mulga] seedpods are lying [there], Viele mit Narben versehene [Mulga]-Schoten liegen [dort]. Many [Mulga] seedpods treated with cicatrices are lying [there].
11 dans les gousses sont là rangées / avec des cicatrices piquées couchées en ordre en ligne {file}	11 In den Schoten der Reihe nach liegen, / Mit Narben versehen in Reihen liegen.	11 In the seedpods in rows are lying, / With scratched scars in rows are lying.	11 In den Schoten liegen [die Körner] der Reihe nach, In the seedpods lie [the kernels] in rows, In den mit Narben geschmückten [Schoten] liegen sie der Reihe nach da. In the seedpods decorated with scars they lie in rows.

---

32 Probably misreading: Strehlow has *jenes*, I suggest that TT has *celui*.

33 In ms.

34 Not in Strehlow's text.

12 "mords, vraiment, oo blanc cacadou / beaucoup beaucoup mange, vraiment, oo blanc cacadou"	12 "Beiß ab, wirklich, o weißer Kakadu! / Sehr viel friss wirklich, o weißer Kakadu!"	12 "Bite off, really, o white Cockatoo! / Much eat, really, o white Cockatoo!"	12 "Beiß doch [die Schoten] ab, o weißer kakadu! "Bite off [the seedpods], o white Cockatoo! Friss doch nur sehr viele, o weißer Kakadu." Eat very many, o white Cockatoo."
III. Tristan Tzara, Oeuvres Complètes I, 451–52[35]	Strehlow I, III.ii, pp. 54–56 The Rain (kapi) Cult [Loritja]	English interlinear version (WV)	Carl Strehlow's translation & English translation (WV)
Tribu Loritja [Lòrage][36]	Carl Strehlow's interlinear version		

---

35 Béhar 1975:716, fn 9; Dada 2, Zurich, Dec. 1917, 12; some variations in the mss. autogr.

36 [Carl Strehlow's] Preliminary note. In contrast to Arrernte rain-songs which depict the rushing of a flood and the final drying up of the water, the rain-cult songs of the Luritja deal with the depiction of a storm which discharges over a vast claypan. The difference in the treatment of the subject matter by both tribes has its reason, as much as I know, in that in the area of the Luritja there are no big rivers like the Finke with its many big and small tributaries which during strong rain turn into torrents. It seems rather as if in early times the Luritja were pushed by the Arrernte into areas in Central Australia less favoured by rain where they had to rely mostly on water collected in claypans and springs emerging from rocks. Introduction to the Songs. These depict in vivid descriptions how the rain man in the west expands in the form of a black cloud; white clouds precede him which unfold like a flower (1,2); soon the rain pours over the mistletoe branches which are illuminated by lightning (3). The rain also streams through the ilbara [Mulga]-trees under which some boys are seeking shelter (4). With the cry "Woe is us! Woe is us!" they search for firewood, howling, because the rain has extinguished their fire; suddenly

1 là l'ouest des nuages végètent {végétant}[37] / se répandre à l'èst	1 Im Westen Regenwolke wachsend, / Nach Osten breitete sie sich aus.	1 In the west rain cloud growing, / Toward the east it extended.	1 Im Westen wuchs die schwarze Wolke an, / In the west a black cloud grew, / Nach Osten breitete [sie] sich aus. / Toward the east it spread out.
2 fleur se déplia /452 / blanc nuage se déplia	2 Blume entfaltet sich / Weiße Wolke entfaltet sich.	2 Flower unfolded itself, / white cloud unfolded itself.	2 Die Wolkenblume entfaltete sich, / The cloud flower unfolded itself, / Die weiße Wolke entfaltete sich. / The white cloud unfolded itself.
3 des branches de gui – pissat couler / éclair branches de gui	3 Mistelzweige Urin heranfließen, / Blitzen Mistelzweige.	3 Mistletoe branches urine flowing down, / Lightning mistletoe branches.	3 Wie Urin fließt [der Regen] von den Mistelzweigen herab, / Like urine flows [the rain] down from the mistletoe branches, / Der Blitz beleuchtet die Mistelzweige. / The lightning lights up the mistletoe branches.
4 coulent arbres ilbara touffus / tua	4 Herniederströmen ilbara [Bäume] dicht. / Erschlug.	4 Pouring down ilbara [trees] dense / Struck down.	4 [Der Regen] strömte hernieder durch die dichten ilbara-Bäume, / [The rain] flowed down through the dense ilbara-trees, / [Der Hagel] erschlug sie. / [The hail] struck them down.

lightning strikes (5–8). But on the claypan, above which the rain clouds have drawn together, there is a big collection of claypan-water. Growling the thunderstorm moves on (9,10). The name of the place where the thunderstorm has discharged is called Ngankali, i.e. "Rain Cloud".

37 Tzara 2006: 76.

5 vehée / pleurant immobile	5 Wehe uns! / Weinend standen.	5 Woe [is] us! / Crying standing.	5 Wehe uns! Woe is us! Heulten sie [indem sie] dastanden. They cried [while] standing there.
6 plus large sětend feu serre[38] / feu ayant vu presse feu[39]	6 Weiterziehend Feuer ausdrücken, / Wenig gesehen habend Feuer ausdrücken.	6 Moving on fire extinguishing, / Little having seen fire extinguishing.	6 Weiter ziehend löscht [der Regenmann] das Feuer aus, Moving on [the rain man] extinguishes the fire, Wo er ein kleines Feuer gesehen hat, löscht ers aus. Where he has seen a small fire, he extinguishes it.
7 couche élargi	7 Feuerholz aufladen, / Lagerplatz ausbreiten.	7 Firewood loading up, Resting place spreading out.	7 Feuerholz laden sie sich [auf den Kopf]. Firewood they load [on their heads], Im Lagerplatz breiten sie es aus. At their resting place they spread it out.
8 éclair frappe casse	8 Es blitzte, / Es schlägt ein.	8 It was lightning, / It strikes.	8 Es blitzte[stark], It flashed [strongly], Es schlägt ein. It strikes.

38 *plus large sětend* [growing larger/increasing]: TT misunderstood German *weiter ziehend*, English moving on.
39 *feu ayant vu*: German *wenig gesehen habend* suggests misreading ms. *feu < peu*.

Chanson du serpent	Carl Strehlow's interlinear version	English interlinear version (WV)	Carl Strehlow's translation & English translation (WV)
9 eau sur la surface d'argile[40]	9 Wasser auf Lehmebene stehend, Einander gegenüber waren.	9 Water on clay pan standing, Opposite each other [they] were.	9 Das Wasser steht auf der Lehmebene, The water is lying on the clay pan, Wo sich [die Wolken] gegenüber gestanden waren. Where [the clouds] stood opposite each other.
10 il rugissa continuellement éclair / tonnerre garde rancune.	10 Es brüllte, Fortwährend blitzen, / Grollen.	10 It roared, Continuously lightning, Growling.	10 Der Donner brüllte, The thunder roared, Es blitzt fortwährend, It flashes continuously, Der Donner grollt. The thunder growls.
IV. Tristan Tzara Oeuvres Complètes I, 452 Tribu Loritja	Strehlow I, III.i, p. 72 [41] [Aranda] Knarinja-Song[42]		

---

40 TT has omitted the next line in CS version, so do Joris and Schrott who, in addition, entitle the song without reason "Gesang der Frösche", [Song of the Frogs].

41 Aranda – obviously wrongly attributed by Tzara. Schrott does not give any reason for entitling the song "Gesang des Krähenwürgers" [Song of the Crow Strangler]. It is quite meaningless.

42 [Carl Strehlow's] Introduction to the tjurunga-song. Verse 1 depicts how the *knarinja*-song (knarinja, a non-poisonous snake; it has three other names: *inturkuna, latnara, latmara, ntalarka*) travels to her homeland, snaking forwards and thrusting her head

1 serpentant jeter en avant / se tordant jeter en avant	1 Schlängelnd voraus-werfen / Sich windend vorauswerfen.	1 Twisting itself throwing ahead / Snaking throwing ahead.	1 Schlängelnd wirft [die knarinja-Schlange ihren Kopf] vorwärts, Snakingly [the knarinja-snake] moves [her head] ahead, Sich windend wirft sie [ihren Kopf] vorwärts. Twisting she throws [her head] ahead.
2 peau de serpent se lève / au ciel se lève	2 Schlangenhaut sich erheben, / Am Himmel sich erheben.	2 Snakeskin lifting up, / At the sky lifting up.	2 Die Schlange erhebt sich, The snake rises, Sie hebt sich hoch in die Höhe. She lifts herself up high.
3 coeur battre continuellement / queue battre continuellement	3 Herz fortwährend schlagen, / Schwanz fortwährend schlagen.	3 Heart continuously beating, / Tail continuously beating.	3 Ihr Herz schlägt fortwährend, Her heart beats continuously, Ihr Schwanz schlägt fortwährend [den Boden]. Her tail beats continuously [the ground].
4 queue veut s'éteindre / queue veut remuer tremblant	4 "Schwanz will ab-sterben, / Schwanz will zitternd bewegen."	4 "Tails wants to die off, / Tails wants to trembling move."	4 "Mein Schwanz will absterben, "My tails wants to die, Mein Schwanz will sich zitternd [hin und her] bewegen." My tails wants to move twitchingly [to and fro]."

forwards; suddenly she jumps through the air (3) and settles down again; traveling on she makes impressions on the ground with her "heart" and her tail (4); dying she still twitches her tail to and fro.

In his reading, translation and interpretation of Australian Aboriginal songs, Tristan Tzara did not have the benefit of either anthropological training, or of adequate knowledge of Australian Aboriginal lore – although Carl Strehlow would have given him a good introduction. He also did not have the benefit of Ted Strehlow's publication of *Songs of Central Australia* (1971),[43] which is one of the few studies of Aboriginal songs that considers them not only in terms of their anthropological interest, but also as poetry. In 1916 there was no comprehensive history of Australian literature, and early literary studies make no reference to Aboriginal poetry (Byrne 1896), although there has been an explosion of Aboriginal literature, particularly since the Referendum in 1967, and it is considered to be a "rapidly developing literature in its own right" (Shoemaker 1989: 7). But even Penguin's more recent popular *The Literature of Australia since 1788* (Dutton 1964) ignores it and everything before that date completely, because "oral poetry" is by definition not literature. This was also the view of Henry Mackenzie Green when writing his massive *History of Australian Literature*, published first in 1962, which mentions Aboriginal poetry when reviewing writings by Australian anthropologists like A.P. Elkin under the rubric of "Philosophy, Psychology, the Sciences" (Green 1962: 892–94, 1452–54). In her revision for the second edition of 1984, Dorothy Green includes the anthropological works that had appeared after 1961, such as Ted Strehlow's *Songs*, under "Sciences". At this point she also introduces Carl Strehlow's works and gives a balanced appraisal of the Spencer-Strehlow controversy. In the *New Literary History of Australia* Stephen Muecke offers a brief but sensitive literary introduction to Aboriginal "oral literature" with reference to collections by anthropologists (Muecke 1988: 27–34). It was left to Rodney Hall in 1981 to include a few Aboriginal songs in *The Collins Book of Australian Poetry*, among them Arrernte chants from Ted Strehlow's book, and to Barry Hill to offer an illuminating introduction to and literary appreciation of *Songs* in his biography of Ted Strehlow (Hill 2002: 12–23). The dilemma in interpreting Aboriginal songs or art – are they

---

43 Theodor Georg Heinrich Strehlow (1908–1978), born in Hermannsburg, Central Australia, was lecturer, then reader of linguistics and finally professor of anthropology, at The University of Adelaide from 1946 to 1973; Hill, 2002, 488–99.

anthropological material only? Who are their owners? Who has the linguistic competence? – is still apparent in Hodge's and Mishra's 1991 postcolonial study (see also Shoemaker 1989: 265–79). The authors attempt, albeit with great hesitation, an interpretation of a more recent Aboriginal poem (Hodge & Mishra 1991: 92–95). They nevertheless fail to recognise its indebtedness to the form and aesthetics of traditional Aboriginal chants.[44] The entry "Song" by Linda Barwick in the 1994 *Encyclopedia of Aboriginal Australia* (Horton 1994: 1005–6, Vol. 2)[45], however, does emphasise their religious significance:

> When songs are performed correctly, in the appropriate ritual context, they are believed to tap the creative power of the Dreaming. Some songs are considered so powerful that they cannot be performed or even heard by people who do not have the appropriate training, for fear that their power may be misused. In Central Australia, there are gender-exclusive song series, and the witnessing of women's performances by men, or men's performances by women, is believed to cause severe illness or even death (Barwick 1994: 1005).

Although referring not to traditional ritual songs but to stories told/written by contemporary writers, I take what Morris has to say in her *EAA* entry "Oral Literature" as a summary of the difficulties an interpreter still encounters today:

> The meaning of Aboriginal 'oral literature' is almost impossible to convey to a non-Aboriginal audience. It contains information on how to live in the world as an intricately connected entity, while the non-Aboriginal world is about how to survive as a discrete entity. In contrast to Western ego-based society, it contains knowledge with no place for the ego. Even the term 'oral literature' is a contradiction, and Aboriginal people find themselves in a dilemma when they are faced

---

44 On earlier translations of Aboriginal chants see Hill 2002: 488 ff.
45 See also "Ceremony" (1, 188), "Religion" (2, 937–40), "Ritual" (2, 943–45) and "Song Cycle" (2, 106–07), "Storytelling" (2, 1033–34). In 1962, C.M. Bowra used the term "primitive song" to describe Aboriginal ritual poetry in *Primitive Song*. London: Weidenfeld and Nicolson, 1962, 42.3, 159.60, 226.38, specifically on Arrernte songs based on the work of Carl Strehlow and T.G.H. Strehlow.

with the arduous task of trying to write a piece of work in a format that Western readers find acceptable. When a Westerner reads, he/she brings a culturally constructed reading strategy to the interpretation of the text ... An area which is most contentious is that of the compilation of traditional stories that have been conveyed orally and then reinterpreted by non-Aboriginal people. There is a fundamental factor missing when this occurs: the association with the land. A story is separated from its roots in the land, changing its very nature. The land is an essential element in a traditional Aboriginal story (Morris 1994: 827–28).

Such statements seem to preclude any "literary" approach to Aboriginal song per se, let alone by a non-Aboriginal person. Thus even Ted Strehlow,[46] who laid claim to a special kind of aboriginality for himself, does not find it easy to jump the perceived divide between anthropology and poetry in his extensive seminal study. Taking his careful analyses of paradigmatic Arrernte chants performed in totemic rituals with regard to their formal, structural poetic devices and thematic elements as our guide, we may examine the composition of the Luritja Kangaroo-Cult Song in Carl Strehlow's and Tristan Tzara's translations to which I shall restrict my observations here. The basic composition is in couplets – other songs are in quatrains – in which the underlying story of the wanderings of the metamorphic, rather than zoomorphic, totemic ancestors, as outlined in Carl Strehlow's introduction, progresses in repetitions and parallelisms in which the second verse adds to or varies specific details of the first, thus enlarging the *visual* impression:

1.1 something moving has been speared,
1.2 it is the tail which has been speared;[47]
2.1 Grass makes them stumble,
2.2 it is Utungu grass;

---

46 See his extensive analyses in *Songs*, particularly Chapter 2, "The Language and Verse Structure", and Chapter 3, "Subject Matter and Themes of Songs", TGH Strehlow, 1971. See Hill's account of the development of the book in Hill, 2002.
47 As indicated earlier, I am at a loss to explain how and why Tzara "misunderstood" the German text.

they move on to the flat ground; they drink and get wet; pebbles rattle while they are moving through the creek-bed, they pass a white mountain quickly seeing a fire there; they take a rest under a mulga tree where they prepare a sleeping place. But assuming red human bodies – replacing the noun in verse 13.1 with a synonym in 13.2 – the Kangaroo-ancestors wander on over hard rock; they walk on until they find the entrance to a rock-cave into which they – showing their sharp backbones – are invited to go. With their long hair hanging down, they stroll under the punpu trees, looking for the gumtrees where they beat the ground with their tails and their elbows.

Sometimes the couplet is used to place a noun and an adjective that belong together into two separate lines:

3.1 flat and good,
3.2 ground;
14.1 rock,
14.2 hard;

alternatively, the second line may provide the reason for or consequence of an event in the first:

4.1 they drink,
4.2 they get wet;
5.1 the stone pebbles rattle,
5.2. (because) they run through the creek bed.

According to Ted Strehlow's observations, and applicable to the Kangaroo song, what remains the same in all ritual songs is that each individual couplet contains a complete thought and one scenic feature. The song is principally and primordially a naming act by the totemic ancestor that not only brings these features into existence, but more significantly, it is an act in which that same ancestor names himself. Because "these songs are believed to contain the actual words of supernatural personages," the "Central Australian clansmen in their ceremonies were interested in watching not human actors, but living impersonations of supernatural beings" (T.G.H. Strehlow 1971: 126f). This is the very reason why these songs are taken to be sacred and secret.

There is, however, on Ted Strehlow's part, a puzzling omission here in that his discussion of the poetical function of metaphor and the absence of simile does not attempt to find reasons for the lack of simile and the significance of this lack for the metaphors developed in the songs. When analysing another Kangaroo-ancestor song, he demonstrates at great length the technique of substituting words with "poetic synonyms," and "native equivalents of metaphors" (1971: 172) with "poetic paraphrases" (1971: 173), finding himself forced to insert " 'like' before such substitute words in order to indicate clearly that such comparison is intended" (1971: 174f). The poetic problem is that such insertion creates a simile where there is none in the original and obliterates the metaphor and its essential function in the song, namely, as asserted earlier, that of calling into being and naming. Representing replaces presenting. From the point of view of poetics, the Kangaroo-song literally realises the presence of the totem ancestors, their epiphany in the landscape of Central Australia.

Obviously, these are details of an interpretation Tristan Tzara would have been interested in only, I would like to argue, in so far as these Australian songs – like all the other songs he translated – presented in form, subject matter and performative quality a poetry totally different from the poetry of his own culture, of an in his view primordial originality untainted by European tradition and, therefore, paradigmatic for the totally new. It is the same poetic strategy great modernist poets after Dada, like Rilke, Pound and Benn among many others, would be using. The 'as if' had to be replaced by 'is.' Appraising Dada in 1919, Walter Serner, one of the most radical Dadaists in Zurich, wrote:

> Dadaism started everything anew. From it issued, finally, again after a long time, creations, a new, strong and genuine feeling for life. Therefore its existence alone was a dangerous front against everything effete that had become a stereotype … Above all its diffidence towards artistry, its contempt of the strictures of particular schools of art, its derision of doctrines (Serner, quoted in Meyer 1990: 119–20).[48]

---

48 See also Milch 1981–84, Vol. 2, 259 ff.

Tzara and the Zurich group were revolting against tradition and looking for originality and primordiality in the sense of "Ursprünglichkeit" [that which is originary], both in language and meaning. For the early phase of Dada in Zurich, nothing could have been more "primitive" and therefore literally more "original" and authentic than the poetry of the oldest living civilisation on earth, as Australian Aboriginal culture was described at the time by anthropologists and missionaries alike. Adapting and introducing its poetry to a world in crisis meant getting hold of the beginning of culture and civilisation and attempting a renewal. The absence of simile and the dominance of metaphor is the decisive element in the new poetry which tries to assert the metaphoricity of every word. For those reasons, Tzara did not translate Carl Strehlow's "normalised" translation, but instead the interlinear version, which offered in its compression a "distorted" syntax and rhythmical stammer close to the original. When Tzara published his *Vingt-cinq poèmes* [*Twenty-five poems*] with woodcuts by Hans Arp in the "Collection Dada" and read from it during the 7th Dada Soirée (23 July 1918), the "Soirée Tristan Tzara", W. Jolles reviewed the book, which did not contain any Indigenous poetry, and the performance the same day in the *Neue Zürcher Zeitung* as follows:

> Tristan Tzara has, together with Hans Arp, issued an attractively designed booklet: *Vingt-cinq poèmes* (published by the authors). It demonstrates that, for one, here the illustrations in the book do not emerge as foreign elements; on the contrary, Arp's woodcuts most definitely aid the reader's understanding. Much in these verses of Tzara is still chaos, a struggle with the word, clumsy stammer. Much too often the essential, the inner rhythm is missing. But even if the language is lost in primeval African sound, nevertheless a will, even if on a wrong track, opens up new vistas, to a formation of meaning in our diversity, an unmediated expression of our world of sensations in lieu of clichés of sensibleness which never come close to the essential things (Jolles, quoted in Meyer 1990: 141).

Furthermore, Dada is also a "performance art," and in the performance of Dada poetry – accompanied by continuous drumming[49] – some
critics recognise a social and political dimension of Dada's creativity of
meaning: "What emerges most clearly is the dissolution of syntax. Such
decay of the language order reflects the ruin of world order." This is the
central argument advanced by William H. Rey when assessing – long
after Dada – the Dada movement in his book *Poesie der Antipoesie*.[50] His
interpretation very much keeps to trends in literary theory of that time,
dominated by theoreticians like Theodor W. Adorno, foregrounding
the relationship between literature and society which manifests itself,
paradoxically, in the ruptures and silences in language (Adorno 1975:
49–68). However, such early form of deconstruction theory in literary
criticism is not invalidated when one realises that Hugo Ball, Richard
Huelsenbeck and Tristan Tzara, the literary protagonists of the Dada
movement in its early phases in Zurich, had – just like contemporary
painters and sculptors from Arp to Picasso – recourse to African and
Oceanian Indigenous art and poetry in order to return to perceived
universal sources of language and culture. Even if we consider their
efforts as an attempt at a cultural critique that failed, emerging during World War I and overrun by World War II, they were keeping to a
search for origins and new beginnings in a struggle for a revolution and
rejuvenation of European civilisation. The search for the "primitive" as
the primordial and starting point for the unknown and unexpected new
is the foundation myth of the Dada movement. The utopian and, given
the historical context of war in Europe, the eschatological foundations
cannot be overlooked. But the lure of the exotic offered more than an
escape from the cataclysm of the beginning of the 20th century.[51] The
poetry of four Australian Aboriginal ritual songs became part of Tristan
Tzara's attempt to gain access to the original sources of humanity and

---

49 For the program notes of the Gallery Dada Evening: *Alte und Neue Kunst* on 12
May 1917 see Schrott 1992: 105. The performance seems to have been a success:
"Der appetit für die mischung von instinktiver zusammenstellung und wilder
buschtrommel, deren vortrag erfolgreich war, zwang uns zur WIEDERHOLUNG
DER SOIRÉE" [The appetite for the mixture of instinctive compilation and primitive bushdrums, presented with success, forced us to REPEAT THE SOIRÉE].
50 Rey 1978; see also Béhar & Carassou 1990.
51 See Huelsenbeck & Tzara 1985.

the beginning of a new life. Marc Dachy's words, with which I wish to finish this essay, point to the importance of the role of Indigenous poetry in the emergence of Modernism in literature:

> Emerging in 1916 from the melting pot of abstract painting and avant-garde poetry, Dada was a crisis in art, a leap outside the ranks of "isms," a complete insurrection. Reinventing the mechanisms of creation and thought, a group of young artists fundamentally changed the world's conception of art. The incandescence and integrity of this individualistic revolt were to become the yardstick for all avant-garde art in the future (Tzara 2006: 11).

Bibliography

Adorno TW (1975). Rede über Literatur und Gesellschaft. In R Tiedermann (Ed), *Gesammelte Schriften*, Vol. 11, 49–68.

The Age, 13 March 2006, 7.

Albert-Birot P (Ed), (1980 [1916–19]). *SIC [Sons Idées Couleurs]*. Paris: Place.

Anderson GH (Ed) (1999). *Biographical Dictionary of Christian Missions*. Grand Rapids: Eerdmans Publishing Company.

Ball H (1919). *Zur Kritik der Deutschen Intelligenz*. Bern: Der Freie Verlag.

Ball H (1974). *Flight Out of Time: A Dada Diary*. J Elderfield (Ed). A Raimes (Trans.). New York: Viking Press.

Ball H (1984). *Der Künstler und die Zeitkrankheit: Ausgewählte Schriften*. HB Schlichting (Ed). Frankfurt: Suhrkamp.

Ball H (1992). *Flucht aus der Zeit*. Zurich: Limmat Verlag (originally Luzern: Stocker, 1946).

Ball H (1993). *Critique of the German Intelligentsia*. Brian L. Harris (Trans.). New York: Columbia University Press.

Barwick L (1994). Song. In D Horton (Ed), *Encyclopedia of Aboriginal Australia*. 2 Vols., Canberra: Aboriginal Studies Press, 1005.

Béhar H (1975). *Tristan Tzara: Oeuvres Complètes.* Paris: Flammarion.

Béhar H & Carassou M (1990). *Dada: Histoire d'une subversion.* Paris: Fayard.

Béhar H (2005). *Tristan Tzara.* Paris: Oxus.

Benjamin W (1966). *Literarische Essays.* Frankfurt: Suhrkamp.

Browning GF (1979). *The Genesis of the Dada Poem or from Dada to Aa.* Stuttgart: Akademischer Verlag Hans-Dieter Heinz.

Byrne D (1896). *Australian Writers.* London: Richard Benley & Son.

Cawthorn M (Ed), (2004). *Traditions in the Midst of change: Communities, Cultures and the Strehlow Legacy in Central Australia.* Proceedings of the Strehlow Conference, Alice Springs, 18–20 September 2002. Northern Territory Government: Strehlow Research Centre.

Clifford J (1988). *The Predicament of Culture: Twentieth Century Ethnography, Literature and Art.* Cambridge: Harvard University Press.

Dachy M (1994). *Dada & les dadaïsmes. Rapport sur l'anéantissement de l'ancienne beauté.* Paris: Éditions Gallimard.

Dachy M (2002). *Dada au Japon.* Paris: puf.

Dachy M (2006a). *Archives Dada: Chronique.* Paris: Éditions Hazan.

Dachy M (2006b). *The Revolt of Art.* London: Thames & Hudson.

Dickey B (Ed) (1994). *Australian Dictionary of Evangelical Biography.* Sydney: Evangelical History Association.

Dutton G (Ed), (1964). *The Literature of Australia.* Hammondsworth, Middlesex: Penguin Books.

Feest CF & Kohl KH (Eds) (2001). *Hauptwerke der Ethnologie.* Stuttgart: Kröner.

Forcer S (2006). *Modernist Song: The Poetry of Trsitan Tzara.* Leeds: Legenda.

Green HM (1962). *A History of Australian Literature Pure and Applied: a Critical Review of All Forms of Literature Produced in Australia from the First Books Published After the Arrival of the First Fleet until 1950.* Sydney: Angus & Robertson.

Hall R (1981). *The Collins Book of Australian Poetry*. Sydney: Collins.

Harms HF (2000). Die Arbeit in Australien und Neuseeland. In EA Lüdemann (Ed), *Vision: Gemeinde weltweit. 150 Jahre Hermannsburger Mission und Ev.-luth. Missionswerk in Niedersachsen*. Hermannsburg: Verlag der Missionshandlung, 445–90.

Hergenhan L (Ed) (1988). *New Literary History of Australia*. Ringwood: Penguin.

Hill B (2002). *Broken Song: TGH Strehlow and Aboriginal Possession*. Sydney: Knopf.

Hodge B & Mishra V (1991). *Dark Side of the Dream: Australian Literature and the Postcolonial Mind*. Sydney: Allen & Unwin.

Horton D (Ed) (1994). *The Encyclopedia of Aboriginal Australia*. 2 Vols., Canberra: Aboriginal Studies Press.

Huelsenbeck R (Ed) (1987). *Dada: Eine literarische Dokumentation*. Hamburg: Rowohlts Enzyklopädie.

Huelsenbeck R & Tzara T (1985 [1920]). *Dada siegt! Bilanz und Erinnerung*. Hamburg: Nautilus.

Janco M. *Revue d'avant-garde*, Part IV, 8.

Joris P (2002). *4 x 1: Tristan Tzara, Rainer Maria Rilke, Jean-Pierre Duprey, Habib Tengour*. Albany: Inconundrum Press.

Kenny A (2005). A Sketch Portrait: Carl Strehlow's German Editor Baron Moritz von Leonhardi. In A Kenny & S Mitchell (Eds), *Collaboration and Language*. Strehlow Research Centre Occasional Paper Number 4. Alice Springs: Northern Territory Government, 54–70.

Kenny A & Mitchell S (Eds) (2005). *Collaboration and Language*. Strehlow Research Centre Occasional Paper Number 4. Alice Springs: Northern Territory Government.

Kneebone H (2001). Was hat die gegenwärtige Mission für die Sprachwissenschaft geleistet? Missionare und die vergleichende Philologie im 19. Jahrhundert. In R Wendt (Ed), *Sammeln, Vernetzen, Auswerten, Missionare und ihr Beitrag zum Wandel europäischer Weltsicht*. Tübingen: Narr, 145–72.

Lee M & Meng H (Eds) (1997). *Cultural Dialogue and Misreading*. Sydney: Wild Peony Press.

Leske E (1986 [1977]). *Hermannsburg: A Vision and a Mission*. Adelaide: Lutheran Publishing House.

Lüdemann EA (Ed) (2000). *Vision: Gemeinde weltweit. 150 Jahre Hermannsburger Mission und Ev.-luth. Missionswerk in Niedersachsen.* Hermannsburg: Verlag der Missionshandlung.

Metzger R (2007). *Berlin in the 20s: Art and Culture 1918–33.* London: Thames & Hudson.

Meyer R (1990). *Dada in Zürich: Die Akteure, die Schauplätze.* Frankfurt: Luchterhand (originally Zurich: Arche, 1985).

Milch T (Ed) (1981–84). *Walter Serner, Gesammelte Werke.* 10 Vols. München: Goldmann.

Moeller MM (Ed), (2002). *Emil Nolde: Expedition in die Südsee.* Berlin: Brücke Archiv.

Moeller MM (Ed) (2006). *Brücke-Museum Berlin: Malerei und Plastik.* Berlin: Publication of the Brücke Museum.

Morris C (1994). Oral Literature. In D Horton (Ed), *Encyclopedia of Aboriginal Australia.* 2 Vols., Canberra: Aboriginal Studies Press, 827–28.

Muecke S (1988). Aboriginal Literature: Oral. In L Hergenhan (Ed), *New Literary History of Australia.* Ringwood: Penguin, 27–34.

Paulhan J (1913). *Les hain-tenys Marinas.* Paris: Genthner.

Petermann W (2004). *Die Geschichte der Ethnologie.* Wuppertal: Hammer.

Reuther JG & Strehlow C (1897). jaura jinkinietja wulana, *Testamenta Marra. Jesuni Christuni Ngantjani Jaura ninaia karitjimalkana wonti Dieri jaurani.* Tanunda: G. Auricht.

Rey WH (1978). Poesie der Antipoesie. Moderne deutsche Lyrik: Genese, Theorie, Struktur. Poesie und Wissenschaft XXI. Heidelberg: Stiehm.

Ritchie J (Ed) (1990). *Australian Dictionary of Biography*, Vol. 12, Melbourne: Melbourne University Press.

Sanouillet M (Ed) (1976). *DADA: Réimpression intégrale et dossier critique de la revue publiée de 1916 à 1922 par Tristan Tzara.* 2 Vols. Nice: Centre du XXe siècle.

Schild M (2004). Heading for Hermannsburg: Notes on Carl Strehlow's Early Career Path. In W Veit (Ed), *The Struggle for Souls and Science. Constructing the Fifth Continent: German Missionaries and Scientists.* Occasional Paper Number 3, Northern Territory Government: Strehlow Research Centre, Alice Springs, 51–58.

Schuhmann K (Ed) (1991). *sankt ziegenzack springt aus dem ei. Texte, Bilder und Dokumente zum Dadismus in Zurich, Berlin, Hannover und Köln.* Köln: Kiepenheuer.

Schrott R (Ed) (1992). *DADA 15/25: Post Scriptum oder die Himmlischen Abenteuer des Hrn Tristan Tzara und ein Suspensarium von Gerald Nitsche zu Elde Steeg & Raoul Hausmann.* Innsbruck: Haymon-Verlag.

Sheppard R (Ed) (1981). *New Studies in Dada: Essays and documents.* Driffield: Hutton Press.

Shoemaker A (1989). *Black Words, White Page. Aboriginal Literature 1929–88.* Brisbane: University of Queensland Press.

Stephen A, McNamara A & Goad P (Eds) (2006). *Modernism in Australia: Documents on Art, Design and Architecture 1917–67.* Melbourne: Miegunyah Press.

Strehlow C (1907–20). *Die Aranda und Loritja-Stämme in Zentral-Australien.* Publications of the Völker-Museum Frankfurt am Main, edited by the directors, 7 Vols. Frankfurt: Baer.

Strehlow TGH (1969). *Journey to Horseshoe Bend.* Sydney: Angus & Robertson.

Strehlow TGH (1971). *Songs of Central Australia.* Sydney: Angus & Robertson.

Tythacott L (2003). *Surrealism and the Exotic.* London: Routledge.

Tzara T (1963). *Lampisteries précédées des Sept manifestes Dada quelques dessins de Francis Picabia.* Paris: J.-J. Pauvert.

Tzara T (1981). *Seven Dada manifestos and lampisteries.* B Wright (Trans.), illustrations by F Pacabia. London: Calder Publications.

Tzara T (1984). *Sieben Dada-Manifeste*. Übers. von Pierre Gallissaires, 3. Verb. Aufl., Hamburg: Ed. Nautilus.

Tzara T (2006). *Découverte des arts dits primitives: Suivi de Poèmes nègres de Tristan Tzara* (Préfacier par M. Dachy). Paris: Éditions Hazan.

Veit W (1990). Strehlow, Carl Friedrich Theodor. In Ritchie (Ed), *Australian Dictionary of Biography*, Vol. 12, Melbourne: Melbourne University Press, 121–22.

Veit W (1997). Misunderstanding as Condition of Intercultural Understanding. In M Lee & H Meng (Eds), *Cultural Dialogue and Misreading*. Sydney: Wild Peony Press, 163–74.

Veit W (2004a). Labourers in the Vineyard or the Uneducated Missionary. In M Cawthorn (Ed), *Traditions in the Midst of Change: Communities, Cultures and the Strehlow Legacy in Central Australia*. Proceedings of the Strehlow Conference, Alice Springs, 18–20 September 2002. Northern Territory Government: Strehlow Research Centre, 136–50.

Veit W (Ed) (2004b). *The Struggle for Souls and Science, Constructing the Fifth Continent: German Missionaries and Scientists*. Occasional Paper Number 3, Northern Territory Government: Strehlow Research Centre, Alice Springs.

Veit W (2005). *"Arbeiter im Weinberg" oder "Der ungebildete Missionar": Aspekte der nicht-theologischen Bildung der Missionare*. Berliner Beiträge zur Missionsgeschichte 8, Berlin: Wichern Verlag.

Verkauf W, Janco M & Bollinger H (Eds) (1958). *Dada: Monographie einer Bewegung*. Teufen: Niggli.

Völker H (2001). Missionare als Ethnologen: Moritz von Leonhardi, australische Mission und europäische Wissenschaft. In R Wendt (Ed), *Sammeln, Vernetzen, Auswerten, Missionare und ihr Beitrag zum Wandel europäischer Weltsicht*. Tübingen: Narr, 173–218.

Weisgerber J (Ed) (1984). *Les Avant-gardes littéraires au XXe siècle*. 2 Vols. Budapest: Akademiai Kiado.

Wendt R (Ed) (2001). *Sammeln, Vernetzen, Auswerten: Missionare und ihr Beitrag zum Wandel europäischer Weltsicht*. Tübingen: Narr.

II
Living the Mission:
Religious Disseminations

3
Carl Strehlow's Mission

Anna Kenny

Although Carl Strehlow's success in converting the Arrernte and Luritja[1] to Christianity at the Lutheran Finke River Mission in Central Australia was modest and a constant frustration to him, he managed to impose strong patriarchal structures deriving from his own cultural setting upon the small flock that had seemingly accepted the gospel around 1900 and stayed voluntarily at the mission. Dr Herbert Basedow described this regime in a report on his medical inspection of Hermannsburg:

> In Pastor Strehlow the Mission possesses a man who during his twenty-five years sojourn at Hermannsburg has mastered the aboriginal's [sic] language and his peculiar ways. As a disciplinarian he has established himself at the head of the tribal group he manages, and even in quarrels and feuds of the bitterest nature his word is and must be final. Moreover the religion taught is sincere and not overdone. I have visited mission-stations in most parts of Australia but must confess that none has impressed me so much as Hermannsburg (Basedow 1920–22: 22).

In the following essay I explore some aspects of the origins of these European authoritarian structures that lasted for the better part of the 20th century at the Finke River Mission, and the likely factors that allowed their effective establishment at Hermannsburg, despite the merely moderate success of the mission work. Carl Strehlow's ideas and views were mainly formed by his training at the Neuendettelsau Mission Seminary, where a specific form of Lutheran mission theology was

---

1 The orthography of Arrernte and Luritja words follows the Western Arrernte and Luritja spelling systems developed by the Institute for Aboriginal Development.

Hermannsburg Mission looking south, Central Australia, circa 1890s. Source:
Strehlow Research Centre.

propagated. The main elements of this theology stemmed from Wilhelm
Löhe's "innere und äußere Mission" [Inner and Outer Mission] theory
and Bauer's concept of "Bedürfnislosigkeit" [lack of needs/desires] and
conversion by individual free choice.

Based on the ideological premises of this theological approach, Carl
Strehlow tried to reproduce a Lutheran world in the Arrernte space to
which he had been posted. The reproduction and reinforcement of social structures from his own background were to a certain degree aided
by his impressive knowledge of the Arrernte and Luritja languages,
cultures and societies. His ethnographic masterpiece, *Die Aranda- und
Loritja-Stämme in Zentral-Australien* [*The Aranda and Loritja Tribes of
Central Australia*], shows that he had engaged profoundly with the people to whom he had been sent to serve. The data he had acquired could
only have been transmitted during a long-term, reciprocal engagement
with an Indigenous society. However, an underlying desire for comfort
and the familiar in an utterly strange world would also have helped to
motivate him to recreate his own world. Nearly ten years after he had
arrived in Central Australia, he still felt foreign:

One sometimes feels rather lonely at such a remote post, even though one knows that God is with us even at the end of the world; one feels very foreign living with a people with completely different views and customs. Our work is not without success, though we often do not see much of it. On the surface the church is present; the church is visited regularly, the sacrament given and received, but Christianity is making little progress here … If one wanted to make a summary of the state of the mission work, one would say: Heathenism is still a great power, towards which Christianity feels still very weak, in particular because heathenism exerts great attraction on the Christians here due to its entertainment value.[2]

Training at the Neuendettelsau Mission Seminary

Entering the Neuendettelsauer Missionsanstalt [Neuendettelsau Mission Seminary] in 1888, Carl Strehlow (1872–1922) was one of the youngest students to be educated and trained there. The pastor of his birthplace Fredersdorf, Carl Seidel, had recognised the outstanding talents and potential of the child. He prepared Strehlow for entering a seminary with great dedication and effort, teaching him the basics of the classical languages, mathematics, geography, world history and correct German syntax and orthography. His protégé needed these in order to be competitive against the other applicants to the seminary who came primarily from the gymnasium stream of schooling – academically demanding secondary schools that provided their students with a classical education. Until World War I, most seminarians at Neuendettelsau had attended a gymnasium (Pilhofer 1967: 29). Strehlow was indebted to Seidel and remained in touch with his early teacher and mentor throughout his life, as he did with the seminary.[3]

The selection process at Neuendettelsau was rigorous (Koller 1924;

---

2 Carl Strehlow to Inspector Deinzer, Hermannsburg 8 January 1901 (Neuendettelsau Archiv, Germany), A. Kenny (Trans.).
3 The seminary was considered a home base. Many missionaries returned to Neuendettelsau to teach or upon their retirement. In the 1950s, Frieda Strehlow went to Neuendettelsau to spend her last days: her brother, Christian Keysser, had become the director of Neuendettelsau. Even today, Neuendettelsau still has

Hermannsburg Mission, Central Australia, circa 1920s.
Source: Strehlow Research Centre 6580.

Pilhofer 1967). The criteria for successful applicants included a high level of secondary education, as well as a strong personality and excellent health. The intense course lasted three years with a very challenging and dense curriculum. The expectations and the pressure were immense, imposed both by the seminary, as well as by the students upon themselves. Nervous breakdowns, it seems, were not unusual (Pilhofer 1967: 29).

Not all institutions that trained missionaries had Neuendettelsau's classical orientation. Neuendettelsau gave its students a broad education in the humanities, including the Classics and languages (Moore 2003: 23). Greek, Latin and Hebrew were taught to prepare the missionaries for their language tasks. This linguistic training laid a solid foundation for the students to recognise and deal with structures of further foreign languages, which facilitated the systemisation of grammars and compilation of dictionaries – essential for the translation of

a number of elderly missionaries who meet on a regular basis; at these gatherings Indigenous languages are often heard.

94

the Holy Scripture[4] and mission preaching and schooling. Byproducts of these intense language studies were not only grammar manuals and dictionaries of Indigenous languages, but also major collections of ethnographic data. The German Lutheran linguistic tradition based on Luther's view that the gospel was to be preached in vernaculars and translated into the mother tongues of peoples (Wendt 2001: 8) influenced their approach towards Indigenous peoples. Among German missionaries, it went without saying that the knowledge of the respective Indigenous language(s) – the vernacular – was the prerequisite for successful mission work.

As a consequence, in the 19th century it was characteristic of German Protestant mission theology and practice to pay particular attention to a people's language and its idiomatic and cultural implications (Schild 2004: 54). German missionaries in Australia brought their linguistic tradition with them. As soon as the mission staff had managed to acquire a moderate proficiency in the vernacular, Lutheran missionaries at Bethesda and Hermannsburg used the Indigenous languages in church services and in schools. Lessons were conducted in German and English as well (Moore 2003: 24). This ready and constant deployment of language meant that the missionaries were constantly developing their proficiency, moving towards the point where their skills would have become sufficiently developed to begin the translation task. Translation required familiarity with idiom, and generally, this came only through immersion and also through trial and error.

Upon arrival at Bethesda Mission near Lake Eyre in 1892, Carl Strehlow immediately started to study the local language and translated the New Testament into Diyari with Missionary J.G. Reuther. According to Otto Siebert, a co-missionary of both Strehlow and Reuther's son, the linguistic achievements at Killalpaninna were predominately Strehlow's.[5] At Hermannsburg he became fluent in Arrernte within months and preached in the vernacular (Schild 2004, Eylmann 1908). In 1896,

---

4 A house tradition of the Neuendettelsau Mission Seminary was to use the Greek source for translation (pers. comm. Dr Hauenstein of the Neuendettelsau Missionswerk, August 2005).
5 Tindale interviewed O. Siebert and J.G. Reuther's son in the 1930s (Tindale Collection Acc No 1538, SA Museum Archives).

Carl Strehlow's winter semester timetable 1890–91.
Source: Archive of Neuendettelsauer Missionswerk.

only two years after Strehlow's arrival on Arrernte territory, Gillen re-
marked in a letter to Spencer that "Rev Strehlow" spoke the language
of the Finke very well (Mulvaney, Morphy & Petch 2001: 118–19). He
compiled an Arrernte Service Book, published in 1904; it was called
Galtjindintjamea-Pepa Aranda Wolambarinjaka and included 100
German hymns translated into Arrernte.[6] By the end of 1909 he had
compiled an ethnographic masterpiece, the above-mentioned *Die
Aranda- und Loritja-Stämme in Zentral-Australien*. In his final period
in Hermannsburg between 1913 and 1919, Carl Strehlow translated the
New Testament into Arrernte.[7] Parts of it were published after his death
(Hebart 1938: 317) as *Ewangelia Lukaka* (1925) and *Ewangelia Tarama-
tara* (1928), without, however, mentioning him as the translator.

6 This work was partially based on Kempe's catechism. Strehlow had been able
to draw on published and unpublished Arrernte language material. The Strehlow
Research Centre (SRC) and Lutheran Archives Adelaide (LAA) hold unpublished
material by Kempe produced between1877–91. See Carl Strehlow's letters to Kaibel (1899–1909), Schild 2004, J. Strehlow 2004: 83.
7 Carl Strehlow's letter to the Mission Friends, 9 January 1920 (Albrecht Collection
Acc. No. AA662, SA Museum Archives).

The Inner and Outer Mission

Neuendettelsau had its own style of mission theology based on Wilhelm Löhe's view of the "innere und äußere Mission" [Inner and Outer Mission]. This approach did not have a mission to Indigenous peoples as its pre-eminent goal.[8] The Inner Mission, according to Löhe, was to hold the Lutheran congregation together through general pastoral care that would keep them from flagging in their commitment. The Outer Mission had the task of finding people to be baptised, which included both Germans and Indigenous peoples. Once baptism was accomplished, the Outer Mission automatically led back into the Inner Mission that saw its role as not only that of recruiting converts, but also of caring for the congregation. This included education, and providing and sustaining pastoral assistance (Weber 1996: 353, 360). It was viewed as a responsibility of the mission. The mission was thus an ongoing commitment that stretched well beyond mere conversion (the result of the Outer Mission).

Wilhelm Löhe (1808–72) seems to have originally founded the Neuendettelsau Mission Seminary with an emphasis on the Inner Mission. Missionaries were sent out to take care of existing Lutherans and their communities in North America. It was thought that the role and practice of religion in these Lutheran communities was deteriorating due to the lack of Lutheran clerics. Löhe was principally concerned with the care of German diaspora communities (Koller 1924; Pilhofer 1967). From North America, disturbing, even shocking reports, had reached Löhe and other Lutheran clerics regarding perfectly righteous and devout Christian parents who had up to 11 unbaptised children due to the absence of qualified clergy. The German migrants were growing up "like the Indians". The dispersion and spiritual "decrepitude" [Verwahrlosung] in America proved to be far greater than initially anticipated, so that the Inner Mission amongst Germans took precedence. However, Löhe could mention Indian and German heathen parents in the

---

8 Wilhelm Löhe is seen today as one of the fathers of World Lutheranism. However, he was also a crucial figure in the development of social institutions and education. During his lifetime, the state was not particularly engaged in social activities and this was largely left to the churches' care. See Weber 1996: 15, Schlichting 1998: 7 and Farnbacher & Weber 2004.

Neuendettelsau Mission House, Southern Germany (Koller 1924: 39).

same breath, indicating that the agenda was set (Weber 1996: 346). The broader pastures of North America were soon beckoning. By 1888, "The Society for the Inner Mission" added 'Outer' to its name (Schlichting 1998: 5). The *Gesellschaft für die Innere (und Äußere) Mission [The Society for the Inner (and Outer) Mission]* still exists today and has again turned its attention to the Inner Mission.[9]

For Löhe the Inner and Outer Mission were parts of the same issue and church (Weber 1996: 343). Hence, missionaries and pastors received the same education at Neuendettelsau. The concepts relating to the Inner Mission would have been transferred immediately into the Indigenous context, in which after the Outer Mission had recruited new members, they would quickly become a Lutheran community with the potential for an Inner Mission. Therefore, the members of such a community were treated similarly to any other member of a Lutheran community, regardless of their colour or culture.

Löhe's mission theology was taught to the students of the Neuendettelsau institution by F. Bauer and later on by the Deinzer brothers, university graduates, who integrated this theology into their broader

---

9 For more information, see www.gesellschaft-fuer-mission.de.

98

academic program. Bauer had gained fame by writing an excellent grammar manual of the German language that was republished 14 times during his lifetime alone (Pilhofer 1967: 11). He also drafted the two basic manuscripts – *Entwurf einer christlichen Dogmatik auf lutherischer Grundlage* [*An Outline of Lutheran Christian Dogmatics*] and *Entwurf einer christlichen Ethik auf lutherischer Grundlage* [*An Outline of Lutheran Christian Ethics*] – pertaining to theological studies in Lutheran dogmatics and ethics. The style was much influenced by Löhe, but also included Bauer's own views on education as the route to individual freedom and "Bedürfnislosigkeit" [lack of needs/desires] (Pilhofer 1967: 18–19). These were regarded as general conditions of ethical value that were equally relevant to both the Inner and Outer Missions. Free will and individual choice were of paramount importance in the educational philosophy at Neuendettelsau, and a key element in its mission theology. During a six-month probation period, recruits had to prove that they were absolutely certain of their calling if they were to be confirmed as permanent.

In Carl Strehlow's mission approach, individual "free choice" and true firm conviction were formative concepts. He perceived the Indigenous people at Hermannsburg as individual human beings who could make free choices regarding their circumstances. Strehlow only accepted converts if they were firmly convinced that they wanted to take this step, that their decision and their commitment were based on free individual choice, or if they could convince him of their sincerity. Conversion and confirmation allowed Indigenous people to participate at Hermannsburg as full members of the Lutheran community (which included rights and responsibilities). In fact, he often discussed free will and conversion in his letters to his superiors in the south between 1895 and 1922, and often referenced it in his contributions to the *Kirchlichen Mitteilungen*.[10] The educational philosophy at the Neuendettelsau Mission Seminary, its theological style and social structure all made a

---

10 The *Kirchlichen Mitteilungen* [*Church Notes*] was Neuendettelsau's monthly church newspaper. It reported on the mission work in North America, Australia and New Guinea. However, it also published letters and sometimes even brief accounts of Indigenous languages, beliefs and customs.

major impression on Strehlow when he entered as a young, bright and enthusiastic 17-year-old.

At the time of Carl Strehlow's attendance there, the seminary's mission theology was taught by Dr Johannes Deinzer. He was particularly interested in the Outer Mission and ethics – in reaching out to those who remained unconverted, and was not so engaged with the Inner Mission that catered for existing and lapsed Lutherans. Thus, linguistic training was prioritised to facilitate this task, and through language an interest in culture could emerge; in both German mainstream thinking as well as in Lutheranism, language was believed to contain the *Volksgeist*[11] of a people.

Johannes Deinzer's particular concern may have led Carl Strehlow in this direction. As the main teacher and director at Neuendettelsau until 1897, Deinzer expanded interest in the Outer Mission to encompass Australia and Papua New Guinea (Koller 1924: 17). It was under him that the first graduates of Neuendettelsau were sent to Australia. By 1914 about 40 had gone to Australia, the majority as pastors for the German immigrants in Australia (Pilhofer 1967: 22). Deinzer had another interest that may have influenced Strehlow: ethics. He placed heavy emphasis on ethics in his classes and favoured students who could follow his intellectual path (Pilhofer 1967: 23). He considered ethics to be more important than dogmatics, because it allowed interpretation. The dogmatic and ethics texts drafted by Bauer were the main texts for the students which he and, to a limited degree, his brother edited and expanded. These works had to be copied by hand by all students, for

---

11 Johann Gottfried Herder (1744–1803), the founder of German historical particularism, was interested in the differences of cultures from age to age, and from one people to another, and coined the term *Volksgeist*. Herder's concepts of *Volk*, a cultural group or entity, and *Volksgeist*, the individual expression of the being of a group which sets it apart from others, provided the basis for this particularism. The *Volksgeist* of a people, he believed, was embodied in their language and their literature, which included the oral traditions of Indigenous peoples. The word *Geist* is very difficult to translate, because its semantic field and the underlying concept is vast. Literally it means ghost or spirit, however in this context it means something like "the essence of a people" or "the mind and spirit of a people". See Kenny 2005: 56.

the *Christliche Ethik auf lutherischer Grundlage*[12] only appeared in print in 1904 (Koller 1924: 82). The treaty on dogmatics was published in 1921 (Pilhofer 1967: 18). Notwithstanding the rigours of these scholarly tasks, Deinzer's interest in ethics, encouraged among his students, may have directed their missionary task to humane engagement with others – an interest in the other person as much as in pious formulae. It is likely that Strehlow's propensity to acknowledge the human dignity of others, including Indigenous Australians, was encouraged by Deinzer's classes. Veit (1991; 2004a) as well as Schild (2004) write that Neuendettelsau advocated a humanistic approach towards others, which was related to Warneckian thinking.

Like many other theologians, clerics and missionaries, Dr Gustav Warneck, a Lutheran professor at Halle University,[13] stressed the importance of learning local languages to enable missionaries to spread God's word (Wendt 2001: 8; Veit 2004a). The nucleus of his thinking on anthropology (Warneck 1897: 278–304) was that Christianity had universal attributes applicable to all peoples and could thus be adapted to all ethnic, social, cultural and state constellations (Warneck 1897: 279). In his view, all humans during all times, climates, and cultures had religion and language (Warneck 1897: 285). He maintained that since there

---

12 The full title reads: *Christliche Ethik auf lutherischer Grundlage. (Zunächst für die Schüler der Neuendettelsauer Missionsanstalt.) Entworfen von Missionsinspektor F. Bauer. Umgearbeitet und vermehrt von Missionsinspektor Joh. Deinzer. Revidiert und in den Druck gegeben von M. Deinzer, Inspektor der Missionsanstalt in Neuendettelsau. Neuendettelsau 1904: Im Selbstverlag der Missionsanstalt.* [*Christian Lutheran Ethics*]. (*In the first instance for pupils of the Neuendettelsau Mission Seminary.*) *Drafted by Mission Inspector F. Bauer. Revised and expanded by Mission Inspector Joh. Deinzer. Edited and published by M. Deinzer, Inspector of the Mission Seminary in Neuendettelsau. Neuendettelsau 1904: Self-published by the Mission Seminary*].

13 Warneck was one of the main Lutheran scholars of mission studies and well known in 19th-century German missionary circles. He was a prolific writer on mission topics. In 1874, he founded the *Allgemeine Missionszeitschrift* [*Global Mission Journal*], and was its editor for decades (*Lueker* 1954: 1120). This journal published ethnographic material from all over the world, as well as theological and other theoretical treatises. Warneck's main thoughts on mission work were synthesised in *Evangelische Missionslehre: Ein missionstheoretischer Versuch* (1897) [*Evangelical Mission Doctrine: From the Perspective of Mission Theory*].

were no peoples in the world who were speechless, there could also be no people who were without religion. This was evident in the fact that the gospel could be preached in all languages and all languages were capable of Bible translation.

Warneck used German anthropological literature of the time by eminent scholars such as Waitz, Ratzel and Müller to support his theological views; he maintained that the unity of mankind was also an ethnological fact. He wrote, "[h]umanity is a unity, despite its multitude" (Warneck 1897: 285). His views were consistent with those of Herder and Humboldt. He maintained that humanity's spiritual and intellectual unity was particularly manifest in languages, which were a common feature among all humankind. He was also of the view that each language is a masterpiece of *"Geist"* [spirit and intellect] (Warneck 1897: 286). He postulated that there were no peoples with an inferior language and that the word of God (due to its universality) could be translated into any language and communicated in any language. Owing to this universality of a spiritual propensity towards Christianity, in Warneck's view it was never necessary to destroy a culture in order for its people to become Christian converts (Warneck 1897: 282). Rather, the objective was to learn about them so that Christian thinking could be conveyed in the appropriate language and through cultural concepts with which the respective people could identify. He wrote that "the Christian mission rejects emphatically the conscious or unconscious amalgamation of Christianisation or Europeanisation (Anglicanisation, Germanisation, etc.) and even the Christianisation and civilisation itself" (Warneck 1897: 279).

Although it is not clear that Strehlow was taught Warneck's principles on language and religion (or ethnography) at the Neuendettelsau Mission Seminary, Veit maintains that it is reasonable to assume that he was at least familiar with some of these Warneckian thoughts about the "foreign and the familiar" (Veit 2004a: 146). Strehlow's approach to language and culture at his two Australian postings and his anthropological work suggests this background. Some of Warneck's earlier writings and pamphlets, such as *Die gegenseitigen Beziehungen zwischen der modernen Mission und Cultur* [*Reciprocal Relations between the Modern Mission and Culture*] (Warneck 1879) or *Die Stellung der evan-*

gelischen Mission zur Sklavenfrage [*The Standpoint of the Evangelical Mission Regarding Slavery*] (Warneck 1889), were and still are available at the Neuendettelsau Mission Seminary's library and Strehlow may have read them.

The Social Structure of the Mission Seminary

Although the training at Neuendettelsau was very demanding and strictly regimented, there was also an emphasis on fellowship and community spirit that gave the students a sense of belonging and security. The seminarians were embedded in the communal life of the village, as well as in the seminary itself, which was perceived as a "family". The strong ideal of family and community was reflected in the practice that the director was seen as the father (patriarch) (Koller 1924: 118). The students helped in community life as well as in the other Neuendettelsau institutions such as the psychiatric clinic (Koller 1924: 90, 99), at the time called "Blödenhaus" [lunatic asylum].[14] They were enjoined to develop empathy for others and practice the true love of "thy neighbour" [Nächstenliebe]. This emphasis on communal spirit was crucial in building a loyal and strong community and in maintaining compassion for others. For those who went to Australia and other areas of Oceania, this approach was to be transferred to the Indigenous context.

The whole curriculum was geared towards the development of strong personalities that would be fit for the demanding tasks and challenges that awaited them at their overseas postings. The hard training was to equip the students with self-discipline, endurance and an inner, spiritual (*geistige*) strength that would carry them through hardships and environments that would push them to their limits. The teachers at Neuendettelsau were well aware of the realities that the young people encountered once out in the field (Pilhofer 1967: 37). At the same time,

---

14 The Mission Seminary [Missionsanstalt] seems to have been better integrated and accepted in the village of Neuendettelsau than Löhe's other institutions (psychiatric clinic, Diakonesenhaus [Diocese House], hospital, Armenhaus [Poor House], etc.) which were for the mid-19th century cutting edge social institutions and very experimental. Indeed, it was at the forefront of female education. The historical context should not be forgotten here, as at the time it was not the state but the Church that took interest in social issues and pursued reforms in the health and education sectors for the general public. See Jenner (2004).

a patriarchally structured community was emphasised to give the individual a context and to provide fraternal support. These ideas helped effect the shift from Outer to Inner Mission within newly formed communities.

These social structures of a Lutheran world that Carl Strehlow tried to replicate – consciously and unconsciously – and the diverse influences of German intellectual life, Lutheran theology and human social ethics all emerged to some degree in the very different and remote context of Carl Strehlow's Finke River Mission in Central Australia. Paradoxically, Löhe's doctrine of the Inner and Outer Mission, and Bauer's emphasis on freedom (from desire) may have had an unexpected consequence in Central Australia's Hermannsburg. In this isolated setting, a lonely one for Strehlow, he came to treat his converts as his community. Despite the inward gaze and authoritarian structure of Strehlow's mission, it gave the community at Hermannsburg some unusual features of humanistic engagement (along with the missionisation) hardly known in other Central Australian frontier settlements. Interestingly, despite disciplinarian features, his Lutheran background carried the seeds of respect, responsibility and commitment. Strehlow treated his congregation as his equals and his family; and not as the "missing link" in an evolutionary chain (Arrernte people working and living with him were made, for instance, godparents of his own children).

In Strehlow's case, his Outer Mission became his Inner Mission so that the missionary became the pastor (*ingkarte* in Arrernte) of, in his view, freely baptised Christians. It was a strange group, not really Lutheran – it more closely resembled a sect – and it formed the basis for an unusual Christian community. In many ways the Lutheran world that he tried to reproduce in Central Australia and the Indigenous world of that place were, and still are, so different; in the course of the 20th century, these worlds have converged and produced a particular kind of Arrernte Lutheranism with corresponding narratives, even making way for the implementation of Lutheran law in the Arrernte landscape (Austin-Broos 1994; 2004).

The mutual engagement between Strehlow and his flock, based on his partial misperception of his congregation, may have helped to facilitate both his linguistic and ethnographic work. Through the thorough study of Indigenous language and oral literature for nearly three decades,

Strehlow had accumulated an unmatched knowledge of Australian Aboriginal cosmology and ontology that generated in him a deep respect and understanding for this particular Aboriginal worldview. He was a scholar, with a positive and intimate appreciation of the biblical and classical worlds, which were older and different from his own; in Australia he came in contact with another different world, which seemed to him in some ways analogous to these remote worlds.[15] This new world opened itself up to him through his intensive study of its languages and his personal interest in myth and song, and allowed him to enter the world of Aboriginal mythology, which gave him a glimpse of the worldviews of the Arrernte and Luritja. Strehlow's Arrernte informants may have sensed in their engagements with him a form of exchange that was not unfamiliar to them. They may perhaps have seen a man bent on building a "portfolio" of knowledge concerning both his own law and that of the Arrernte (Austin-Broos 2004: 61). He had become the *ingkarte*[16] of Christian law and *altyerre* (the Western Arrernte word for "Christian God" today; this was the word used for the ancestral beings significant in Western Arrernte religion around the turn of the century). At the same time, it seems likely that Strehlow's senior informants "hoped that this form of inscription might be more enduring than their revered *tywerrenge*,[17] which were abused by settlers and some of their own, and then de-legitimised by missionaries" (Austin-Broos 2003: 314).

Although his status as an *ingkarte* and his Indigenous portfolio of knowledge reinforced and strengthened his standing as the keeper of social order, his decade-long efforts to understand the Arrernte and Luritja on their own terms seem to have undermined his main task: to

---

15 C. Strehlow, Missionary, Hermannsburg. In: *The Register* (Adelaide), 7 December 1921.
16 The word *ingkarte* has changed its meaning significantly over the past century. According to Strehlow (1915: 1), it used to mean "the chief" of a traditional country (termed "estate" in anthropological literature) or "father of all". Today it is used for "pastor". It is likely that this shift of meaning started to occur during Carl Strehlow's period, because he seems to have been their first white *ingkarte*.
17 Referred to as *tjurunga* in Carl Strehlow's work. This term has a number of very complex meanings depending on its context. It can mean songs, stories, dances, paraphernalia, sacred object, etc. associated with the ancestral dreaming beings.

convert them. We can only imagine what kind of impression he made on the Arrernte. His preaching of the gospel must have stood in obvious tension or even complete contrast to his intense interest in their culture and views. So, while social structures were successfully transplanted, according to his own account, his mission work and thus Christianisation was not making much progress and was a great frustration to him (Albrecht 2002: 347–48). He felt at times that he wanted to drop it all, run away, that it would have been better that Hermannsburg had never been re-established as a mission after the first group of missionaries had had to abandon it:

> Whether the mission is ever going to have any success, only God knows. The present looks bleak. The ways of the blacks are not improving; of late they have been fighting more often than ever about trivialities. A woman made a big hole in the head of another just because of a small piece of meat; a man, a Christian, hit his wife, wounding her badly, today just before mass, because she allegedly spoke with another man. These feelings on a Sunday morning, when the Christians are behaving like savages, are often very difficult to describe. And when one punishes this behaviour according to God's word, they only look in amusement at us. If it had been known what kind of hardships and annoyances would be met with at this station, it would have been better not to take it up again, as it is still going to take many years before the mission work shows any kind of success).[18]

After 26 years at Hermannsburg, Strehlow had baptised only 46 adults.[19] He conducted a survey for the census authorities in 1921. From the grand total of 176 Aboriginal adults at Hermannsburg, 66 were labelled as "Lutherans", the rest were retaining their own religion. Of these, 29 were men and 37 women (T.G.H. Strehlow 1969–70: 119–50). It seems that he had compromised his status as a missionary, and his attempts to convert the Indigenous peoples at Hermannsburg, with his intense study of their cultures. Strehlow's behaviour must have appeared ambiguous to his informants. On the one hand he preached the gospel

---

18 Carl Strehlow to Pastor Rechner, Hermannsburg 2 October 1898 (LAA).
19 Carl Strehlow, Kirchen- und Missionszeitung, 9 January 1920.

(in their languages), but on the other hand, he spent years meticulously recording their languages and talking about and listening to their religious beliefs. He is likely to have spent as much time talking with senior Arrernte men about their own beliefs as he did about the gospel. The recording of the myth, song and language data was extremely time-consuming. Not only the recording of the myths and songs, but also the interlinear and free translations and annotations of his data were very time-consuming[20] and required long and repeated consultations and discussions about semantics. And what kind of impression did it make on his Arrernte and Luritja informants when he was trying to explain to them that Christian teaching had effected their cosmological beliefs (C. Strehlow 1908: 2)?[21] Sometimes he had to make detailed and persistent inquiries, to the point that he had to convince and nearly argue with his informants that Christian beliefs had made their way into their cosmology:

> That God created humanity by dropping a tjurunga-stone on earth during a visit, I read in Kempe; some Christians who grew up on the station confirmed this. This is definitely a skewing of Biblical[22] and heathen creation beliefs; for this reason I retreat from this view. In the meantime, I had to concede that this view is wrong, after consulting heathens who have grown up in heathenism and have been in influential positions (one of them is a famous magic-doctor).[23]

In an ironic twist, on 4 January 1923, one year after Strehlow's death at Horseshoe Bend, a mass-baptism seems to have taken place at Hermannsburg (T.G.H. Strehlow 1969–70: 178–80). Moses Tjalkabota and H.A. Heinrich had continued Strehlow's pre-baptismal instructions that resulted in the baptism of 26 adults and 14 children on that day. H.A. Heinrich (1926: 75) wrote in the *Lutheran Herald*:

---

20 Carl Strehlow to von Leonhardi, 19 September 1906 (SH-SP-3-1).
21 Carl Strehlow to von Leonhardi, 2 June 1906 (SH-SP-2-1).
22 Although the word is not quite readable, the context makes it clear that it is biblical.
23 Carl Strehlow to von Leonhardi, possibly 8 April 1906 (SH-SP-1-1). This was almost certainly Loatjira.

Not long after the death of the late Rev. Strehlow, it was indeed perceptible how a spiritual awakening stirred not only our natives at Hermannsburg, but all Aranda people. All seemed to feel and realise, that by devoting his whole life to it, even laying down his life in the service, there must be something great and true in what Rev. Strehlow taught, to thus enable him to unselfishly work for them, in contrast to most other white folks they knew.

Among these converts was Loatjira, who had been christened Abraham. He had been Strehlow's main informant on Western Arrernte culture, and the main upholder of Arrernte religion. According to T.G.H. Strehlow, he "remained strongly opposed to Christianity throughout the lifetime of my father, and in fact came to Hermannsburg very rarely after the completion of my father's book" (T.G.H. Strehlow 1971: xxi). He died shortly after his conversion on 4 October 1924 from Spanish influenza. He is said to have been by that time a broken man (T.G.H. Strehlow 1969: 125, 211; 1971: xxi). There are no reliable records of either Carl Strehlow's or Loatjira's state of mind towards the end of their lives. Both men had been devoted to their faiths, but were troubled. They had both reached the edge of knowing, and began entertaining doubts. Loatjira seems to have wavered in his faith and, according to T.G.H. Strehlow (1969: 174–79), so had Carl.

Acknowledgment

I would like to thank Shane Mulcahy, Michael Cawthorn and Urs Kenny for comments on earlier drafts of this essay.

Bibliography

The letters written by Carl Strehlow to Inspector Deinzer and Pastor Rechner are held in the Archive of the Neuendettelsauer Missionswerk and the letters to von Leonhardi are held at the Strehlow Research Centre in Alice Springs. Carl Strehlow's letter to the Mission Friends dated 9 January 1920 is held in the Albrecht Collection in the South Australian Museum Archives.

Albrecht PGE (2002). *From Mission to Church, 1877–2002.* Adelaide: Finke River Mission.

Applegate C (1990). *A Nation of Provincials: The German Idea of Heimat.* Berkley: University of California Press.

Austin-Broos D (1994). Narratives of the Encounter at Ntaria. In J Beckett (Ed), *Aboriginal Histories, Aboriginal Myths.* Oceania, 65: 131–50.

Austin-Broos D (1996). 'Right Way' 'Til I die': Christianity and kin on country at Hermannsburg. In L Olson (Ed), *Religious Change, Conversion and Culture.* Sydney: Sydney Association for Studies in Society and Culture, 226–53.

Austin-Broos D (1996). Two Laws, Ontologies, Histories: Ways of Being Aranda Today. *The Australian Journal of Anthropology* 7(1): 1–20.

Austin-Broos D (2003). The Meaning of Pepe: God's Law and the Western Arrernte. In *The Journal of Religious History* 27(3): 311–28.

Austin-Broos D (2004). Western Arrernte Endogenous Change and the Impact of Settlement. In M Cawthorn (Ed), *Proceedings of the Strehlow Conference 2002* (pp. 60–65). Alice Springs: Northern Territory Government.

Basedow H (1920–22). *Hermannsburg Mission. 'Medical Inspection of Natives of Southern Portion of N.T.'* In Department of External Affairs, Correspondence files, N.T. Series.

Breen G (2000). *Introductory Dictionary of Western Arrernte.* Alice Springs: IAD Press.

Deinzer M (Ed) (1904). *Christliche Ethik auf lutherischer Grundlage. (Zunächst für die Schüler der Neuendettelsauer Missionsanstalt.) Entworfen von Missionsinspektor F. Bauer. Umgearbeietet und vermehrt von Missionsinspektor Joh. Deinzer. Revidiert und in den Druck gegeben von M. Deinzer, Inspektor der Missionsanstalt in Neuendettelsau.* Neuendettelsau: Im Selbstverlag der Missionsanstalt.

Eylmann E (1908). *Die Eingeborenen der Kolonie Sudaustralien.* Berlin: Dietrich Reimer (Ernst Vohsen).

Farnbacher T & Weber C (2004). *Ein Zentrum für Weltmission: Neuendettelsau.* Neuendettelsau: Missionswerk Neuendettelsau.

Harms HF (2003). *Träume and Tränen*. Hermannsburg: Verlag Ludwig-Harms-Haus.

Hebart T (1938). *The United Lutheran Church in Australia: Its History, Activities, and Characteristics*. Adelaide: Lutheran Book Depot.

Heinrich HA (1926). *Lutheran Herold*. 1926, 25.

Jenner H (2004). *Von Neuendettelsau in alle Welt*. Neuendettelsau: Diakonie Neuendettelsau.

Kenny A (2005). A Sketch Portrait: Carl Strehlow's Editor Baron Moritz von Leonhardi. In A Kenny & S Mitchell (Eds), Collaboration and Language. Strehlow Research Centre Occasional Paper 4. Darwin: NT Government Press, 54–70.

Kenny A (2008). From Missionary to Frontier Scholar: An Introduction to Carl Strehlow's Marsterpiece *Aranda-und Loritja Stämme in Zentral-Australien*. Phd Thesis. University of Sydney.

Koller W (1924). *Die Missionsanstalt in Neuendettelsau: Ihre Geschichte und das Leben in ihr*. Neuedettelsau: Verlag des Missionshauses, Nummer 7.

Leske E (Ed) (1977). *Hermannsburg: A Vision and a Mission*, Adelaide: Lutheran Publishing House.

Liebermeister B (1998). Leben und Werk Carl Strehlows, des Erforschers der Aranda-und Loritja Stämme in Zentralaustralien. MA thesis. München: University of München.

Lueker EL (Ed) (1954). *Lutheran Cyclopedia*. Saint Louis, Missouri: Concordia Publishing House.

Mulvaney J, Morphy H & Petch A (Eds) (2001). 'My Dear Spencer': The Letters of FJ Gillen to Baldwin Spencer. Melbourne: Hyland House.

Moore DC (2003). TGH Strehlow and the Linguistic Landscape of Australia 1930–60. Honours Thesis. University of New England.

Nobbs C (2005). A Missionary's Defence. In A Kenny & S Mitchell (Eds), Collaboration and Language. Strehlow Research Centre Occasional Paper 4. Darwin: NT Government Press.

Pilhofer G (1967). *Geschichte des Neuendettelsauer Missionshauses.* Neuendettelsau: Freimund-Verlag Neuendettelsau.

Scherer PA (1963). *Venture of Faith: An Epic in Australian Missionary History.* Tanunda (SA): Auricht's Printing Office.

Scherer PA (1995). *The Hermannsburg chronicle, 1877–1933.* Tanunda (SA): PA Scherer.

Schild M (2004). Heading for Hermannsburg: Notes on Carl Strehlow's Early Career Path. In W Veit (Ed), The Struggle for Souls and Science; Constructing the Fifth Continent: German Missionaries and Scientists in Australia. Occasional Papers 3: 51–8. Darwin: NT Government Press.

Schlichting W (1998). *Die Erneuerung Lutherischen Lebens durch Wilhelm Löhe: "… unter dem Winterschnee hervorgeholt"; 150 Jahre "Gesellschaft für Innere (und Äußere) Mission im Sinne der Lutherischen Kirche".* Neuendettelsau: Freimund-Verlag.

Stevens C (1994). *White Man's Dreaming: Killalpaninna Mission 1866–1915.* Melbourne: Oxford University Press.

Strehlow C (1907–20). *Die Aranda- und Loritja-Stämme in Zentral-Australien,* 7 Vols. Frankfurt am Main: Joseph Baer & Co.

Strehlow C (1921). In *The Register* (Adelaide), 7 December 1921.

Strehlow TGH (1969). *Journey to Horseshoe Bend.* Sydney: Angus & Robertson.

Strehlow TGH (1971). *Songs of Central Australia.* Sydney: Angus & Robertson.

Strehlow J (2004). Reappraising Carl Strehlow: through the Spencer-Strehlow debate. In W Veit (Ed), The Struggle for Souls and Science; Constructing the Fifth Continent: German Missionaries and Scientists in Australia. Occasional Papers 3: 59–91. Darwin: NT Government Press.

Veit WF (1991). In Search of Carl Strehlow: Lutheran Missionary and Australian Anthropologist. In J Tampke & D Walker (Eds), *From Berlin to Burdekin: The German Contribution to the Development of Australian Science, Exploration and the Arts.* Sydney: UNSW Press.

Veit WF (1994). Carl Strehlow, Ethnologist: The Arunta and Aranda Tribes in Australia Ethnology. In TR Finlayson & GL McMullen (Eds), *The Australian Experience of Germany*. Adelaide: Australian Association of von Humboldt Fellows, Flinders University, 77–100.

Veit WF (2004a). Labourers in the Vineyard or The Uneducated Missionary. In M Cawthorn (Ed), *Strehlow Conference 2002 Proceedings of the Strehlow Conference*. Darwin: NT Government Press.

Veit WF (2004b). Social anthropology versus cultural anthropology: Baldwin Walter Spencer and Carl Friedrich Theodor Strehlow in central Australia. IIn W Veit (Ed), The Struggle for Souls and Science; Constructing the Fifth Continent: German Missionaries and Scientists in Australia. Occasional Papers 3: 92–110. Darwin: NT Government Press.

Warneck G (1897). *Evangelische Missionslehre*. 3 Vols. Gotha: Friedrich Andreas Berthes.

Weber C (1996). *Missionstheologie bei Wilhelm Löhe: Aufbruch zur Kirche der Zukunft*. Gütersloh: Güntersloher Verlagshaus.

Wendt R (2001). Einleitung: Missionare als Reporter un Wissenschaftler in Übersee. In R Wendt (Ed), *Sammeln, Vernetzen, Auswerten: Missionare und ihr Beitrag zum Wandel europäischer Weltsicht*. Tübingen: Gunter Narr Verlag, 7–22.

4
Missionary Love and Duty: Frieda Keysser's and Carl Strehlow's Letters of Courtship 1894–1895

Andrea Bandhauer and Maria Veber

> Sagt, was wollt Ihr drüben schaffen
> Zarte Jungfrauen welche Waffen
> nehmt Ihr mit zum heilgen Streit?
> Gerok, Das Missionsschiff

> Say, what do you want to embark on over there
> Young maidens what weapons
> Are you taking to the holy battle?

In response to the fears the young Frieda Keysser (1875–1957) expressed before embarking on her long journey from Germany to Australia to be united in marriage with her missionary fiancé Carl Strehlow (1871–1922), his words of comfort include a poem by the Lutheran preacher Friedrich Karl (von) Gerok (1815–90),[1] who was particularly widely read by those involved in Lutheran missionary activity.

---

1 (Carl Strehlow to Frieda Keysser, 16 May 1895). The publisher's foreword to an 1881 edition of *Palmblätter* refers to the "more than 50 editions" of the work to that point (Gerok 1881: vii); Carl Strehlow's 1894 Christmas gift from his teacher in Neuendettelsau is a deluxe edition – "Prachtausgabe" – of the volume (Carl Strehlow to Frieda Keysser, 5 March 1895). The poem *"Das Missionsschiff"* [The Mission Ship] is dedicated "in farewell to a missionary bride in Spring 1860" (Gerok 1881: 376–80, here 376).

Gerok's poem *The Mission Ship* evokes the missionary project as an imaginary undertaking, and sets up fundamental tropes of the Lutheran "holy battle" to be fought by virginal brides-to-be travelling alone to distant and dangerous lands to marry their missionary fiancés. The poem comforts and celebrates these young women, who are exposed to the dangers of the elements on a long sea voyage that has at its end a marriage ceremony far from their family and homeland. Faced with the dangers presented by lions, snakes and dark heathens, they are offered the ultimate consolation of the God in whose name they travel and who emphatically affirms their undertaking. By reminding his reader how Jesus calmed the waters of Lake Genezareth and that he is the one who blesses the marital bond, Gerok repeatedly emphasises the fact that Jesus underwrites these women's sea journey and mission and is ever present to offer them succour.

Many of the poem's themes, such as the loss of one's family and of material security, the horrors of the unknown, and Jesus' eternal beneficence, resonate in the couple's letters of courtship, exchanged over a 21-month period and functioning as the medium through which they established their relationship.

Carl and Frieda first met in a three-day encounter at her uncle's vicarage in the Franconian village of Obersulzbach during Easter 1892, just before the 22-year old Carl set out to his first posting at the Bethesda mission station in Killalpaninna, South Australia. Carl's proposal of marriage to Frieda in a letter to her uncle/guardian soon after (Carl Strehlow to August Omeis, 23 November 1892), was rejected by the latter (August Omeis to Carl Strehlow, 3 January 1893), who stated that the 17-year old Frieda was too young to entertain even the thought of marriage. Carl persisted, Frieda seems to have been interested, and more than a year after their initial meeting, the two were finally given permission to enter into a correspondence with view to marriage. They exchanged letters between January 1894 and their second meeting in South Australia in September 1895, when they married.

Their letters thus both represent and enact the courtship between Frieda, writing from Germany, and Carl, writing first from Bethesda in the salt-lake areas of north-eastern South Australia, and then from Hermannsburg in Central Australia.

Frieda and Pastor Carl Strehlow, recently married, at Point Pass, SA 1895.

While literary and textual scholarship is yet to produce a survey of and analytical framework for letters exchanged by missionaries and their brides-to-be, Frieda's and Carl's letters can certainly be viewed in the context – unique for its time – of Luther's cultivation of the exchange of letters as an expression of personal feelings and private thoughts (Nickisch 1991: 35). There is of course a well-established tradition of love letters exchanged between German male writers and their fiancées, and letters of friendship that evolve into a relationship of greater intimacy such as those between Bettina Brentano and Achim von Arnim (see Ledanff 1991). Such letters, that include those exchanged by the author and critic Johann Christoph Gottsched (1700–66) and Luise Kulmus (1713–62), as well as later exchanges in the circle of the German Romantics, enabled both partners in a couple to develop a closer relationship and share their most intimate thoughts. Some of these exchanges had a stronger pedagogical inflection, reflecting the practice initiated in Rousseau's *Emile ou L'Education* (1762), of a male mentor writing letters of pedagogical instruction for the education of young people. In Germany, Campe's *Briefe an meine Tochter* [*Letters to my Daughter*], written in alignment with Rousseau's text, became a highly-influential reference book for the education and upbringing of young women. Widely read women's journals also printed letters intended for the same purpose. As we will see, Frieda's and Carl's letters were both a means through which the couple forged a more intimate relationship, and a means by which Carl could educate his fiancée for their life as a married couple.

However, Frieda's and Carl's correspondence is marked by the acute sense that that they were separated by a vast distance. As Georg Simmel writes, in situations in which two people are separated from each other by force of circumstance, letters take on a surrogate function, providing their writers with continuing psychic contact with each other, and occupy the space of continuing conversations. This is particularly the case for individuals who have been driven into isolation and separated from their closest intimates (Simmel 1908: 380). Although Carl's vocation determined that he live in cultural isolation, and the couple chose to breach the distance and continue their relationship despite the difficult conditions, the distance between them, the lack of physical contact, and the concomitant lack of opportunity to cultivate the physical dimension of their relationship, such as the *Verlobungskuß* [engagement kiss], are recurring motifs of their letters.

In this context, Frieda's and Carl's letters over the period of separation are the sole constituents of their relationship and indeed its only manifestation. Moreover, the rhythm of their correspondence was determined by the mechanics of the postal delivery system, which meant that their communication occurred in fits and starts. They could never establish a linear reciprocal dialogue, as the delivery was characterised by extended delays, particularly since their letters were carried by ship, train and camel-train. They would thus receive two or three letters at once, or not until well after the expected date, in the case of a delay due to floods or delivery mishaps. This unpredictability of the postal system, that disrupted the development of a smoothly flowing dialogue, also impeded the development of intimacy. A quite concrete example of this was that delivery delays and the chronological crossing of their letters meant that Carl's suggestion that they move from the formal *Sie* form of address to the informal and intimate *du*, made in April 1894, was not implemented by Frieda until two months later (10 June 1894). In keeping with her role, she had waited for her fiancé to initiate this move. In addition, lengthier postal delays caused each of them to fear for the safety and wellbeing of the other. In one instance, Frieda's fears were intensified by reports in missionary newspapers about a near fatal incident of unrest at Bethesda (19 August 1894).

Under these unique circumstances, their relationship as a couple and their intimacy begins and is first developed as a textual narrative, which Frieda writes about with a note of regret on the third anniversary of their first meeting:

> On the 14th, 15th, and 16th of April I had a vivid recollection of the beautiful days at the Obersulzbach vicarage. It's a great pity that in our case the (beautiful) [inserted by Frieda as an afterthought] time of first love was so short. I sometimes envy my friends when they tell me how they slowly got to know and love each other [their fiancés] before telling each other about their feelings. If only we had met sooner. Well, for us, telling each other about our feelings and the first kiss are still to come (18 April 1895).[2] [Our English translations of Frieda's and Carl's letters reflect the idiosyncrasies of their writing styles].

As their relationship develops in the course of their correspondence, they revisit this scene in the Obersulzbach vicarage again and again, Carl in particular constructing an increasingly elaborate account

---

2 "Am 14., 15. und 16. April, dachte ich wieder lebhaft an die schönen Tage im Obersulzbacher Pfarrhaus zurück. Es ist sehr schade, dass bei uns die (schöne) Zeit der ersten Liebe so kurz war. Ich beneide manchmal meine Freundinnen wenn sie mir erzählen, wie sie sich so nach und nach kennen und lieben lernten bis es endlich zur Aussprache kam. Wenn wir uns doch auch schon früher kennen gelernt hätten. Nun ja, die Aussprache und der erste Kuß steht uns ja noch bevor. Ich freue mich ganz unsagbar."

that can be viewed as the foundational myth of their coming together, their love for each other and their shared sense of duty:

> I still can't really understand how we knew that we belong together and how we fell in love so quickly. But love, first love, also has something wonderful, mysterious, about it … But I loved you straight away, the moment uncle introduced us. You can feel love in the pressure of someone's hand. In order to test you I even asked you while we were having a relaxed conversation in the evening, whether you would consider going to Australia. I believe you didn't even think then about the meaning of this question. If you had said "no" then, even jokingly, I would never have asked for your hand, as I really would have taken that as a kind of refusal. But since you happily replied: "Yes", I was full of hope and in my heart I only said farewell until we see each other again [Auf Wiedersehen] (31 January 1895).[3]

When Carl proposes to Frieda (16 January 1894), he writes to her from within a shared social, cultural and religious context. They first met when Frieda's uncle invited the ambitious and dedicated young missionary to visit his vicarage before Carl's departure to his first missionary posting in Australia. Frieda, whose parents were both deceased, and who had spent longer intervals living at her uncle's, was knowledgeable about the missionary work supported and carried out by the Neuendettelsau seminary. Indeed, as she writes to her fiancé, her central

---

3 "Wie wir uns so schnell zusammengefunden und herzlich lieb gewonnen haben, kann ich selber nicht recht begreifen. Doch die Liebe, die erste, hat auch etwas wunderbares, geheimnisvolles an sich. Mit manchen Leuten kann man Jahre lang zusammen leben, doch sie bleiben einem mehr oder weniger gleichgültig. Ich habe Dich aber schon gleich geliebt, als uns Onkel einander vorstellte. Man kann die Liebe auch schon im Händedruck fühlen. Um Dich zu prüfen, stellte ich auch einmal, als wir am Abend uns gemütlich unterhielten über Australien u.s.w. an Dich die Frage: ob Du auch wohl nach Australien gingest. Ich glaube, damals hast Du gar nicht daran gedacht, welche Bedeutung diese Frage hatte. Hättest Du damals geantwortet 'Nein', auch nur scherzweise, so hätte ich Dich niemals um Deine Hand gebeten, da ich dieses schon für eine halbe Absageantwort aufgefasst hätte. Da Du aber fröhlich antwortest [sic]: 'Ja', so war ich voller Hoffnung und nahm in meinem Herzen nur Abschied 'Auf Wiedersehen.' "

longing had always been focused on Africa: "Even as a child I wanted to be a grown-up and to be allowed to be among the heathens in Africa. I'm now very much looking forward [sic] and am very happy that I'm allowed to travel to the heathens."[4] In this sense, leaving her homeland to become a missionary's wife was already present in her imaginings of her future. The environment in which she had spent the most time was one in which she was exposed to Lutheran missionary ideas, both through the intellectual milieu of her upbringing, as well as the regular visits of mission candidates and missionaries to her uncle's vicarage.

Besides functioning as the means by which the two established intimacy, the letters, as indicated above, are the medium through which Frieda both prepares, and is prepared for, her role as missionary wife. In his letter of proposal, Carl clearly sets out the foundations for their relationship. He asks if she will commit herself to him and leave her homeland to live at his side, sharing everything; happiness, suffering and sorrow; that the Lord sends them. He expresses his confidence that if Frieda puts everything into the hands of the Lord as he, Carl, already has, then the Lord will bless their marriage. From the very beginning, Carl appeals to Frieda's strong piety and sense of duty by invoking the Lord as the figure who determines their path by joining them together to successfully serve the missionary enterprise with His support.

Frieda has already independently set out upon this path, as she demonstrates in an extensive quotation she has copied from a discussion of the phrase "My friend is mine and I am his" from Luther's version of the "Song of Songs" (23 March 1895). The unnamed author of this discussion provides gender-specific definitions of love and duty in a marital relationship in terminology typical of behavioural manuals for young people or couples written from the late 18th century onwards:

> If a man belongs to the world with respect to his profession, his office, his work, so too does he belong to his wife in a special way. To her shall he dedicate his entire love and loyalty, her love shall accompany him on all paths and after his work

---

4 "Afrika war immer das Ziel meiner Sehnsucht und Wünsche. Schon als Kind wünschte ich groß zu sein und nach Afrika unter die Heiden zu dürfen. Ich freue mich nun sehr [sic] und bin glücklich, dass ich nun doch zu den Heiden darf."

and struggle he shall seek and find peace and refreshment in
their faithful union.[5]

That Frieda considers this view of the ideal marriage as an apt description of their relationship to each other, with respect to the status of
marital love and the function of marital intimacy, shows the degree to
which her thinking conformed with ideas about gender roles and the
gendered division of labour in the family that were common in 19th-
century Germany.

At the Hermannsburg station, the model of the Lutheran Holy
Family serves as a further reference point in our discussion of Frieda's
role within the marriage, the family and the household, which was the
mission station. Lutheran missions were run according to a workshop
model harking back to the guild structures of Reformation Germany:
Frieda would be responsible for the internal organisation of the station
and the care, instruction and supervision of the Indigenous women,
while Carl would oversee station business and spiritual affairs. As the
historian Lyndal Roper states in her discussion of the Holy Family:

> discipline and order ... elevated to the status of moral and
> religious values, were thought of as the defining character-
> istics of the pious household, where the distinct offices of
> master, mistress, children, and servants were structured in
> a hierarchy of benign authority of age over youth, master
> over servant, and man over woman. It was a patriarchal ideal
> which sanctified the existing exclusion of women from in-
> dependent ... enterprise, and from political power (Roper
> 1989: 252).

In the case of Frieda, who had grown up surrounded by the values
of Lutheran "Rechtschaffenheit" [righteousness and virtuousness], Carl
had no cause for worry. In her answer to his proposal, which she gladly
accepts, she immediately defines herself as his bride-to-be and faithful
helpmate in the same terms and from within the same framework of

---

5 "Gehört der Mann auch seinem Berufe, seinem Amte, seiner Arbeit für die Welt,
so gehört er zugleich doch auch seinem Weibe in besonderem Sinne. Ihr soll er
seine ganze Liebe und Treue weihen, ihre Liebe soll ihn begleiten auf allen Wegen
und in ihrer trauten Gemeinschaft soll er Ruhe u. Erquickung suchen und finden
nach Arbeit und Kampf."

Lutheran marriage and the working household that is implicit in his proposal, and that is analysed by Roper above. Frieda's subordination of herself is an expression of the explicitly gendered hierarchy that under- pins the German Lutheran missionary project and its particular form of colonisation. Her very first questions about her Australian future dem- onstrate this. Her main interest is in the interior of their future house and her tasks in the mission household. Frieda, who has grown up in the gentle landscape of Bavarian Franconia, has only a passing interest in the foreign and strange space of the Australian outback: "so I'd like you to tell me about the snakes and bats which I've heard are around in large numbers. Tell me, what furniture is in the rooms?"[6] Her next ques- tion, which asks for the names of the "blacks" in a photograph Carl had sent, already concerns her future domain of work. This attitude is typi- cal of all the letters written before Frieda's arrival in Australia. Aspects of her new home that lay outside her immediate area of interest, such as Australia as a foreign country and the exotic landscape, remained only of peripheral importance to her.

As a woman whose vocation was unequivocally that of mission- ary wife, Frieda's focus on the internal space comprised of her home and the mission household enables her to insert herself seamlessly into the Australian version of the Lutheran hierarchy explicated above. This hierarchy was: God, Carl's employer the Immanuel Synod in South Aus- tralia as well as the Neuendettelsau mission seminary, Frieda's husband the missionary, Frieda in her supporting role as the missionary wife, and the "blacks" [die Schwarzen] who are to be guided towards the true path and schooled in the Lutheran work ethic as well as in Lutheran Christian beliefs. As Carl writes from Bethesda, the "Schwarzen" would be instructed to be faithful servants to her, as they already are to Frau Reuther, the wife of the mission head:

> You will get 4–6 black women or girls, who will take care of the washing up, milking the goats, mopping the rooms, etc.;

6 (1 March 1894) "so bitte ich um Antwort darüber[,] wie es mit den Schlangen und Fledermäusen aussieht[,] die in ziemlicher Anzahl vorhanden sein sollen. Mit welchen Möbeln sind denn die Zimmer versehen? Es wäre uns auch interessant[,] einige [Namen] von den Schwarzen zu erfahren, die auf dem Bilde sind."

if you wanted more women, you can have more servants, as the blacks ought to be given as much to do as possible. A black [man] will get the water for you, chop wood, etc., so that besides the cooking and the gardening you will mostly only have to give instructions to the blacks and keep them occupied (5 June 1894).[7]

Despite the exploitative and instrumentalising authoritarian stance indicated here, which was typical of his behaviour as the head and patriarch of the Hermannsburg Mission, there is evidence that Carl Strehlow also at the same time had a relatively humane approach to his flock in Hermannsburg, as is for example elaborated in Kenny's contribution in this volume. The concept fundamental to the Christian Lutheran mission that the indigenes have a soul to be won over for the Lutheran God, and therefore could not be the "missing link" from the evolutionary chain, determined this attitude. As a result, and due to their incorporation into the greater Lutheran family of the mission station, Arrernte Christians were for instance made godparents of Carl's and Frieda's children, and thus given a status of some significance within the Lutheran framework.

However, the missionary enterprise was nevertheless a manifestation of the colonial attitude that assumes European and Christian values as normative parameters of "civilisation" to be forced on the Other. The extent to which this attitude informs Carl Strehlow's perceptions of the Diyari may be illustrated by his slip of the pen in the letter cited above, when he appears to mistakenly use the term "Kulturvolk" [civilised people] instead of "Naturvolk" [primitive people]. In the course of urging Frieda to travel to Australia as soon as possible, as she is needed in Bethesda to help with the women, Carl mentions that "the black women are also urging me to have my wife come soon". He then explains that their language does not have the word fiancée and so they simply refer

---

7 "Du bekommst 4–6 schwarze Frauen oder Mädchen, die das Abwaschen, Melken der Ziegen, das Aufwischen der Zimmer u.s.w. besorgen; wenn Du noch mehr Frauen wünschest, kannst Du noch mehr Dienerinnen haben, da die Schwarzen soviel als [sic] möglich beschäftigt werden sollen. Ein schwarzer Mann holt dir das Wasser, haut Holz u.s.w., sodaß du außer dem Kochen u. Backen mehr [nur – inserted] den Schwarzen die Arbeit anzugeben und zu beschäftigen hast".

to her as "*noa*", or "woman". The slip comes when he states that as a "Kulturvolk", the Diyari do not distinguish between the formal *Sie* and informal *du* form of address, but rather refer to everyone as *du*. Ironically it is while Carl is describing the Diyari language from a perspective that assumes its lack, that the slip describing them as a civilised people occurs. We would argue that this unconsciously produced inconsistency brings to the fore the "language of lack" typical of colonial descriptions of the foreign Other.

The appropriateness of the structure of the Lutheran Holy Family for Frieda's understanding of herself as a missionary wife is illustrated in her correspondence during her years at Hermannsburg. For example, in a letter to the wife of the head of the Lutheran Synod, Margarete Stolz, who has just given birth, Frieda writes:

> Do you have a washing machine? Because doing the washing is of course far too strenuous and also hanging it on the line. In this respect it's easier here with the blacks (15 May 1919).[8]

This passage, in which sympathy with Margarete coincides with the instrumentalisation of the "black women", demonstrates unequivocally that Frieda operates from a position of authority within the mission station's white colonial hegemony. The letter evokes the white women's common suffering and presents a world in which European "civilisation" – in the form of a washing machine – lightens their load. This allows Frieda to confirm her European and "civilised" Self, and stands in stark contrast to her lack of consideration for the "black women". In this context, in which the dominant culture asserts its identity through the discursive displacement of the Other, cultural contact is clearly cultural conflict. On the mission stations of Bethesda and Hermannsburg, the Indigenous people are to be brought to their Christian spiritual home through the exercise of discipline and control, thereby suffering a loss of agency.

The physical locations of the Bethesda and Hermannsburg Missions thus exemplify the conditions of Pratt's "contact zone", and are namely:

---

8 "Denn das Waschen sollte doch eine zu große Anstrengung sein und das Aufhängen auf der Leine. In dieser Beziehung hat man es hier leichter mit den Schwarzen." See Bandhauer & Veber 2007: 35f.

the space of colonial encounters, the space in which peoples geographically and historically separated come into contact with each other and establish on-going relations, usually involving conditions of coercion, radical inequality and intractable conflict (Pratt 1993: 6–7).

In the context of Carl's and Frieda's correspondence, the contact zone is the space from within which Carl Strehlow writes and which he seeks to represent to his future bride. Within this space they have to confront, and, in their mission roles, bring under control, that which is foreign to them. During the first nine months of their correspondence, Carl prepares Frieda for conditions at Bethesda. From December 1894 onwards, he writes from Hermannsburg. The mission there, which the Immanuel Synod charged Carl to re-establish after its failure in 1891, was in ruins. The distance from an established white settlement, lack of the comforts of European civilisation, and the limited numbers of white people on the station, meant it was one of the most isolated missionary destinations of the time. Yet, this absolutely foreign setting was the place they were to make their home for an unspecified length of time. Carl's letters from the Hermannsburg Mission seek to represent this place to his future bride and make it as familiar as possible in order to present Frieda's future home and workplace, as ordained by the will of God, in a positive light. He describes their future home with particular attention to its interior, providing details about the shape of rooms and windows, as well as the furniture.

Rather than exoticising the foreign, Carl's letters veil the unknown by translating its conditions into a language of social organisation that is familiar to Frieda. In this sense, Carl's project cannot be to represent her migration to the Australian desert as an adventure of discovery that could potentially disrupt the trajectory of her life as she would have lived it in Germany. Rather, he seeks to present the migration as a journey to a new home in which she would continue to dedicate her life to the fulfilment of God's will in much the same way as she would have done in Germany.

In a theoretical contribution on the representation of foreignness in literature, Gutjahr discusses the significance of boundaries and ways in which they are drawn, in order to define the Self by excluding the foreign Other – or in more explicitly spatial terms, to define the home-land as the space of the Self in opposition to the foreign as the unknown territory inhabited by the foreign Other. The spatial model of inside and outside thus defines the place of the Self and of the foreign Other respec-tively. According to Gutjahr, the foreign is "conceived as the unknown outside, which is juxtaposed and thus contrasted with the horizon of the Self's experience. In addition, the foreign may also be described as the invasion of the unknown into the 'inside' space that defines the Self." Moreover, Gutjahr states that

> just as the foreign and that which belongs to the Self are in-terdependent relational terms, so too are the concepts of the unknown outside and the invasion of the unknown into the 'inside' space that defines the Self. The logical consequence of this is that that which is experienced as foreign is defined in terms of whether the Self conceives of itself as being situated "at home" or "inside the foreign space" (Gutjahr 2002a: 50).

Gutjahr further makes the point that in literary representations, language becomes the foundation of what belongs to the Self, as even that which is most distant and unreachable can be captured in language and thus made accessible to understanding. Thus the foreign as the unknown outside is expressed as that which lies beyond the spatially defined border of the Self, the family, the village, the city, the country, etc. In these terms, foreignness is made comprehensible as that which is still not known, but which at the same time contains the possibility of becoming known. The structure and topos of the journey are de-finitive for the literary representation of the Self and the foreign in this sense. The prototypical figures in such representations are adventurers, explorers and conquerors, who leave their homeland in order to seek the unknown and to compare it with the homeland, which they have for the most part only left temporarily (Gutjahr 2002a: 51).

Whereas the trajectory of a Lutheran missionary's life can be likened to that of such figures in the sense that each travels to unknown parts in a spirit of inquiry which is coupled with an overtly stated colonialising impulse, the trajectory of a missionary wife's life is to travel to unknown parts in order to reproduce conditions at home by transposing the ritu-als of day-to-day life and its organisation from the homeland to the new space, and in so doing, she enacts her own form of colonialisation. Carl therefore, from the beginning of their correspondence, seeks to present the foreign to Frieda using familiar tropes from their common German culture. The missionary and his wife in effect travel to the foreign in gender-specific ways that are determined by the male and female roles of Restoration Germany and the Lutheran church.

While Carl had the benefit of three-years training for work in the missionary field, Frieda did not undergo the kind of preparation normally given to later missionary wives whose husbands worked in the African mission, for example. Her training was, in effect, provided by Carl's letters. We may ask: What instructions were given, then, with respect to the work in the field? And slightly rephrasing Walter Veit, we may further ask: What was the missionary wife taught first of all to see? (Veit 2002: 136) In preparing Frieda for her journey, Carl strongly determines her access to information about the unknown living conditions and actively shapes her view of the respective mission stations. In doing so, he assumes the role of pedagogue to the willing Frieda, who writes in an early letter (22 July 1894):

> I'm always, and have always been, looking forward to my home, to the time when we sit together cosily, and when you then teach me as my master.[9]

In Germany, waiting to join her fiancé in Australia, Frieda, with Carl's help, is hard at work defining her homeland within the imagined foreign space.

Bibliography

The letters written by Frieda Keysser, August Omeis and Carl Strehlow that are referred to in this article are all held in the Strehlow Research Centre, Alice Springs, Northern Territory in folders organised according to the year the letter was written. The letter from Frieda Strehlow to Margarete Stolz is held at the Lutheran Archive, Adelaide, South Australia.

---

9 "Ich freue mich nämlich schon immer auf mein Heim, wenn wir beide vertraulich beisammen sitzen, und wenn du mich dann als mein Herr belehrst."

Bandhauer A & Veber M (2007). Frisda Strehlow: Eine Missionarsfrau in Australian. *Akten des internationalen Germanistenverbandes*, 29–36.

Gerok K (1881). *Palmblätter*. Philadelphia: Verlag von Jg. Kohler.

Gutjahr O (2002a). Fremde als literarische Inszenierung. In O Gutjahr (Ed), *Fremde: Freiburger literaturpsychologische Gespräche*. Jahrbuch für Literatur und Psychoanalyse, Band 21. Würzburg: Könighausen & Neumann, 47–67.

Gutjahr O (Ed) (2002b). *Fremde – Freiburger literaturpsychologische Gespräche: Jahrbuch für Literatur und Psychoanalyse, Band 21*. Würzburg: Könighausen & Neumann.

Ledanff S (1991). *"Bist Du Luftbild oder Leben?" Brautbriefe aus zwei Jahrhunderten (1750–1833)*. Berlin: Ullstein Taschenbuch.

Nickisch RMG (1991). *Der Brief*. Stuttgart: J.B. Metzlersche Verlagsbuchhandlung.

Pratt ML (1993). *Imperial Eyes: Travel Writing and Transculturation*. New York/London: Routledge.

Roper L (1989). *The Holy Household: Women and Morals in Reformation Augsburg*. Oxford University Press.

Simmel G (1908). Exkurs über den schriftlichen Verkehr. In G Simmel, *Soziologie: Untersuchungen über die Formen der Vergesellschaftung*. Leipzig: Duncker & Humblot, 379–82.

Veit W (2002). Labourers in the Vineyard or the Uneducated Missionary: Aspects of the Non-Theological Education of Missionaries. In *Traditions in the Midst of Change: Communities, Cultures and the Strehlow Legacy in Central Australia*. Proceedings of the Strehlow Conference Alice Springs, 18–20 September 2002. Strehlow Research Centre, Alice Springs, Northern Territory, 136–50.

III
Narratives of National and Cultural Identity

5
Debating the "German Presence" in Australia: Notes on Research and Research Desiderata

Gerhard Fischer

I

A year before his death at the age of 78 on 23 April 2005, Al Grassby, the former Minister of Immigration of the Whitlam government who had supposedly "launched Australian multiculturalism in 1973", was asked by the *Sydney Morning Herald* how one could explain the dramatic increase in the number of Germans in Australia over the previous two decades. According to data collected by the Australian Bureau of Statistics in the last two national censuses (1986 and 2001), the number of Australians or Australian residents who claimed to be of German ancestry had risen by 230,000, or 45 per cent, in just 15 years: a remarkable figure which, however, bears no resemblance at all to the actual number of new arrivals from Germany during this period. Grassby attributed the apparent discrepancy to a newly found willingness of German-Australians – the "hidden migrants" in James Jupp's words (Jupp 1995) – to identify with their past, to come out of the closet of their assimilationist denial and to embrace their ethnic identity. "All those John Smiths," Al Grassby is quoted as having surmised, "who could be Hermann Schmidts, had emerged from hiding." He added: "After two world wars, who would have wanted to be German?" (Gibbs, 26 April 2005).

Grassby's observation raises a number of interesting questions. Could it be that recent developments in Germany, notably the collapse of the Berlin Wall and the peaceful reunification that followed in 1989/90, also had repercussions in Australia? Did the resurgence of an enthusiastic "national movement" in Germany have an impact on German migrants overseas? Could it be that the census figures are indicative of a re-emergence of a new community spirit 80 years after German-Australians were being branded for the first time as "enemy aliens" during World War I? Could it be that at the turn of the new century, German-Australians no longer felt that they had to be afraid of being vilified – more than five decades after the horrors of Nazism and World War II, with which people of German origin had been associated, if not stigmatised, over the subsequent decades? Could they now have the confidence to proclaim their ethnic identity in public as a matter of course, just like most other groups that make up the mosaic of Australia's multiethnic and multicultural population patchwork?

A somewhat different picture, along with other questions, emerges when one looks at the statistics of language usage and maintenance. In his latest book, *Australia's Language Potential*, Michael Clyne reports that in 2001 the number of German speakers in Australia was 76,444, a figure nearly 33 per cent lower than in 1991. The rate of decline is more than twice as high as that of other, comparable European languages; the corresponding figures for the decline in the number of Dutch, French and Italian speakers are 15, 13 and 16 per cent, respectively (Clyne 2005: 6). The statistics regarding language maintenance confirm the record decline of German as a community language. Migrants from Austria and Germany (along with their Dutch neighbours) represent by far the highest number of Australian residents of non-English speaking background who use "only English at home" (Clyne 2005: 70), while a comparison of language shift patterns among first and second generation migrants reveals an equally clear picture. With an aggregate figure (covering first and second generation migrants) of nearly 40 per cent, the number of German speakers who trade in their native language for English is far higher than that of comparable groups. Of course, one could cite a number of reasons for this: a perhaps higher degree of affinity with the mainstream Anglo-Celtic culture, the rapid dispersal of migrants from Germany into the wider community, a ready knowledge and application of the English language among more recent arrivals, etc. Nevertheless, the figures are striking enough to suggest that the German migrants are somehow different in comparison with other ethnic groups in Australia. Could the fact that they do not seem to make up a readily identifiable community be a reason, or a contributing factor, for German speakers in Australia appearing to be so keen to give up their language?[1]

Language teachers in Australia, both on the secondary and tertiary level, have witnessed the weakening of German as a second language in schools and universities over the last decades, which has paralleled the shrinking numbers of German speakers in the wider Australian community. The introduction of new, mainly Asian language programs as a result of government policy has led to significant curriculum changes, with the result that German, once one of the privileged foreign languages taught in Australia, has lost much of its traditional clientele. In many secondary schools, German has dropped out of the curriculum altogether. In universities, the study of German language and literature – or German Studies as an area based, interdisciplinary course of study – has largely been absorbed by other units, such as Applied Linguistics or European Studies. In an academic environment where language teaching has become part of a business culture, in which "exporting" means attracting to the home campus full fee paying overseas students mainly from Asia, "non-competitive" languages like German are facing the dire prospect of being declared "unviable".

Clyne observes that the decline of German in the curriculum "has been very substantial in New South Wales and Western Australia, but the language is still doing relatively well in Queensland and South Australia" (Clyne 2005: 115–16). That may be so, but considering that the decline is occurring in an educational environment where, across the nation, "languages are the cinderellas of the school curriculum" (Clyne 2005: 22) – still awaiting rescue by their princes, one might add – there seems to be little reason to be optimistic about the possibility of a re-

1 Clyne's statistics, of course, do not come as a complete surprise. There is a long tradition, particularly among German speakers who consider themselves "cosmopolitan", to adopt foreign language expressions and patterns. As early as 1848, Heinrich Hoffmann, then a member of the revolutionary *Vorparlament* in Frankfurt and otherwise better known as the author of the original *Slovenly Peter [Struwwelpeter]*, observed that, "nobody finds it easier to become a German citizen than a foreign word" [Niemand wird leichter deutscher Staatsbürger als ein fremdes Wort] (Hoffmann 1848).

naissance of German as a community language or of German regaining a stable position in the educational sector. Queensland and South Australia are traditionally the states with the highest number of German migrants. But in Queensland, only 5.8 per cent of all Year 12 students are taking a language other than English. The corresponding figure for South Australia is 11.4 per cent, also below the national average of 13.1 per cent (Clyne 2005: 117).

Where does all this leave us with regard to the question of a "German presence" in Australia? The numbers suggesting an increase in ethnic awareness and decreasing language use clearly do not correlate. We are presented with a curious dichotomy: while the number of persons who identify themselves as being German-Australians appears to have risen sharply over the last two decades or so, there has been a simultaneous and serious decline of German as an Australian community language, with immigrants from Germany, Austria and the German-speaking part of Switzerland shifting to English as their preferred means of communication, both inside and outside their homes, within a very short time. Is language maintenance unrelated to the existence or resurgence of an ethnic group as a culturally autonomous, identifiable entity within Australian society? And who are the people whose stories are hidden behind the anonymous statistics? Does the German-Australian community, if indeed it can be said to exist at this time in history, have a future, or does it only have a past?

II

What does it mean if scholars are said to be investigating a "German presence" as part of a research program in social, historical, linguistic or other studies in Australia? It appears that the papers presented at Lee Kersten's 2005 Adelaide conference on "The German Presence in South Australia" and at the 2006 University of Sydney colloqium "Germans in Australia" are about resuming a scholarly debate that flourished briefly during the 1980s but that seems to have been more or less abandoned after or around 1990. A large number of articles, monographs and edited collections appeared during that period. The first to set the scene was Joseph Vondra's *German Speaking Settlers in Australia*, published in Melbourne in 1981. From Germany, Johannes H. Voigt, Professor for overseas history at Stuttgart University, contributed with *New Beginnings: The Germans in New South Wales and Queensland*, published in 1983. The book is in many ways typical of the volumes that were to follow. It commemorated a number of centenaries: of the foundation of the German clubs in Sydney and Brisbane, the consecration of the Lutheran German Church in Goulburn Street, Sydney, the founding of the city of Broken Hill by the German emigrant Charles Rasp and, finally, the arrival in Australia of Heinrich Niemeyer who was to become the founding father and head of the (German language) Apostolic Church of Queensland. Voigt's multifaceted volume already presents an impressive picture of the breadth and width of early migration from Germany to the east coast of Australia. A similar volume was published in 1985 on the occasion of the 150th anniversary of the first settlement in Victoria and the 125th anniversary of the German Club in Melbourne. Entitled *The German Connection: Sesquicentenary Essays on German-Victorian Crosscurrents 1835–1985*, it was edited by Leslie Bodi and Stephen Jeffries of the German Department at Monash University. Their colleagues Manfred Jurgensen and Alan Corkhill from the University of Queensland followed suit three years later with a volume on Queensland (*The German Presence in Queensland*), while Jürgen Tampke and David Walker of the University of New South Wales were the editors of yet another commemorative collection, *From Berlin to the Burdekin*, published in 1991, which was not restricted to developments in that particular state, however.

In South Australia, a similar scholarly collection was not produced, but the writings of Ian Harmstorf filled in the gap to some extent. Harmstorf's "Some Observations on South Australian German History" presented material from his PhD thesis on German migration to South Australia. His subsequent monograph (written together with M. Cigler) on *The Germans in Australia* was part of a series of government-sponsored publications featuring accounts of the contributions of various ethnic groups to the development of a multicultural Australian society in the context of the country's bicentennial celebrations. Similarly, Johannes H. Voigt's study, *Australien und Deutschland: 200 Jahre Begegnungen, Beziehungen und Verbindungen* [*Australia and Germany: 200 Years of Encounters, Relationships and Connections*], published in

135

1988 with a Grußwort [Greeting Note] by Germany's President, Richard von Weizsäcker, was presented as a kind of official bicentennial volume for German readers. In the same year, *The German Experience of Australia 1833–1938* was published by the Australian Association of von Humboldt Fellows, jointly edited by Ian Harmstorf and Paul Schwerdtfeger. Also in 1988, Marlene Norst and Johanna McBride contributed to this collection with a book on the story of Austrian migrants, entitled *Austrians and Australia*. Finally, *Australia, 'Willkommen'. A History of the Germans in Australia* by Jürgen Tampke and Colin Doxford, published in 1990 by UNSW Press, was the last of the series of monographs published around the date of the Australian Bicentenary. A relative latecomer was *The Germans in Western Australia* by Mary Mennicken-Coley, published in 1993. To complete this survey, mention should also be made of the more specialised research of Walter Veit of Monash University, who edited a number of studies on the European perception and exploration of the Pacific (notably two volumes on *Captain Cook: Image and Impact*, published in Melbourne in 1972 and 1979, respectively) and on *The German Contribution to Australian Anthropology and Science* (Alice Springs, 2003), with special emphasis on the work of Carl Strehlow.

The aforementioned studies on Germans in Australia, to which must be added a number of smaller articles in journals and other publications, testify to the lively interest in German-Australian issues during the 1980s.[2] It was an interest that was fuelled on the one hand by the official bicentennial celebrations and the funding possibilities made available during this period, and on the other hand, by the increasing multicultural awareness that had its origins in the policy changes of the 1970s. Similarly, one might argue that the lack of a continuing engagement with this area of research since the early 1990s attests to the relative disinterest of Commonwealth funding bodies (which largely drive research trends and initiatives), which in turn reflects

---

2 I am concentrating here on book-length studies. For further material, see the bibliographies in Voigt 1983: 279–86 and Tampke & Walker 1991: 241–42. These bibliographies also list the earlier studies on Germans in Australia, notably by Augustin Lodewyckx (1932), Wilfried Borrie (1954) and Charles A. Price (1957, 1972, 1975).

on the minimal governmental commitment to promoting Australian multiculturalism during the Howard years, except perhaps by way of lip service. The Howard government's lack of concern in multicultural matters could be observed in many areas, for instance in its relation to the work of United Nations agencies. In 2005, the Australian government under John Howard was one of only six nations who refused to sign the Universal Declaration on Cultural Diversity, an initiative of the General Conference of UNESCO. The document, "designed to save unique cultures from rampaging homogeneity" in the wake of galloping globalisation, was adopted by 148 nations, suggesting to at least one Australian observer that Australia may have become a "cultural pariah" within the international community (Creagh, 3 February 2006).

Not surprisingly, the 1980s volumes on Germans in Australia have a number of features in common. Some of the authors or editors seek a kind of semi-official status for their works by prefacing them with forewords and addresses from various public figures or patrons, such as consuls, ambassadors, German as well as Australian politicians, or university officials. The collection of the Queensland University German Department takes the cake in this respect, with no less than seven introductory addresses. The edited collections arose out of conferences organised mainly by the various German departments mentioned; they brought together "Germanists" who had embarked on a program to redefine their traditional, philological-literary discipline into a more historically and socioculturally accentuated German Studies concept, along with Australian historians, anthropologists and scholars in the natural sciences.

These studies are predominantly commemorative and celebratory in nature. Their publication dates were usually linked to coincide with foundation dates or anniversaries to emphasise the continuity of German immigration and its impact on the development of Australian society; the preferred term is usually "the German (or Austrian) contribution" to Australian arts, science, education, business, etc. The contributions focused mainly on the 19th and early 20th centuries; they covered the work of the early German settlers, notably in the traditional areas of German settlement such as the Barossa Valley or Southeast Queensland, the role of the churches and clubs as community institutions, the influence of the 1848 liberal-democratic migrants through their journalistic work (Püttman in Melbourne and Muecke in South Australia), as well as the contributions of eminent scientists and artists such as von Müller, Neumaier, Leichhardt or Becker. Less attention was paid to the war years and the interwar period of the 20th century, and the second half of the century remains even less researched.

As a rule, the authors go to pains to stress the positive influence of German immigrants, the achievements of explorers and scientists, as well as of the pioneering farmers and businessmen. The narratives follow mostly biographical or genealogical patterns; they are often anecdotal rather than concerned with structural, larger social or political issues and questions. These are histories that favour the stories of individuals. A characteristic example is the Tampke/Doxford volume *Australia, 'Willkommen'* that, according to its programmatic dust jacket text "documents the rich and varying contributions made by Germans in Australia and breathes life into the stories of their hardships, triumphs and quiet achievements." The Germans, the readers are told, are indeed the "quiet achievers" in Australian society. The coffee table format of this particular volume, with its glossy front cover depicting the schoolhouse at the Hermannsburg Mission, along with the book's abundant illustrations, seems itself a sign of the celebratory nature of this kind of historical writing.

My own study of 1989, *Enemy Aliens: Internment and the Homefront Conflict in Australia 1914–20*, took a different approach. The analysis of the treatment of German-speaking migrants during wartime was meant to offer a contribution to a multicultural Australian history in which the "war at home" was seen as a violent conflict over the future identity, character and composition of Australian society at large. It did not aim to present a contribution to a narrow "ethnic history" with an affirmative view of Australian history as a story of inevitable progress towards multiculturalism, but it chose instead to investigate the dynamics of sociocultural and political interaction between a majority and a minority in a society that was at a difficult phase in its emergence from a colonial past. Rather than playing down areas of conflict and issues of contention, the book focused on the persecution of the German-Australian minority during World War I as a result of policy differences and internal cleavages within Australian society at a time of crisis. This change in treatment of migrants who had previously been regarded as model immigrants and neighbours, as "our Germans", was seen as part of the larger Australian war effort, a psychological reaction to a danger that was unfolding far away but that had profound repercussions on a transplanted "British" society at the very fringe of the Empire. The war to be fought at home was seen as part of a larger policy objective of the Australian government that used the war effort for its partisan purposes, both in order to shape the nature of Australian society and to influence its development towards a certain kind of modernity. In this, ironically, the Hughes government followed a "German model" of "negative integration", by stigmatising and persecuting an imaginary enemy against which the majority could be rallied to present a united front, a process which attempted to gloss over existing social conflicts and contradictions (Fischer 1995). The "war at home" conducted by the government, which called on the Australian people to assist in every way possible, fuelled a jingoistic atmosphere of demarcation; its aim was to emphasise the "Britishness" of Australian society and to reinforce its links to the Empire.

This particular experience of "Australians at war" at home needs to be contrasted with the development of an Australian nationalism generated by the Anzac (Australian and New Zealand Army Corps) story, arguably the most significant foundation myth of Australian nationhood. The invention of an internal enemy, which in the end included not only German nationals and naturalised or native-born German-Australian residents, but also a variety of socialists, Irish republicans, pacifists and other anti-war campaigners, was not fully successful, as the two failed conscription referenda show. However, it was effective enough to put a stop to the continuing development of an original multicultural – or at least, seen from the German-Australian perspective bi-cultural – society which had been in full swing by the end of the 19th century when the German-Australian community was by far the largest of the non-British immigrant groups. The aim of emphasising a homogenous society that was clearly and exclusively British in its ethnic, "racial" and cultural make-up, while also and at the same time independently Australian in national character, was largely realised. World War

I confirmed the "White" and British "destiny" of the Australian people; it was to be a home for Australian "Britishers", monocultural and
monolingual – there was no room for anything else. Seen in this light,
I argue in *Enemy Aliens* that World War I was the end of a period, not
a beginning. The war brought about the disintegration of the German-
Australian community, which had previously been a strong and proud,
highly visible, yet fully accepted, integrated and valued part of Australian society. By the end of the war, German-Australians had largely gone
underground, into assimilationist hiding, and their community had
been destroyed as a public, autonomous, sociocultural entity. Whether
it has now recovered, half a century after the World War II that in many
ways meant a carbon copy repetition of the homefront experience during 1914–18, is very much an open question.

III

Enemy Aliens was received with a lot of interest and with positive re-
views by critics in Australia and overseas.[3] To my surprise, however,
the concluding thesis of the book, namely that World War I meant the
end of the German-Australian community, has never been taken up by
commentators, even though it seemed to me to be the most provocative
supposition of the study. What has happened to the cultural presence of
German-Australians in the public life of Australia and to its traditions
that were instituted before 1914? If there was no German community

---

3 An exception is John Moses who has argued that the treatment of the German-
Australian minority during World War I was justified on national security
grounds. Cf. John A. Moses, *Australia and the 'Kaiser's War' 1914–1918: On
Understanding the ANZAC Tradition. Argument and Theses*. Brisbane, 1993;
*Prussian-German Militarism 1914–1918 in Australian Perspective: The Thought of
George Arnold Wood*. Bern, 1991. A similar line is followed by a group of authors
(Anthony Cooper, Peter Overlack, Craig Wilcox and Jürgen Tampke) whose work
was published in a special cluster in *The Australian Journal of Politics and History*,
Vol. 40, no. 1 (1994). I think the argument of Moses et al. misses the point: es-
sentially they treat the German-Australians as "aliens", rather than as Australian
citizens (either native born or naturalised) or permanent residents loyal to their
new country and to its political institutions including the Crown. I have commented on the debate that followed the publication of *Enemy Aliens* in my article
" 'Negative Integration' and an Australian Road to Modernity: Interpreting the
Australian Homefront Experience in World War I" (Fischer 1995).

during most of the 20th century, then what does that mean with regard to the experiences of German migrants in this period? How have
German migrants "survived" without a community? How do their experiences differ from other migrant groups? The scholars who wrote about
the "German presence" in the 1980s were perhaps still too close to the
experience of World War II and to the generations of postwar migrants
to conduct in-depth studies along these lines of enquiry, but it seems
that perhaps today, after half a century of peaceful relations between
Germany and Australia, the time has come for a new wave of research
that would focus on German migration during the second half of the
last century. This appears all the more imperative when one considers
that the migrants who arrived around 1950 and later are now aged at
least in their 70s: the sources and opportunities for research projects in
oral history will rapidly shrink over the next few years.

The argument set out in *Enemy Aliens* also has repercussions with
regard to the study of a number of issues in Australian history that have
become topical again fairly recently, such as the question of citizenship.
Government practices instituted under wartime emergency regulations,
such as restrictions on free speech and freedom of organisation, or even
more drastically, the removal of naturalisation certificates by adminis-
trative *fiat* and the subsequent mass deportation of civilian internees
who had been held in detention without trial, must be seen as having
been unprecedented measures with regard to a traditional political cli-
mate that had seemed to guarantee a fair degree of individual protection
under British common law. Now, all of a sudden, this had proven to be
illusionary. According to David Dutton, the Federal government's civil
rights policies (or rather the lack thereof) during World War I constituted an important turning point in Australian citizenship policy: its
repercussions are as relevant today as they were then (Dutton 2002). As
Alison Holland has observed:

> The war set a precedent: once established, actions and pro-
> cesses could be, and were, replicated in times of national
> emergency or apparent threat … The war, therefore, demon-
> strated how far the national government was prepared to go
> to override the civil and political rights of citizens in the inter-
> ests of national security and defence – internal and external.

It showed how ideas of race and nationality underpinned and legitimised violations of such rights. It demonstrated at once the significance (from a liberal governance perspective) and potential insignificance (from a citizen's perspective) of citizenship to the nation state. It demonstrated that the state was not beyond using violence in the interests of social cohesion, and that difference (racial, cultural, political) constituted the biggest threat to it (Holland 2005: 159–60).

Holland also points to the precedents of civil rights violations during World War I in the area of industrial organisation and their implications in the decades following the war up until the 1950s (Holland 2005: 160; Davidson 1997), as well as to "the practice of alien internment" as having "provided the setting for the mass incarceration without trial of people who had committed no crime" (Holland 2005: 160).

The destruction of the German-Australian community as a watershed experience of World War I also offers new insights into Australian multiculturalism and its history. For one thing, it puts into question the triadic paradigm of assimilation-integration-multiculturalism. According to this scheme, which seems to be generally accepted by writers on Australian multiculturalism, attitudes and policies in Australia towards non-British migrants can be defined by a "shift from assimilation through integration to multiculturalism" (Wooden et al. 1994: 317).[4] In terms of periodisation, assimilationism is thought to express the prevailing attitude until the mid-1960s, while "pluralistic integration" appears as a kind of transitory stage, from the 60s to the early 70s, which ushers in the present phase of multiculturalism (Lippmann-Report 1975: 51). In a key study on *Multiculturalism and the Demise of Nationalism in Australia*, the period of 1945–72 is summarised under the heading "Assimilation to Integration" (Castles et al. 1992: 43–56). The term integration is thus used to distinguish a specific, innovative phase in the development of Australian society. In the earlier period,

---

4 The material on "integration" is in part taken from my article "Integration, 'Negative Integration', Disintegration: The Destruction of the German-Australian Community during the First World War" (Fischer 2000). An earlier German version of this is "Desintegration: Über die Zerstörung der deutsch-australischen Community während des Ersten Weltkrieges" (Fischer 1997).

assimilation is said to have aimed at creating a homogeneous, uniform society in which ethnic differences were supposed to disappear and immigrants were presumed to become socially and culturally invisible, indistinguishable from other residents of the mainstream Anglo-Celtic Australian society. As an alternative policy, integration presupposed a model of a "plural society", which allowed for the recognition of ethnicity and distinct ethnic identities that could "co-exist" within "a common realm" defined by equal political and civil rights and shared "social valuations" (Lippmann-Report 1975: 49). This policy promoted, in the words of Nick Bolkus, the former Minister for Immigration in the Keating government, the "acceptance as full equals [of] all people living legally in Australia and recognised immigrants' legitimate desire to retain their languages and cultures" (Bolkus 1994: 453). Multiculturalism, finally, is said to acknowledge the existence of different ethnic communities as a factor of societal enrichment. As a post-nationalist "state ideology", it is primarily interested in safeguarding and managing the ethnic, linguistic and cultural diversity of Australian society as an important "national resource" and as part of the country's identity, of its "national distinctiveness" (Castles et al. 1992: 44). The historical experience of German migration does not seem to support this model, however, except perhaps as the exception that proves the rule (but why, again, do the Germans again seem to be following a *Sonderweg*, in other words, present a different ethnic profile or a unique and special way of integration into Australian society in comparison with other migrant groups?). In any case, further theoretical clarification as to exactly what it is that constitutes integration and further analysis of the particular historical circumstances of the integration and disintegration of the German community in the early 20th century seems very much desirable.

Finally, the argument put forward in *Enemy Aliens* that Australian society during and after World War I became less "civil" and less firm in its commitment to its liberal-democratic traditions and to upholding basic civil rights and liberties, also seems to be a useful point of departure for a discussion of current developments in Australia. The questions involved in this debate entail the making of a significant judgment on a key issue regarding Australian history in the 20th century,

143

namely, which period might be considered the formative, dominant paradigm which will set the mode for the sociocultural development of Australia over the next few decades. Is it the exclusionary, assimilationist and monocultural period of the 1920s–1960s, or is it the open, inclusionary, multicultural era of the 1970s and 1980s?

At a time when new social cleavages are emerging and when existing tensions newly erupt along the faultlines of perceived "ethnic" and "racial" differences and prejudices, which somehow seem to belong to a previous era, it might be appropriate to remember that such conflicts are not new in Australian history. Following the brief appearance of "Hansonism" in the 1990s, we are currently witnessing the introduction of "innovative" policies of surveillance, practices regarding the identification of suspects, of the pre-emptive arrest and detention of alleged enemies of the state, whether Australian citizens, residents or otherwise. These government practices, relating for instance to the so-called war on terror or the policy of mandatory and indefinite detention of asylum seekers, are sometimes seen as unprecedented, but such practices, or similar ones, have in fact a prehistory which might tell us something about the nature of Australian society and its historical development today. To give only one concrete example: during World War I, police and military personnel routinely searched asylums for the mentally ill to identify so-called enemy aliens who were then arrested, interned for the duration of the war and subsequently deported, or "repatriated", as the official language used at the time had it. This was not because they were seen as hostile or as a threat to the security of the nation, but in the interest of social and national efficiency and homogeneity. Recent cases of mistreatment by government officials of similarly disadvantaged immigrants, like that of German migrant Cornelia Rau and of Australian citizen Vivian Solon, originally a migrant from the Philippines, may seem to suggest that the political culture that determines the actions of individual policy officers in government departments, or indeed the corporate culture of key government agencies dealing with migrant affairs, has not kept up with the country's propagated self-image as an enlightened, liberal-democratic and non-racist multicultural nation. The study of migration, of migration history and of current practices regarding immigration policies and multiculturalism as they affect some of the nation's most vulnerable people, is important because it could provide something similar to a litmus test to determine the status of Australia as a country on the road to an enlightened, truly multicultural and inclusive civil society. But such studies cannot be undertaken in isolation, as in the earlier affirmative "ethnic histories". Instead, they should investigate the inevitably, albeit to various degrees, problematic and conflictual interaction of migrant communities and individual migrants with other migrant groups as well as with the majority of Anglo-Australians, both within the greater Australian society and its body politic.

IV

I would like to conclude by referring to two recent publications on the topic of Germans in Australia, which could be of interest to readers in Australia generally and the scholarly community in particular. The first one is *A German Church in the Garden of God: Melbourne's Trinity Lutheran Church 1853–2003*, published by the *Arbeitskreis für Kirchengeschichte* – Trinity Church Historical Society under the general editorship of Herbert D. Mees (Mees 2004). This is a massive book, more than 700 pages long, written by 17 different authors, richly illustrated and meticulously documented, with extensive references and bibliographical documentation. It is a history of a single church and its pastors and congregation over one and a half centuries. On the one hand it is a commemorative volume like the earlier ones mentioned above, complete with an introductory greeting by the German ambassador; but its singular focus as well as its sheer size, scope and attention to detail set it apart and make it a contribution that is quite unique in the literature on the German presence in Australia.

The *Dreifaltigkeitskirche*, a modest building situated at Parliament Square in East Melbourne between the imposing structures of St Patrick's Cathedral and the Victorian State Parliament, began life as a "church in a paddock" in the early years of the goldrush, when growing numbers of German-speaking migrants came to Melbourne along with fortune seekers from all parts of the globe. As can be expected, *A German Church in the Garden of God* is to a large extent concerned with church matters, including accounts of the sometimes bewildering succession of schisms and alliances among the various Lutheran synods in Australia and Germany and their – often seemingly petty – doctrinal theological differences. But the book is much more than merely a church history. Its first 12 chapters, in which are embedded biographical narratives of its 20 pastors, are chronologically arranged. Some follow the eras of service of individual pastors, while others more pointedly link the fate of the congregation to that of the history of the surrounding city and society. The last three chapters are devoted to an account of the buildings, the social and cultural life of the congregation, and to the relationship between the Melbourne Trinity parish and the parishes established under its tutelage in other parts of Victoria. The book provides a wealth of information on the social and cultural life of German migrants and their involvement in the civic and social affairs of their new home country, meticulously documenting continuity and changes. There are fascinating and colourful glimpses into the early days of the German-Australian communities. Mention is made of some Germans "who have turned altogether into Englishmen" (Mees 2004: 161) within a short time after their arrival. There is the appearance in Melbourne in the 1880s of a pastor from America who set up a new congregation but was eventually found out to be an imposter and bigamist. The daily life of pioneering German migrants is vividly recounted, as for instance in the heroic "Trek of 1869" by South Australian Lutheran farmers in their horse-drawn wagons from Light's Pass along the Murray River, to the Riverina district of New South Wales where they took up land and opened up the area for intensive cultivation. Regarding more recent developments, the book documents the ageing of the German Lutheran congregation, but it also draws attention to the new face of Australian multiculturalism, for example by reporting on the foundation in 1991 of a Chinese-speaking Lutheran congregation at Trinity Church in Doncaster, established in cooperation with the Hong Kong Lutheran Synod and with Cantonese-speaking pastors (Mees 2004: 409, 565).

In a book with 17 contributors there are bound to be some uneven patches, and that is certainly the case here. The chapters on the period between 1914–34 and "The Dark Days of War: 1935–45", for instance, could do with some more rigorous scholarship. However, such a critique is not by any means intended to detract from the value and merits of a remarkable publication. In his foreword to *A German Church in the Garden of God*, Geoffrey Blainey writes:

> This book weaves together important threads in the religious and social history of this land. In most pages the pastors and their flocks are viewed in the context of their times – times that were both turbulent and tranquil – and that sympathetic context is a special merit of this book (Mees 2004: ix).

One might add that another special merit of *A German Church in the Garden of God* lies in its exhaustive and fastidious documentation, which opens up a number of avenues for further research, notably with regard to questions that would link aspects of local history with a larger view of Australian history.

The second publication is Jürgen Tampke's *The Germans in Australia*, published in 2006. Regrettably, this is a book in an entirely different league. It is a miserly volume (not only in comparison to *A German Church in the Garden of God*): 167 pages of text with sketchy notes and a slim bibliography. Of course it is desirable and practical to read a book that is concise and to the point, with a tightly structured and succinctly developed argument. Tampke's book, however, is neither: it is anecdotal, repetitive and meandering. There is little that is not already covered in Tampke's study *Australia, 'Willkommen'*. As in this earlier book, the author plays down the effects of World War I, arguing that only a minority of German migrants were interned and that the threat posed by imperial Germany's war objectives justified the measures taken, even though he acknowledges some isolated cases of harsh treatment. However, the social and political function of the repressive measures against imagined "enemy aliens" and political dissidents in terms of defining the nature of Australian political culture and identity during and after the war is never questioned. Most curious is the book's cover illustration, which shows a group of Germans in *Lederhosen* and traditional folkloric dress marching down some suburban street; the caption reads "Australia Day ceremony at St Kilda (ca. 1954)". One can only wonder what kind of image of the "Germans in Australia" this picture is meant to convey to readers at the beginning of the 21st century. Perhaps, like the inconclusive speculation about how to "assess" the "German contribution to Australia" (Tampke 2006: 167) at the end of the book, Tampke's cover illustration simply points to an historical consciousness that seems trapped in a time warp.[5]

Bibliography

Bodi L & Jeffries S (Eds) (1985). *The German Connection: Sesquicentenary Essays on German-Victorian Crosscurrents 1835–1985*. Monash University: German Department.

Bolkus N (1994). Multiculturalism: The Australian Way. In M Jurgensen (Ed), *Riding Out: New Writing from Around the World*. Brisbane: Outrider/Phoenix Publications, 451–63.

Castles S, Kalantzis M, Cope B & Morissey M (1992). *Mistaken Identity: Multiculturalism and the Demise of Nationalism in Australia*. Leichhardt: Pluto Press.

Clyne M (2005). *Australia's Language Potential*. Sydney: UNSW Press.

Creagh S (2006). The Optimist Versus the PM in the Chase for a Renaissance. In *Sydney Morning Herald*, 3 February 2006.

Davidson A (1997). *From Subject to Citizen: Australian Citizenship in the 20th Century*. Melbourne: Cambridge University Press.

Dutton D (2002). *One of Us? A Century of Australian Citizenship*. Sydney: UNSW Press.

---

5 It would be easy to pass over Tampke's book in silence if it were not for the fact that it was published by Cambridge University Press. A publication of this kind does not make a serious contribution that would help fill the "ethnic gap" within modern Australian historiography. Historical writing in Australia today is still dominated by an overwhelming majority of professionals writing from an Anglo-Celtic Australian perspective. The publication by CUP of Tampke's *The Germans in Australia* does the profession a disservice: if a reputable academic publisher might suggest to potential readers that its product presents the results of research that is "state of the art", historians might legitimately wonder whether there is much to be missed by the absence of contributions that represent genuinely scholarly "ethnic voices" and that offer more than superficially multicultural views of Australian history.

Fischer G (1989). *Enemy Aliens. Internment and the Homefront Conflict in Australia 1914–20.* St Lucia, Qld.: University of Queensland Press.

Fischer G (1995). 'Negative Integration' and an Australian Road to Modernity: Interpreting the Australian Homefront Experience in World War I. *Australian Historical Studies.* 26(104): 452–76.

Fischer G (1997). Desintegration: Über die Zerstörung der deutschaustralischen Community während des Ersten Weltkrieges. In M Beer, M Kintzinger & M Krauss (Eds), *Migration und Integration: Aufnahme und Eingliederung im historischen Wandel.* Stuttgart: Franz Steiner Verlag, 121–44.

Fischer G (2000). Integration, 'Negative Integration', Disintegration: the Destruction of the German-Australian Community During the First World War. In K Saunders & R Daniels (Eds), *Alien Justice: Wartime Internment in Australia and North America.* St Lucia, Qld.: University of Queensland Press, 1–27.

Gibbs S (2005). Wannabes and Ethnicity. In *Sydney Morning Herald*, 26 April 2005.

Harmstorf I & Cigler M (1985). *The Germans in Australia.* Melbourne: AE Press.

Harmstorf I & Schwerdtfeger P (Eds) (1988). *The German Experience of Australia 1833–1938.* Melbourne: Australian Association of von Humboldt Fellows.

Harmstorf I (1985). *Some information on South Australian German history.* Adelaide: South Australian College of Advanced Education.

Hoffmann H (1848). Handbüchlein für Wühler oder kurzgefaßte Anleitung in wenigen Tagen ein Volksmann zu werden. Von Peter Struwwel, Demagog. Frankfurt [Online]. Available: http://gutenberg.spiegel.de/hoffmann/wuehler.

Holland A (2005). The Common Bond? Australian Citizenship. In M Lyons & P Russell (Eds), *Australia's History: Themes and Debates.* Sydney: UNSW Press, 152–71.

Jurgensen M & Corkhill A (Eds) (1988). *The German Presence in Queensland.* University of Queensland: German Department.

Jupp J (1995). The Hidden Migrants: German-speakers in Australia Since 1950. In M Jurgensen (Ed), *German-Australian Cultural Relations Since 1945*. Bern: Peter Lang, 63–75.

Lippmann–Report (1975). *Committee on Community Relations: Final Report*. Department of Labour and Immigration, Parliamentary Papers No. 298/1975, Canberra.

Moses JA (1991). *Prussian-German Militarism 1914–18 in Australian Perspective: The Thought of George Arnold Wood*. Bern: Peter Lang.

Moses JA (1993). *Australia and the 'Kaiser's War' 1914–18: On Understanding the ANZAC Tradition. Argument and Theses*. St Lucia, Qld.: Broughton Press.

Mees HD (Ed) (2004). *A German Church in the Garden of God: Melbourne's Trinity Lutheran Church 1853-2003*. Melbourne: *Arbeitskreis für Kirchengeschichte*, Trinity Church Historical Society.

Mennicken-Coley M (1993). *The Germans in Western Australia: Innovators, Immigrants, Internees*. Mt Lawley: Edith Cowan University.

Norst M & McBride J (1988). *Austrians and Australia*. Potts Point, NSW: Athena Press.

Tampke J & Doxford C (199). *Australia, 'Willkommen': A History of the Germans in Australia*. Kensington: UNSW Press.

Tampke J & Walker D (Eds) (1991). *From Berlin to the Burdekin: The German Contribution to the Development of Australian Science, Exploration and the Arts*. Kensington: UNSW Press.

Tampke J (2006). *The Germans in Australia*. Melbourne: Cambridge University Press.

Veit W (Ed) (1972; 1979). *Captain James Cook: Image and Impact*, 2 Vols. Melbourne: Hawthorn Press.

Veit W (1994). Carl Strehlow, Ethnologist: The Arunta and Aranda Tribes in Australian ethnology. In TR Finlayson & G McMullen (Eds), *The Australian Experience of Germany: Proceedings of the Fifth Biennial Conference of the Australian Association of Humboldt Fellows*. Melbourne: Monash PS, 77–100.

Veit W (2003). *The German Contribution to Australian Anthropology and Science*. Strehlow Research Centre, Occasional Paper 3. Alice Springs: Strehlow Research Centre.

Voigt JH (Ed) (1983). *New Beginnings: The Germans in New South Wales and Queensland*. Stuttgart: Institut für Auslandsbeziehungen.

Voigt JH (1988). *Australien und Deutschland: 200 Jahre Begegnungen, Beziehungen und Verbindungen*. Hamburg: Insitut für Asienkunde.

Vondra J (1981). *German Speaking Settlers in Australia*. Melbourne: Cavalier Press.

Wooden M, Holton R, Hugo G & Sloan J (1994). *Australian Immigration: A Survey of the Issues*. Canberra: Australian Government Publishing Service.

6
German Anzacs and the First World War

John F. Williams

The Anzacs and "Kaiser" Schmidt

A prevailing image of Australia's treatment of its German minority in World War I, one occasionally encouraged by academics and fed into popular culture, centres on internment (justified or otherwise) and persecution. Many German-Australians did suffer degrees of persecution, and this was even directed at families who had sons, brothers or husbands who were fighting and dying at the front in the Australian Imperial Force (AIF). There is also no doubt that in the interwar years, attempts to disguise the contribution of German-Australians to the national effort in World War I – which occasionally extended to chiselling out names of obvious German origin from small-town war memorials – were relatively successful. By the 1980s, a more sympathetic and less sensationalist treatment of a relatively neglected episode in 20th-century Australian history was beginning to surface – at least in the popular culture. To describe the sensitive and positive treatment of a German Anzac in the television mini-series *Anzacs* of the late 1980s as groundbreaking is hardly an exaggeration. At least it would have come as a surprise to Australians fed on the belief that internment and persecution was the fate of most "enemy aliens" in World War I.[1]

Anzacs is no *War and Peace*. Nor does it pretend to be. Dealing with the adventures, from Gallipoli in 1915 to the Somme in 1918, of a group of mates who serve in the same platoon, *Anzacs* is essentially a

---

1 Recent works dealing with internment and/or social conflict in Australia, principally during World War I include Gerhard Fischer, 1989; Marilyn Lake, 1975; Michael McKernan, 1980; Raymond Evans, 1987; Manfred Jurgensen & Alan Corkhill, "The Pen and the Sword: Anti-Germanism in Queensland During the Great War, and the Worker." In Jurgensen & Corkhill, 1988.

long "Buddy" movie in the form of television soap. While much care, research and funding obviously went into making the battle scenes and historical ambience as realistic as possible, the characters are two-dimensional and clichéd. Even so, on occasion *Anzacs* does offer insights that are unexpected and subtle, especially when dealing with the character of the German-born Wilhelm Schmidt. Since his was the "same name as the Kaiser", his mates decide he will be "Kaiser" Schmidt. To a good-natured enquiry, Schmidt replies, "My father who brought us out from Germany, he always taught us that freedom had its price" (Burrowes & Dixon 1985).

In one of the most remarkable and (dare it be said) moving scenes of the series, Schmidt, who by late 1916 has established himself as a courageous and capable soldier, is on patrol on the Somme with his squad in no-man's-land when suddenly he finds himself with a clear shot at a German soldier standing almost motionless in a gap in the opposing trenches. He raises his rifle and sights along the barrel: a sitting duck. Kaiser allows doubt to flicker across his face, waits to consider his options, then lets his barrel drop slowly to the ground. In a scene lasting barely 60 seconds, the dilemma that must have faced Australians "of enemy origin", in action against men who might be their cousins, is convincingly portrayed (Burrowes & Dixon 1985). Yet the Kaiser Schmidt figure in this series is not presented as unique; the clear implication being, and rightly so, that similar figures could be found in many a platoon in the 1st AIF. Nonetheless, such a depiction must surely have been an eye-opener to Anglo-Celtic Australians brought up on C.E.W. Bean's image of an AIF made up of "almost pure British stock – English, Irish, Scottish and Welsh, not so separate as in the British Isles, but blended" (Bean 1940: 3).

But if *Anzacs* encouraged a more open and positive view of the part played by German-Australians in World War I, the mini-series ignored their suffering on the home front. Internment was, however, addressed rather sensationally in *1915* (another Great War mini-series from the same era) (Yeldham 1982). Yet *1915* unknowingly reflects a view held in Germany; that Australia was "an even more bitter enemy of *Deutschtum* than its English mother-country and after the war did more than any other country to demonstrate antipathy towards all German expression" (Fuchs 1936: 61). This quotation, in a pan-German work with a foreword by Hermann Göring, was expressed by the captain of the *Köln*, a German light-cruiser which visited Australian ports shortly before World War II. Photographs of crowds welcoming and farewelling the ship and its crew suggest that, despite the hardships and persecutions of World War I, Australian *Deutschtum* had not been extinguished. It is easy to dismiss such comments as Nazi propaganda, but in truth they echoed views held since 1919 by Germans of various political shades, particularly those who remembered W.M. Hughes' wartime speeches and could read his anti-German outbursts at the Versailles Peace Conference. Australian *Deutschtum* and Irish Catholic Australia had been the principal victims of Hughes' savage "Those who are not for us are against us" war-winning campaign (Hughes quoted in *Times*, 27 August 1918).

The internment episodes of 1914–18 and 1939–45 were sorry blots on Australian 20th-century history. Not because these "concentration camps" (sometimes capitalised) remotely resembled those of the Third Reich, rather because internees were often unjustly deprived of liberty by the maliciousness of petty officialdom, or as a result of rumour-mongering by a business competitor, local politician or community elder with a grudge to settle or a profit in mind. Yet the internment saga is only a small part of the story. Some 4,500 German-born Australian residents were interned out of a German-born population of 36,000 in a German-Australian community of 150,000 or perhaps 200,000 souls. Seven hundred internees were British subjects and 70 were Australian born. In addition, some 2,500 German war prisoners were interned in Australia.[2] Thus, internment in a "concentration camp" was but one, statistically minor, German-Australian experience in World War I. And even then, not all internees were incarcerated without reason. As Geoffrey Serle has pointed out, while "the great majority of the Australian-born of German origins were entirely loyal, a few of them and

---

2 Population statistics from the Commonwealth Bureau of Census and Statistics, *Census of the Commonwealth of Australia 1911* and on the internment of civilians and prisoners of war etc. (principally from the cruiser SMS *Emden*) in National Archives of Australia (NAA): A11803, 1918/89/279; A11803, 1917/89/261; A11803, 1917/89/859 and MP16/1, 1916/1479. Also Fuchs 1936: 61–65.

some of the older generation of migrants were markedly pro-German" (Serle 1982: 205).

Stirred by media hate-mongers, Anglo-Australians inflicted some gross indignities on their fellow citizens, particularly in cities or towns where German-Australian numbers were small and where their customs and accents stood out in the local community.[3] In places where those of German descent were numerous or in the majority, they were far less likely to be picked on. Irrespective of location however, official state policy weighed heavily on citizens who now found themselves described as "enemy aliens" and regarded as pariahs or even potential traitors. While only a comparative handful of them ever saw an internment camp, after 1916 the threat of internment hung over the heads of thousands of non-naturalised and naturalised Germans in Australia. Having a son in the AIF was seen (sometimes incorrectly) as a guarantee against the break-up of a family and the suffering and indignities that even the most benign form of imprisonment was bound to cause. After the failure of the first conscription referendum, the threat that internment posed to older German-Australians acted as a spur to their sons to demonstrate loyalty to their adopted motherland by volunteering to become cannon-fodder for the armies of the British Empire.

---

3 For the first six months of the war, Australian newspapers had tended to restrict hostile criticisms to attacks on the Kaiser and what was commonly called "Prussian Militarism". In October 1914, the *Sydney Morning Herald (SMH)* was still proclaiming that "Our quarrel is not with the German people, it is with the sword of Prussian militarism." The *SMH* hoped that from the war "a regenerated Germany will arise, and we in Australia will welcome an accession to the ranks of the industrious German settlers we already have" (*SMH*, 10 October 1914). The appearance of the official British *Report of the British Committee on Alleged German Outrages presented to both Houses of Parliament by Viscount Bryce* (Sydney 1915) materially changed this. Although the report was based exclusively on the hearsay evidence of refugees – describing outrages for which scarcely a sole "eyewitness" was to be found – it sold in Australia in the tens of thousands, with its more sensational extracts being widely reprinted in the mass media. Perhaps the most famous Australian "anti-Hun" propaganda was created not by journalists or correspondents, but by cartoonists, of whom Norman Lindsay remains the best known exponent. Manning Clark believed Lindsay had "portrayed the Germans as the monsters inside himself, and then painted naked women to tickle the madness of the puritans in Australia" (Clark 1983: 403).

Some German-Australians endorsed the idealistic reasons for enlisting given by Kaiser in *Anzacs*, but whatever their reasons, the part played by German-Australians in the 1st AIF was substantial.

Australia, Germany and the Last Years of Peace

In 1913, few Australians except close followers of the Balkan War had even heard of Gallipoli.4 And although visiting British imperialists had a vested interest in saying otherwise, on the eve of the Great War, Australia had a perceptible national identity. And although Australians still often regarded themselves as "overseas" Britons, Australia by 1913 was already an important world trader – no longer identified as a collection of British colonies or a British appendage, but one of the world's up-and-coming new societies. It is true that over half of Australian trade was with Britain, for there were still strong "commercial and sentimental preferences in favour of the Mother Country", but Australia, on the eve of the Great War, was also fifth among the nations from which Germany imported; a relative position of influence and importance which it would never again attain.[5]

In 1913, what was grandly called the "Empire", "Dominions" or "Imperial" Trade Commission – or sometimes "Dominions Royal Commission"– toured the more lush and fertile fringes of the Australian continent. No matter what it was called, in retrospect this enterprise seems more like an exercise in public relations. Comprising an odd mixture of pensionable and beknighted Tory politicians, Whitehall bureaucrats and one very prominent novelist, the Commission's aims were to affirm the links that bound "John Bull and Company [through] trade and intercourse with the Mother-country and amongst the British Dominions" (*Daily Telegraph* [Sydney], 18 April & 21 April 1913). One of the clear, if understated, implications behind this visit was that the dominions were buying a little too much from the upstart Hohenzollern

---

4 In February 1913, Australians had been advised that Bulgarian cavalry was "attacking the Turkish outposts at Gallipoli, a town on the Dardanelles, 132 miles south-west of Constantinople" (*SMH*, 6 February 1913).

5 Economic data in "Australia" (supplement published by the High Commission for Australia) in *The Times*, 30 July 1914.

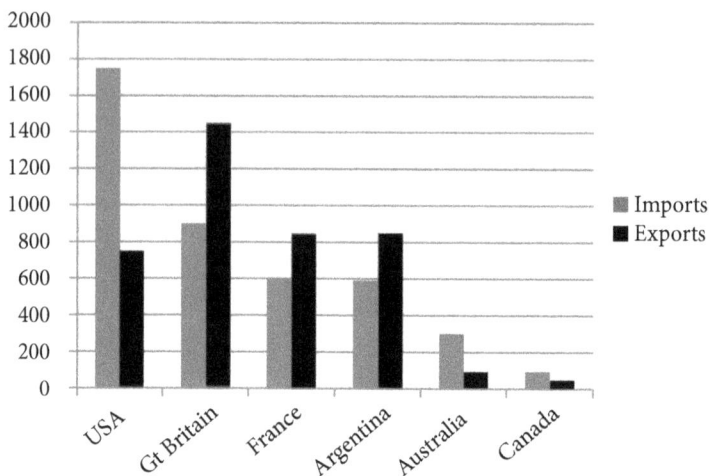

Germany, Six Principal Trading Partners – Marks Millions – 1913[6]

Empire, and that too much was being invested in the tools of production that the Germans had become expert in designing and manufacturing. In the Imperial scheme of things, the role of the dominions was to populate their lands in great numbers, then farm, mine or fell forests as raw materials for the factories of Mother England, from where the recycled material might be bought back by the dominions in the form of manufactured goods.

The trade commissioners of 1913 are now mostly footnotes in history. But one, Sir Rider Haggard, was already a post-Edwardian Imperial media star in his own right. The celebrated author of *She* (1887) and *King Solomon's Mines* (1885), Haggard was in Australia, not in the role of cultural luminary, rather, in his own words, as "a practical farmer, and one who knows the agricultural conditions throughout the world"; virtues that evidently qualified him to lecture Australians about their tendency to cluster too much in the big coastal cities. It was to "the man

---

6 From "La 'carte de guerre' économique, par André Fribourg", *L'Illustration*, 20 July 1918.

on the land that you must look for your wealth and your strength. (Hear, hear.) ... If you do not nurture and people your land, then the country must decay, as other nations have decayed." Haggard was convinced that deserts could be converted into arable land, and that Australia's supposedly Dead Heart "could maintain 40 to 50 millions of white people." But first, something would have to be done about the towns of Australia that were "already too big for the country (Cheers.)". There were two Australias – that of the towns, and that of the land – and it was the "Australia of the land that urgently needed developing (Cheers.)" (Haggard quoted in *SMH*, 31 March & 20 May 1913). Despite all the enthusiastic "Cheers!" and "Hear, Hears!", when Haggard and his fellow commissioners sought to criticise the usually sycophantic Australian Britons for daring to buy German manufactured and manufacturing products at the expense of those "Made in England", they received a chastening and quite unexpected response:

> Sir Rider Haggard ... received an unhesitating affirmative in reply to the suggestion that the goods supplied by the German traders were equal to, if not better, that those supplied by British merchants, that the arrangements made for the dissemination of information were better, that they were more obliging, and that, therefore, the natural tendency was for trade to go to Germany (*Daily Telegraph* [Sydney], 26 April 1913).[7]

The days of confusing loyalty to the Empire with good business were passing. Trade with the Reich in 1913 was lucrative and in Australia's favour, so much so that Australia ranked behind only the United States, Great Britain, France and Argentina in the value of its exports to Germany. The Germans were seen by many as a people to be admired. The

---

7 Sir H.R. Haggard (1856–1925) became Secretary to the Governor of Natal at the age of 19. In 1880, in Transvaal, he "witnessed its surrender to the Boers", returned to England, read for the Bar, but "soon discovered that literature was to be his career." The two interests in his life would be agriculture and romantic writing. In later years, much of Haggard's time was occupied with matters concerning the welfare of the British Empire. From 1912 to 1917 he travelled round the world as a member of the Dominions Royal Commission; in 1916 he visited all the dominions in connection with the post-war settlement of ex-servicemen.

British-born Australian High Commissioner in London, and former prime minister, Sir George Reid acclaimed them as one "of the finest peoples"; their nation the "fairest trader in the world" (Reid quoted in *SMH*, 15 November 1913).

Admiration for Germany in the last years of peace manifested itself in countless ways. Germany's technical education system was already an exemplar to more than one Australian state. "Modern civilisation", it was noted in the *Technical Gazette of New South Wales* in 1912, was "becoming every day more industrially efficient. It is leaving the battlefield and the forum, and wins its victories in the workshop" (Vol. 2, pt. 1; 4). No modern nation was having greater success than Germany, not only in training its workers, but also in inculcating in them "the basic conception of true education", the ancient "Greek ideal of human perfection in absolute mental and physical balance" (Vol. 2, pt. 1; 5). The German system of technical education had made of the Reich "that great and puissant modern nation whose power and influence are practically ungaugeable", an example Australia could only follow:

> Throughout Germany, the school, the polytechnic, the college, the university – each constitutes a unit, a rallying point, a focalising centre. Our Technical College should likewise be our Alma Mater (Our Benign Mother), our Collegiate Commonwealth ... [Every] member of our College can work to a standard worthy of the whole of us, as we expect our Australian cadets to do when the Compulsory Military Defence Scheme develops (Vol. 2, pt. 1; 9).

Civic leaders, such as the Victorian premier, James Watt, chose to look to German cities for inspiration rather than the run-down metropoles of the mother-country. Watt saw Berlin's "very modernity" as inspirational for Melbourne: the aims "being worked for in the great Australian cities", he believed, were exactly "those that have inspired the makers of Berlin" (Watt quoted in *Argus*, 14 July 1913). The city of the future would borrow from other cities already showing the way, but not it seems, British cities. Nor did American skyscrapers have many Australian admirers; it was thought that the tenement-block lifestyle of New York or Chicago must inevitably produce a race of feeble physique that could never be the backbone of a nation. To avoid this calamity, what Sydney needed was a "dispersion from the centre and [the] development of suburban areas" (*Bulletin*, 6 November 1913). It was to Germany "where scientific principles have been applied to municipal methods as perhaps nowhere else in Europe" that Sydney must look, to Germany where "cities and towns have solved the housing problems" (*Bulletin*, 6 November 1913).

Nonetheless, there was no gainsaying that Germany had become, over the 25-year reign of the present Kaiser, the greatest economic and potential military threat to the British Empire. While Germany's large-standing, conscript army could be accepted and tolerated, its decision to challenge Britannia's domination of the waves was another matter. As Germany's maritime power increased, the British dominions responded with due imperial patriotism, purchasing British-built battle-cruisers, which then became the flagships of the dominion-branch fleets of the Royal Navy. But Australia, alone in the British Empire, introduced compulsory military training for teenage youths. That these boys would one day have to fight seemed likely, even if there was no consensus as to who might be the enemy. "There is no fear that helmeted frown, with its brushed-up moustache is going to Teutonize or Prussianize the world", the *Bulletin* warned in August 1913. "It is the browny-yellow grin in a smooth, slant-eyed face that we must watch" (*Bulletin*, 21 August 1913).

The Germans were not only admired for their efficiency and industrial might. Few world figures received more Australian attention, at least in the conservative press, than the Kaiser. On the anniversary of his 25th year as Kaiser, the Sydney *Daily Telegraph* claimed he had "qualified himself as King Edward's successor to the 'Prince of Peace' ":

> It has been his dream since youth that England and Germany should march shoulder to shoulder for their common good in the field of international politics. Joining in that happy sentiment, Australians could yesterday have joined in the toast to the Kaiser with a "Hoch! Noch ein Mal! – Hoch!! Zum dritte [sic] Mal – Hoch!!!" (*Daily Telegraph* [Sydney], 17 June 1913)

The qualified affection that English men (and women in particular) held for Queen Victoria's crippled but dashing grandson did not extend to include the German people. The English had been brought up for too long on images (and music-hall jokes) about blockheaded, overweight (and ruthless) German commercial travellers, arrogant and cadaverous officer types with monocles screwed firmly into place above cruel, sneering faces, and clumsy dumb-witted students coming to work as part-time waiters in order to improve their English at seaside holiday restaurants. These were clichéd impressions that Australians could only share, if they chose, from afar. In contrast to that of their British kith and kin, the direct Australian experience of Germans was of industrious migrants who had come to live beside the Britishers; people valued for being a notch above the wayward Irish; exceptional racial stock with which the Australian Briton might profitably interbreed. By 1913, Germans – despite Germany's bans on emigration – still represented the Commonwealth's fourth-largest immigrant group, at almost 50 per cent that of the Irish and three times that of the Welsh.

The Coming of the Apocalypse

Australians have long been told that their parents and grandparents were "terrifyingly willing to go to war. Their only anxiety was that Britain was not" (Robson 1970: 21). If Australians were as enthusiastic as Lloyd Robson proposes, why then was it so difficult to fill the ranks of the first Expeditionary Force? Or, as Eric Andrews puts it: "Historians who make much of the 'rush to enlist' might do better to ask why 93.6 per cent of eligibles did not enlist" (Andrews 1993: 45). Nor is there much evidence to support Robson's claim that the "daily metropolitan newspapers were enthusiastically imperialist" (Robson 1982: 21). Indeed, Australians were being asked to do their best in an unwanted war, which the stridently imperialistic Sydney *Daily Telegraph* warned "would ultimately involve all the great Powers of Europe, drench their territories with blood, and possibly pave the way – by bringing about the complete exhaustion of the white nations – for the supremacy of the coloured races of the world" (28 July 1914). Not all papers were so alarmist, but few working journalists seemed to observe milling crowds and hordes of enthusiastic volunteers. The outbreak of war had come as a bolt from the blue, leaving most Australians bewildered and uncomprehending. Many viewed the implications with apprehension. No

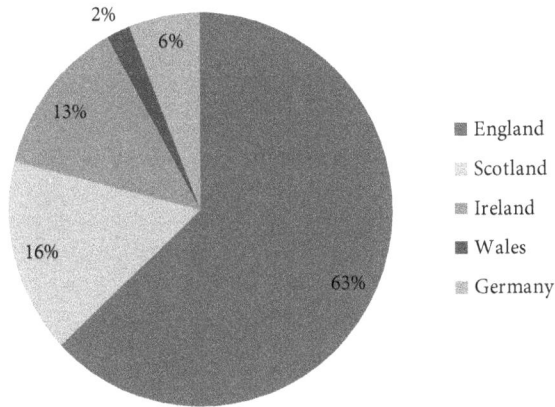

Australian birth rates 1912: of UK or German parentage (Knibbs 1914: 152).

one caught this feeling better than C.E.W. Bean. Writing years later and in the third person, he related, "as he walked home in the small hours" from his newspaper office, that

> [the] clouds, dimly piled high in the four quarters of the dark sky above seemed … like the pillared structure of the world's civilisation, of which some shock had broken the keystone. The wide gap overhead seemed to show where one great pillar after another had crashed as the mutual support had failed; and, as the sky peered through, the last masses seemed to sway above the abyss. The stable world of the nineteenth century was coming down in chaos: security was gone (Bean 1946: 22).

The idea that the outbreak of World War I was greeted by outpourings of enthusiasm by the populations of all the belligerent powers – and British dominions like Australia – is increasingly disputed by historians. Niall Ferguson points to research "which qualifies [the] thesis of mass bellicosity. Crowds there may have been but to describe their mood as simply one of 'enthusiasm' or 'euphoria' is misleading … [F]eelings of anxiety, panic and even millenarian religiosity were equally common responses to the outbreak of war" (Ferguson 1998: 177).[8] Indeed, once war was announced, newspapers that had been pessimistic and described apathy or anxiety, switched to reporting enthusiastic pro-war gatherings in patriotic terms. The "spirit of 1914" became idealised as mythical history, to be recalled throughout World War I at times when war weariness became apparent or morale seemed to be crumbling. Yet there were disputing voices in the mass media even in 1916. That year, while the Somme battle raged, Theodor Wolff, the esteemed editor-in-chief of the *Berliner Tageblatt*, recalled the German people learning of the declarations of war "with heavy hearts":

> [They] experienced it through sleepless nights as a giant, clutching spectre, and the resolution with which they embarked, arose not from joy, but a deep feeling of duty. There were still some who spoke of a "fresh, joyous war", and there were among the great multitude a few more, who immediately after the Austrian ultimatum was announced marched out into the streets with flags unfurled [and] yelled themselves hoarse in front of the Reich Chancellor's Palace (*Berliner Tageblatt*, 31 July 1916).

The agonies that gripped the hearts of many a German, Briton, Frenchman, Austrian or Russian must surely have been compounded in the case of an Australian of German ethnicity, language and culture, whose new homeland had now become the enemy of his ancestral *Heimat* and that of his kinfolk. Or, as the *Australische Zeitung* was obliged to put it, "what was not held to be possible" had come to pass: "England and Germany have declared war" ("Vom Kriegsschauplatz", *Australische Zeitung*, 12 August 1914). In this terrible predicament that the Australian-German community now faced, this German-language newspaper was in no doubt where its duty, and that of its readership, must lie:

> [It] is our duty, all Germans who have become Australian citizens, to remember that even if they might have father or mother, brother or sister, or other relatives over there in the old homeland [*Heimat*], that they, now that they have pledged their oath of loyalty to King George, adhere to the

---

8 See also Verhey, 1992.

new homeland, to which they owe so much and in which they were so freely and readily accepted … From the political standpoint, the English and the Germans have always lived peacefully with one another in all the countries of the world … Both peoples are too closely bound to one another in religion, culture and in family life, for any deeply entrenched antipathy to be able to take root, and in the expanded field of international business they are one another's best customers. Up until now, world history has never recorded a war between England and Germany, they have always fenced beside one another and this is the first time that they have stood as enemies against one another. God let it be the last time! ("Vom Kriegsschauplatz", *Australische Zeitung*, 12 August 1914)

1914

On 18 August 1914, the first draft of the new expeditionary force "showed itself to the citizens of Sydney" (*Daily Telegraph* [Sydney], 19 August 1914). These were described as "strapping, powerful and youthful men" who would "worthily uphold the reputation already won by Australian troops in the cause of Empire" (*Daily Telegraph* [Sydney], 19 August 1914). Even so, a headline in the Sydney *Daily Telegraph* stated still "More Men Wanted", even if they had to come from an unlikely source:

A German presented himself during the day. The officer asked him where he came from. "Well, I was born in Australia, Sir." "Where were your parents born?" "In Germany; they are pure German, but they settled in Australia." "What do you want to fight against your country for?" "Well, Sir, all my parents and myself have in the world is in Australia; all our interests and our home are here." "I don't much care about enrolling you." "But I demand to be enrolled; I want to defend what we've got." "Right, I'll enrol you," said the colonel, as he initialled the man's paper (*Daily Telegraph* [Sydney], 20 August 1914).

Other authorities seemed more at a loss to know how to deal with people who had been part of the local community but were now officially "enemy aliens". The Australian correspondent of the *Berliner Tageblatt* was strictly in this category. In a dispatch to Berlin sent well after the outbreak of the war, he commended the Australians for treating the "Germans living here with civility and respect" (*Berliner Tageblatt*, 16 October 1914). German citizens were "obliged under oath [to] report to the police that we wouldn't undertake anything hostile", and since it was "unacceptable for one of the Censors to open private letters", the *Tageblatt*'s representative was free to describe his impressions of Australia in the first month of war. To the Australian, all "notion of 'war' is unfamiliar." His land had:

> never seen a military campaign, never seen corpses on the field, never seen smoking wreckage or crushed crops. He can do all kinds of things, but not with flushed cheeks. He collects for wounded soldiers, attempts in vain to catch the tune of the Marseillaise [and] fits out an expeditionary corps of voluntary troops. The Federal Government promised 22,000 men. Three weeks ago, although married men were accepted, London had to accept less than 4,000 enlistments (*Berliner Tageblatt*, 16 October 1914).

While Germans still living in Australia were being treated with respect and even kindness – sentiments they appeared to reciprocate – more responsible local journals, like the *Sydney Morning Herald*, were at pains to point out that "Australia's quarrel is not with the German people, it is with the sword hand of Prussian militarism" (*SMH*, 9 September 1914). The *Herald* insisted that "we in Australia will welcome an accession to the ranks of the industrious German settlers we already have" from the regenerated Germany arising after its defeat in the war. Indeed, industrious settlers were already seeking to assert that loyalty publicly:

> A meeting was held to-day at Walla Walla, one of the principal centres of German settlement in Riverina. [The] following resolution was carried unanimously, with much enthusiasm … "That the German residents of Walla Walla and district express their unswerving loyalty to the British flag, and, as

Australian-born, are prepared at any moment if required, to stand shoulder to shoulder with their fellow Australian subjects in the defence of the British flag, and would be prepared to give their money or their blood, if required, in the defence of this country and the British flag, no matter who the invader may be" (*SMH*, 9 September 1914).

In the first month of the war, newspapers like the *Sydney Morning Herald* and Melbourne's *Argus* and *Age*, tended to be scathing in their treatment of journalists, editors and press barons who sought "to make a temporary profit out of the most bitter sufferings by pretending to satisfy a thirst for knowledge which is constant and insatiable, or by recalling descriptions of the horrors of war which only intensify the anxiety of those who are driven to read them" (*SMH*, 6 August 1914). Indeed, the restraint shown by the more serious Australian papers induced Sir Charles Lucas, on his return to London in October 1914, to praise the "standard of the leading newspapers in Australia" for being "as high as anywhere in the world" (*Times*, 20 October 1914). He was pleased to note the absence of a "violent outbreak of anti-German feeling" or anything that could be seen as "boastful or bombastic" (*Times*, 20 October 1914). In Australia, "as elsewhere, the war produced big headlines and sensational paragraphs", but the "general tone of the first-class journals left little to be desired" (*Times*, 20 October 1914).

While the tale of the German schoolboy thrown under a train at Stanmore (Sydney) station by his classmates is a myth, there were still sporadic outbreaks of anti-German feeling in those first months. In September 1914, the *Sydney Morning Herald* reported on strained feelings "between naturalised Germans and British [sic!] members of the Victorian Stevedoring association", which led to violence "when a German who was in the precincts of the club's premises at Port Melbourne threatened to trample down the British flag" (*SMH*, 9 September 1914).

> A fight immediately followed in which others took part, the Germans receiving a rough handling … Further fighting occurred this afternoon in which three Germans received a severe thrashing. They were then followed by a large crowd. Two escaped, and the other took refuge in the Port Melbourne police station. A placard was placed outside the club

rooms this afternoon stating "No Germans need apply." The police are taking action to those who have been concerned in the assaults (*SMH*, 9 September 1914).

Even while the *Herald* was warning its readership not to take atrocity stories seriously, its own headlines told of "German Outrages – Cold-Blooded Butchery", as a lead in to descriptions of the German destruction of the "town of Dint, between Namur and the French border. The women took refuge in a convent, but hundreds of men were shot" (*SMH*, 6 August 1914).

By New Year's Eve 1914, the German-language press in Australia was coming under even closer scrutiny. German-language newspapers, German-language schools and even German-language religious services would soon become things of the past. With all this in mind, as well as the four years of bloodshed and suffering that lay ahead, the *Australische Zeitung*'s final leader for 1914 seems hopelessly, almost pathetically optimistic, yet at the same time profoundly moving:

> The year that lies behind us was so over rich in fighting and sorrow as scarcely any before it … The whole world fervently hopes, along with us, that the New Year above all may soon bring about an end to this tragic war and bring the peace that is so yearned for. [But] the future might not be so confused as it appears, for we can with all confidence assert that the All Mighty, who guides the hearts of nations like streams of water, will guide also the events of the New Year to a wonderful and glorious conclusion ("Das Jahr 1914", *Australische Zeitung*, 30 December 1914).

This was wishful thinking. The best hopes of the *Australische Zeitung* came crashing down with the appearance of the now infamous Bryce Report in April/May 1915. For German-Australians, the appearance of the *Report of the British Committee on Alleged German Outrages presented to both Houses of Parliament by Viscount Bryce* – coming on the heels of the use of poison gas at Ypres, the sinking of the *Lusitania* and the tale of the "crucified Canadian"[9] – was a disaster. If the Bryce Report

---

9 The "crucified Canadian" first saw the light of day in the London *Times*. By-lined 'From Our Special Correspondent', the story appeared on 15 May 1915, almost a

and what the papers were now saying was to be accepted at face value, it must have seemed that there was something in the blood of ordinary Germans that impelled them to commit crimes against humanity. And if Reich Germans had an innate capacity to sink to the depths of depravity, why should German-Australians be different? If anything, the contents of the Bryce Report became better known to Australians than their British kinfolk. Supporters of the *Australian Statesman and Mining Standard* had seen to this, being "so impressed by the work" Bryce and his committee had "done in connection with the war" that they had

> come forward with an amount of money sufficient to enable it to be issued at a merely nominal price for the instruction of Australians and to counteract the attempt on the part of pro-Germans to discredit the tales told of atrocities by German troops. It may be mentioned that this work, which is here published at 6d., has been issued in Great Britain at 2/3 [two shillings and three pence] (Bryce 1915: 3).

The British price was cheap for a work that ran to over 430 pages. Its Australian price was barely more than a week's supply of daily newspapers. With its graphic descriptions of rape, torture and mutilation, Lord Bryce's report not only provided Australians with the "instruction" its supporters envisaged, but with a dangerously high dose of official

---

week after the Aubers Ridge debacle and just two days after the same paper's leader on the Bryce Report. The alleged victim, a sergeant, was "found transfixed to the wooden fence of a farm building. Bayonets were thrust, through the palms of his hands and his feet, pinning him to the fence. He had been repeatedly stabbed with bayonets, and there were many punctured wounds in his body." The correspondent admitted that he had "not heard that any of our men saw the crime committed", but still believed "that the man was dead before he was pinned to the fence, and that the enemy in his insensate rage and hate of the English wreaked his vengeance on the lifeless body of his foe" (*Times*, 15 May 1915). Another British correspondent, Philip Gibbs, accepted that "no Canadians were crucified." But so powerful was the myth, that he assumed it would be "believed in Canada for all time," despite being "analyzed and rejected by our General Headquarters" (Gibbs 1923: 165–66). Robert Graves likewise disbelieved the story, but credited it with causing the Canadians to share, along with Australians "the worst reputation for violence against prisoners." Graves excused Australians on the grounds of convict ancestry, they being "only two generations removed from the days of Ralph Rashleigh and Marcus Clarke" (Graves 1929: 235–36).

pornography for those ready to take out their misplaced loathing on fellow Australians who, for the main part, were peace-loving, loyal and industrious.

Some German Anzacs

German-Australians, a few German-born among them, were in the first waves ashore at Gallipoli and active in all the campaigns fought by the Australian Imperial Force in World War I. Names on gravestones or on the official roll only partly tell the story. Many German-Australians had anglicised their names in peacetime and, particularly in the first two years of the war when they might still be rejected, some chose to enlist under anglicised names or to adopt a pseudonym. Other German-Australians bore an Anglo-Saxon or Celtic name simply because their German descent was maternal. Among them was Alex Buckley VC, who joined up with his cousin Syd Falkenhagen. Buckley was killed in the action that won him his VC barely a week after the death of his younger cousin.

Nothing in the names Buckley and Falkenhagen suggests that the two young men who enlisted together at Dubbo (NSW) on 3 February 1916, were cousins. Alex Buckley, aged 24 and Syd Falkenhagen, aged 22, stemmed from a close-knit rural family that had established itself in the Bourke district of mid-western New South Wales. Buckley's German-ness was in the maternal line, his mother and Falkenhagen's father being two of ten children of German immigrants. The cousins enlisted together in 1916 and were assigned to the 54th Battalion. They trained together in England and, when they made it across the Channel to France, at the infamous Etaples base.[10] In November, Syd was made acting corporal during the final Passchendaele offensive in which he

---

10 "Etaples, about 15 miles south of Boulogne, was a notorious British Army base camp for those on their way to the front. Under atrocious conditions, both raw recruits from England and battle-weary veterans were subjected to intensive training in gas warfare, bayonet drill, and long sessions of marching at the double across the dunes. After two weeks at Etaples many of the wounded were only too glad to return to the front with unhealed wounds. Conditions in the hospital were punitive rather than therapeutic and there had been incidents at the hospital between military police and patients" (Libcom Group, *1917: The Etaples Mutiny*, www.libcom.org).

was wounded. Not seriously it appears, for he remained in France with his unit until early 1918 (Knight 1999).[11]

Syd Falkenhagen was made temporary corporal on 3 August 1918, and barely three weeks later was dead, killed in action.[12] On the day of his death, 23 August, his brigade was in the vanguard of what C.E.W. Bean described as an "attack, south of the Somme [which] though delivered by only two divisions, was one of the hardest blows ever struck by Australian troops" (Bean 1942: 746–47, 760 fn; Vol. VI). Falkenhagen was one of four officers and 139 other ranks lost by the 1st Battalion between 23 and 26 August 1918. At the time of Falkenhagen's death, Buckley's 14th Brigade had not been in serious fighting since late July. On 1 September 1918, the brigade "was in excellent fettle, having been in no serious fight for over a month." In the fighting following that for Mont St Quentin, the 54th Battalion had "raced the Germans to Pérrone."

> The town was surrounded by low grassy ramparts in front of which lay the watery moat crossed in the 54th by two bridges – that carrying the Cléry road into Péronne [and] a wooden footbridge [which] as the Germans disappeared across it … blew up. But the footbridge half a mile south was unbroken and the foremost Australians in that region … went down to it. The right company commander Lieut. McArthur, was examining it when a machine-gun high on the battlements of the old castles killed him and then Corpl. Buckley and two other men (Bean 1942: 836 fn 89, 838–48).

The Corpl. Buckley mentioned by Bean was Alex Buckley; his part in this action won him a posthumous Victoria Cross. The version promulgated in the *Commonwealth of Australia Gazette*, No. 61, of 23 May 1919, elaborates considerably on Bean's account.

> With one man [Buckley] rushed the post, shooting four of the occupants and taking twenty-two prisoners. Later on, reaching a moat, it was found that another machine-gun

---

11 ANA Service Record and Papers for #1876 Buckley A.H. and #1916 Falkenhagen Sydney Colin.
12 ANA Service Record and Papers for Falkenhagen.

nest commanded the only available footbridge. Whilst this was being engaged from a flank, Corporal Buckley endeavoured to cross the bridge and rush the post, but was killed in the attempt. Throughout the advance he had displayed great initiative, resource and courage, and by his effort to save his comrades from casualties he set a fine example of self-sacrificing devotion to duty.

If anything, the recommendation by the commander of the 14th Brigade was more glowing. This stated, that in order "to avert casualties amongst his comrades and to permit of their advance he voluntarily essayed a task which practically meant certain death" (Tivey 1918).

It seems unlikely that Buckley is the only German-Australian among the 100 or so Australian Victoria Cross recipients in World War I. And we do know that not all those nominated actually were awarded the decoration. Such was apparently the case with Erik Kleinschmidt, who was born out of wedlock in Berlin in 1891. Erik and his mother Maria Gurwell arrived in Australia in the mid-1890s, after she had accepted a proposal of marriage by the widower Ferdinand Kleinschmidt, a German national living in Brisbane. After their marriage, Ferdinand adopted the boy who legally became Erik Kleinschmidt and who, aged about 12, joined the Naval Brigade as a cadet and at 16 became a rating.[13] At the outbreak of war the young Kleinschmidt "imagined that, as a marine engineer and a speaker of German, his services would be of value in the Expeditionary Force being assembled to seize the German colonies in New Guinea and the adjacent islands" (Rost 2000: 38–41). But by then, the brief New Guinea campaign was over and Kleinschmidt had to cool his heels until a chance came to join "the proposed Royal Australian Naval Bridging Train which was to be sent to France" (Rost 2000). In May 1915 he sought to join this newly formed outfit. But Kleinschmidt stated that he had been born at sea and was therefore a British subject. Kleinschmidt was now advised to change his name, claiming that "in the event of capture by the Germans, he could expect harsh treatment." Kleinschmidt now took his mother's name of Gurwell and anglicised it to Gowell; a surname "which he was to use for the rest of his life" (Rost 2000). The naval train set off for England on 3 June 1915 but was

---

13 ANA Service Record and Papers for #213 Gowell, Eric.

diverted to the Dardanelles in support of the planned landing at Suvla Bay. The Suvla Bay campaign could almost serve as a prime example of military incompetence. The men of the naval train were thrown in at the deep end and expected to manage as best they could, learning the hard way "exposed to Turkish shrapnel from the heights above Suvla Bay while they laboured to build pontoon piers stretching out from the beach into water deep enough to float lighters from which supplies could be unloaded" (Rost 2000).

Gowell-Kleinschmidt's story was only beginning. When he applied for naturalisation in 1918, he stated that "I was recommended for a Victoria Cross for rescuing 2 wounded under enemy fire in no-man's-land at Gallipoli and my case is still being considered in Melbourne" (Gowell-Kleinschmidt quoted in Rost 2000). The case in question related to an event in which two Australians, under heavy fire, had brought in a wounded corporal to a British Field Ambulance station. The "Tommy" had been pinned down near Jefferson's Post by fire from five Turkish snipers. "After accounting for four of the Turks they managed to extricate him. Upon being thanked for their efforts, the Australians asked that their exploits not be mentioned to their command as they are not meant to be up there. They belong to the bridge-building section and do not carry rifles. They just borrowed two rifles to have an afternoon's sport" (Jose 1935: 390). That may have been so, but they had also broken military discipline. In Kleinschmidt's "Casualty Form – Active Service" the events of 16 October 1915 at Suvla are written up as follows: "Wilful disobedience of Orders. Did break out of Camp. 14 Days detention forfeiting pay & Time. N.D. Act. 22 & 17. Portion of Sentence namely Detention is cancelled. No Detention quarters available but loss of pay to take effect."[14] Needless to say, the Victoria Cross was never awarded. The fact that Kleinschmidt and his mate were disobeying orders was probably just as well. It is not difficult to imagine the hue and cry that must have followed if one of the first Victoria Crosses to be awarded at Gallipoli had been won by a man who was still, technically, an "enemy alien"!

How many men like Alex Buckley, Syd Falkenhagen or Erik Kleinschmidt were to be found in the ranks of the 1st AIF? The Nominal Roll

---

14 Casualty Form – Active Service, in ANA Service Record and Papers for Gowell.

provides no more than a rough (and minimum) guide. Adding to the problem is the uncertainty existing about the true size of the German community, i.e. Australians of German origin or descent, who most likely spoke at least some German and bore affection for their German heritage and culture. In this respect the aforenoted chart, based on the Commonwealth Year Books of 1912, can likewise function as little more than a guide. Given this uncertainty attached to the German community's size in pre-1914 Australia, we will probably never know how many young Australians of German (or Austro-German) birth or descent fought for Australia and the British Empire.

It seems ironic, that in a war against Germany the most famous Australian soldier of them all should himself be of German descent. From 1914 until his death, Sir John Monash had no good reason to attract attention to his German background, which may in part explain why he is so often described as a Jewish Australian of Polish extraction.[15] Monash was as Polish as *Schwarzwälderkirschtorte*. The assumption that his parents were Polish seems to be based on the fact that they originated from a part of Silesia (near the birthplace of the German general Erich Ludendorff) which, since World War II, has been part of Poland. Monash's parents had been in Australia for two years when young John was born. He was brought up in a predominantly German-speaking environment in a West Melbourne house named (by Monash senior) "Germania Cottage" (Serle 1982: 7). Monash's father became a pillar of the German community, and for a time, president of the *Deutscher Verein* [German Club]. So strong was the German influence upon him, that aged 19 at university, John was still conscious of "pronouncing the gutturals in a distinctly Teutonic accent" and sought aid to "correct" this fault. Monash was bi-, but not trilingual. He had a rudimentary knowledge of Hebrew, but Geoffrey Serle notes that neither John nor his siblings "acquired even a smattering" of Yiddish (Serle 1982: 8). Monash's command of both spoken and written German was so fluent that when war broke out in 1914, he was already translating the German

---

15 Even the Australian War Memorial gets this wrong, with the claim that Monash "was born in Melbourne on 27 June 1865, to a family of Polish Jewish origin." 1918: Australians in France – General Sir John Monash, http://www.awm.gov. au/1918/people/genmonash.asp.

Kavalleristische Monatshefte (*Cavalry Monthly*) for the British General Staff (Serle 1982: 193).

Monash's position and social standing offered protection from the worst excesses of anti-Germanism, particularly after the publication of the Bryce Report in 1915. Others were not so fortunate. Nonetheless, the names of senior officers – like Bruche, Sellheim and Rosenthal – suggest the prominent role played by Australians of German descent in the upper echelons of the AIF. At various times, many of them were the subjects of rumour, innuendo and hate campaigns, as were, in Monash's own words, "crowds of junior officers of the AIF [whose] names are a sure and certain index of foreign descent" (Monash quoted in Serle 1982: 203). Originally the Military Board used British citizenship as its sole criterium, but such was public pressure that by late 1915 it had "ceased to commission officers of foreign extraction" (Serle 1982: 204). Since Germans were, by a considerable margin, the highest non-British immigrant group in Australian society, "foreign" was mostly a euphemism for "German". Nor were only junior officers affected in the first year of the war. Young German-Australians seeking to join the AIF were often rejected out of hand, or, even if accepted, still had a chance of being discharged, on the grounds of German descent, from training camp within a matter of weeks.

In Adelaide, Australian-born Max Johann Gerlach first sought to enlist in 1914, and during the next three years was accepted once (then promptly tossed out of camp) and rejected three more times without even the chance to *fail* the medical examination.[16] In between he suffered humiliations, abuse and the indignities of white feathers in the mail.[17] With the recruiting situation desperate, he was finally accepted

---

16 ANA Service Record and Papers for #2117, Gerlach, M.J.
17 White feathers were often sent by womenfolk to apparently fit young men who had not enlisted – as a symbol of their cowardice. They were not always sent anonymously under the cloak of the postal service. Sometimes these were handed out publicly to inappropriate subjects. Late in his life my father – who served with the Kings Liverpool Regiment (55th West Lancs Divn.) on the Western Front from 1916 to 1918 – described how he had been handed one while wearing "civvies" on home leave in 1917. Such was his anger and embarrassment that he chose to wear his tattered and sometimes dirty service uniform on home leave, in preference to his civilian clothes, for the duration of the war. He was not the only serviceman so

in 1917, received a "Blighty One" in the leg on his first taste of action, was repatriated home a cripple and walked with a limp for the rest of his life (Musgrave 1999). But the Australian recruiting system was nothing if not inconsistent. Where the authorities were easier going and the potential recruit known to them, admission to the AIF could be immediate. From a respected family (with known links to Germany nevertheless), South Australia's Edward Mattner enlisted under his own name in early 1915. Mattner (subsequently a Federal Senator) won the Military Medal (MM), Military Cross (MC), Distinguished Conduct Medal (DCM) and received a field commission. Even this did not save his Australian-born mother from police harassment and accusations of pro-German sympathies when she sought to vote in one of the conscription referenda (Dolling 1999).

The successes of the "No" campaigns in the conscription referenda (see Holloway 1966) meant that after early 1917, the authorities had little choice but to accept volunteers they would previously have rejected on the grounds of physique, health or ethnicity. The AIF no longer comprised men of the outstanding physical stamp eulogised by C.E.W. Bean even before the landing at Gallipoli on 25 April 1915.[18] Two years later by the time of the first fighting at Bullecourt, E.J. Rule was writing of his platoon that it "seemed to be composed of school-children [they] were so small" (Rule 1933: 210). There is no indication that this reduction in physical stature, or the increasing presence of German (and Irish) Australians reduced the effectiveness of the AIF, rather the

---

affected. Recounted by ex-sergeant Francis Edward Williams to John F. Williams ca. 1964. The relevant entry in www.spartacus.schoolnet.co.uk states: "In August 1914, Admiral Charles Fitzgerald founded the Order of the White Feather. With the support of leading writers such as Mary Ward and Emma Orczy, the organisation encouraged women to give out white feathers to young men who had not joined the British Army. One young woman remembers her father, Robert Smith, being given a feather on his way home from work: 'That night he came home and cried his heart out. My father was no coward, but had been reluctant to leave his family. He was thirty-four and my mother, who had two young children, had been suffering from a serious illness. Soon after this incident my father joined the army.' "

18 See for example C.E.W. Bean, dispatches published in *The Age* (Melbourne), 21 January 1915 and *Register* (Adelaide), 23 April 1915.

contrary. Nonetheless, Australia was compelled to liberalise its recruitment practice at the moment where the rest of the white British Empire
began discharging loyal volunteers of allegedly suspect ethnicity in favour of conscripts of British stock. A conscripted man was universally
considered the lesser soldier to the volunteer, so from a purely military
standpoint this made no sense. By mid-1918, of the principal national
forces on the Western Front, Australia's was the only one uniquely of
volunteers and was beginning to be ranked by the Germans as one of
the most effective fighting units in the British Army. After Monash's
début battle at Hamel in July that year, German leaders acknowledged
(in private) that an Australian Corps (with perhaps seven per cent of its
men of German heritage), had "acquired a moral ascendancy over their
[German] opponents" (von Bose 1930: 19–21).

By the end of World War I, the AIF was representative of the Australian ethnic diversity of that time to an extent that could never be
claimed for the force that landed at Gallipoli.[19] At least one quarter of the
men who went ashore on 25 April 1915 were born in the British Isles, a
per centage roughly double that which might have been expected, given
the numbers of British born in Australia (Andrews 1993: 45). Embarka-
tion details also suggest that names identifiable as Irish or German are
disproportionately fewer than would be expected. At this early stage of
a war presented as an Imperial crusade, Irish-Australian Catholics were
unlikely to be attracted at the thought of rallying to the aid of an empire
repressing kinfolk in Ireland, where talk of civil war had been mounting
since the failure of negotiations in July 1914. Although a few German-
Australians were among the first troops to land at Gallipoli, most, like
the Irish, were maintaining a wait-and-see attitude before deciding to
fight for an abstract concept of the British Empire, where the enemy was

---

19 There are apparently no recorded statistics of the AIF's ethnicity, only the
empirical evidence of the Nominal Roll and military cemeteries. A search of the
former will produce comparatively fewer names of obvious Irish or Teutonic origin (compared with those of obvious Anglo-Saxon origin) until after 1916, when
the Imperial thrust of the early war propaganda gave way to stronger emphasis on
the danger to Australia. A similar tendency towards the mid- to late war enlistment of Australians of non Anglo-Saxon descent is observable in a most poignant
form on the tombstones of men buried throughout the chronologically ordered
military cemeteries on the Western Front.

from an ancestral homeland with which cultural ties were still strong (Andrews 1993: 45; Williams 1995: 219–33).

But while the parts played by Irish-Australians and Australia's Indigenous diggers have gradually come to be recognised, that of German-Australians – like the "Polish" Monash – goes mostly unacknowledged. There was no place in C.E.W. Bean's heart for anything less than an idealised vision of the Austral-Briton Anzac. His followers have tended to be equally exclusive and chauvinistic. In the intervening six or seven decades since Bean sought to define Anzac and Australian superiority, few historians have given consideration to the *active* role played in World War I by the largest non-British immigrant group – the fourth-largest of the non-immigrant groups – in Australian society. Government-inspired propaganda, presenting the German community as a proto "fifth column"[20] helped ensure that it would be years before other views began to gain currency. Even then, the tendency to present German-Australians almost exclusively as civil victims and not military participants has impeded the development of more rational and realistic appraisals.

Why?

Why would young German-Australian men, themselves often victims of pointed hostility, volunteer to serve and fight against ethnic kinfolk in the forces of an empire which often persecuted their parents? Most, like Monash, undoubtedly felt themselves British. For them, the professions of loyalty made on behalf of the German community or passed at mass meetings in communities like Walla Walla were no empty gestures. German settlers had made their commitment to Australia. They had set up farms, workshops and business, or found work in regular jobs. And in any case, there were no subsidised return fares, even if they wanted

---

20 The phrase, "fifth column" had no particular meaning in 1914–18. In fact, it wasn't coined until 1936, when the Spanish Nationalist General, Emilio Mola, broadcast a message to the inhabitants of (Republican) Madrid, claiming that the four columns of his armies about to besiege the city would be supported by a "fifth column" of Nationalist supporters, intent on sabotaging the Republic from within. The term thus came to be used to describe any ethnic or political minority whose allegiances lay with nations or political ideologies beyond the borders of the society with which they resided. See, for example, Preston 1983: 4–10.

to return. The war could not last forever. Nor, from what was said in the media sources available to them, could Germany win. In the meantime, most of them sought to protest their loyalty as best they could and by whatever means that was available, in the belief that after the war the insults and petty tribulations would surely pass and that they would be able to reassert their place in the Australian community.

Bill Gammage and Richard White have investigated what White calls the "motives for joining-up" – self-sacrifice, self-interest and social class – among Australian Britons (Gammage 1974; White 1986). While neither Gammage nor White exactly spell this out, it seems clear enough that many factors motivating young men of British stock to enlist would have no less applied – particularly after 1916 when "British-Australian" loyalties began to be qualified – particularly by those of Irish or German descent. By then many Anglo-Australians would have been as little inspired by the thought of coming to "the aid of the Mother Country & fighting for Old England" as was C.E.W. Bean, who derisively coined the phrase in 1915 (Bean 1916). The "Old Dart" mattered as little to German-Australians as it did to Bean, but the Empire was another matter and Australia's future within the reborn Empire that must come to pass after the war's victorious conclusion was commonly seen to be boundless.[21]

For the Monashes and the Mattners the choice was clear and their duty obvious. For others, the reasons for enlistment could be as complicated and unclear as they were for thousands of Anglo-Australians. Purely patriotic emotions were not the sole driving forces: young men joined up for adventure, travel, because their mates were joining up, because it was the thing to do, because of the stigma attached to being fit and still out of uniform, because of white feathers in the mail, because six bob a day and keep offered a viable way out for young men facing rural unemployment, or because they simply wanted to escape the boredom or pressures of day-to-day family life. One can only speculate on what impelled Heinrich Otto (Harry) Zink in October 1914, then aged 16, to add three years to his age and present himself as Frank Raynor (Bonney 2000). He served at Gallipoli and was killed at Villers-

---

21 Never more so than by Bean himself. See for example Bean 1918: 47–51.

Bretonneux shortly after his actual 20th birthday. Zink-Raynor was one "disguised" German-Australian who saw action at Gallipoli, Leopold Novak Augstein (Leo Austen) another. He changed his name for what he called "obvious reasons", was wounded at Pozières and promoted to lieutenant in the field. His two brothers also took the name "Austen" and served in France (Sainsbury 2000).

The Australian public knew little about the inconsistencies and unfairness of the recruitment system. They could see young men from German families wearing civilian clothes in the street, while their own sons, brothers and sometimes husbands were suffering or dying at Gallipoli and (later) France. If these men were really loyal Britishers – or loyal Australians – what was holding them back? Serving soldiers were also critical of men of German descent who they felt were not pulling their weight. "It is pleasing to know that Tumba [Tumbarumba] has done its part so well in sending recruits from the district," one wrote from France in May 1916. "I suppose the Heineckes were getting too bad a time to stay back any longer" (Campbell, in Frew 1988: 60). The phrase "too bad a time" needs no explanation; the Heineckes in question being two brothers from a successful gold-mining and entrepreneurial family in a district where the German-born and those of German descent had made a substantial contribution. Contribution turned to sacrifice in World War I. Both Heinecke boys are buried in France; Herbert was killed in action on 6 March 1917, while his brother George died of wounds some six weeks later (Frew 1988: 61).

There was one incentive for young German-Australians to enlist that was unknown to those of British descent – the protection of one's parents. The belief developed that a son in the Australian forces might save his family from internment, or at least where an "alien" could claim a fighting son, it could be a mitigating factor. The *War Precautions Aliens Registrations Regulations* of 1916 required all non-naturalised German-born persons to fill in a Form of Application for Registration. On 22 December 1916 the registering officer wrote of Jonas Reibelt from Artarmon, Sydney, that he "always considered himself an Australian", desired "to avoid any trouble" and had "a son at the front."[22] Reibelt

---

22 *War Precautions (Aliens Registration) Regulations 1916*. Form of Application for Registration by Jonas Reibelt, Palmer St., Artarmon NSW, 22 December 1916.

was left in peace. As was Phillip Kiem of Singleton: "a quiet inoffensive man", Kiem was not "an associate of other Germans, and [had] a son in camp who recently enlisted for Military Service."[23]

A German-Australian's sense of bi-culturality could be burdensome, but sometimes it seems to have been a blessing. Sydney-born Ekkehard Beinssen was no Anzac, rather a young man who, through circumstances, found himself fighting for the other side. His ties to Australia however, remained strong; he felt not so much burdened by his "dual loyalties", but somehow "magically protected". Beinssen had returned with his parents to Germany a year or two before the outbreak of war and, as one of the "Class of 17", aged 18, he joined an elite German regiment in time for Third Ypres. On his way to the front in 1917, he met a group of Australian prisoners. Their surprise at meeting a friendly German who chatted to them in Australian-accented English can be imagined. Beinssen fought the Anzacs at Passchendaele, was awarded the Iron Cross First Class, and forwarded letters found on a dead Australian major to an address which showed that he and the Beinssens had almost been neighbours in Sydney. After the war, the call of the land of his birth must have been strong. When small-scale German immigration recommenced in the 1920s, Beinssen returned to Australia. He suffered prejudice and was interned for a time during World War II (Beinssen-Hesse 2002).[24]

Beinssen was one of a bare handful of eligible German-Australians who felt obliged or duty-bound to fight for "the other side". Others however, experienced life in the land of their ancestors, or even their birth, from behind the wire of a prisoner-of-war camp. Frederick Klingner was captured at Dernancourt in spring 1918 and because of his obvious knowledge of the language, was for a time isolated from the other prisoners. He had no love for the "Boches" but was treated no less fairly

---

ANA Service Record and Papers for #3875, CQMS, Reibelt, R and #16830 Dvr. Reibelt G.E.

23 *War Precautions (Aliens Registration) Regulations 1916*. Form of Application for Registration. Kiem, Phillip. Issued 22 October 1916. Aliens Registration Officer I.D. Burton-Campbell; Police Station Lochinvar NSW.

24 Sourced also from a draft chapter of Beinssen-Hesse's forthcoming biography of Ekkehard Beinssen.

than other "English" prisoners.[25] Klingner's name was not immediately recognisable as German and he felt under no pressure to anglicise it. Yet the fear of brutal treatment at the hands of German captors remained a compelling factor in encouraging German-Australians to anglicise their names or take pseudonyms, as in the case of Erik Kleinschmidt mentioned above.

The men whose life, background and experiences are considered here are all either German or Australian-born – or of German heritage. Many had some knowledge of the German language and in most cases, their decision, or that of their parents, to call Australia "home" was not taken as a denial of cultural identity. In 1914, among the so-called Anglo-Saxon societies, Australia had the second highest percentage of German migrants (after the United States) of any comparable immigrant society. German-Australian soldiers can be seen as having made a distinct, even unique contribution among settlers of non-British ethnicity to Allied victory in World War I.

Bibliography

The Age (Melbourne), 21 January 1915.

ANA Service Record and Papers, #1876, Buckley A.H.

ANA Service Record and Papers, #1916, Falkenhagen Sydney Colin.

ANA Service Record and Papers, #2117, Gerlach M.J.

ANA Service Record and Papers, #213, Gowell, Eric.

ANA Service Record and Papers, #2892, Klingner F.W.

ANA Service Record and Papers, #3875, CQMS, Reibelt, R.

ANA Service Record and Papers, #16830, Dvr. Reibelt, G.E.

Andrews EM (1993). *The Anzac Illusion: Anglo-Australian Relations During World War I*. Melbourne: Cambridge University Press.

---

25 Diary and letter from Frederick Klingner to his mother at the *AWM*. ANA Service Record and Papers for #2892, Klingner F.W. PR 91/099. Papers of F. Klingner, *AWM* 91/0508.

Argus Office (1913). *The Argus*, 14 July 1913, Melbourne: Argus Office.

Australian War Memorial. *AWM 38 3DRL 606*, item 60[2], undated, ca. October 1916 – C.E.W. Bean.

Australian War Memorial. *1918: Australians in France: General Sir John Monash* [online]. Available: www.awm.gov.au/1918/people/genmonash. asp.

Bean CEW (1916). In Australian War Memorial, *AWM 38 3DRL 606*, item 60[2], undated, ca. October 1916.

Bean CEW (1918). *In Your Hands, Australians*. London: Cassel.

Bean CEW (1940). *The Old A.I.F. and the New*. No. 4 of Through Australian eyes, Sydney: Angus & Robertson.

Bean CEW (1942). *The Official History of Australia in the War of 1914– 1918, Vol. VI: The A.I.F. in France: May 1918 – The Armistice*. Sydney: Angus & Robertson.

Bean CEW (1946). *Anzacs to Amiens: A Shorter History of the Australian Fighting Services in the 1st World War*. Sydney: Halstead Press.

Beinssen-Hesse S (2002). Information about her father Ekkehard Beinssen provided in e-mail, 5 March 2002.

Bonney D (2000). Information about her grand-uncle Heinrich Zink provided in Townsville (Qld.), 8 June 2000.

Bulletin, 21 August 1913.

Bulletin, 6 November 1913.

Burrowes G & Dixon J (1985). *Anzacs ©*. Burrowes Dixon Company Ltd.

Bryce V (1915). *Report of the British Committee on Alleged German Outrages*. Presented to both Houses of Parliament.

Clark CHM (1983). *A History of Australia,* Vol. VI, Melbourne: Melbourne University Press.

Commonwealth Bureau of Census and Statistics (1911). *Census of the Commonwealth of Australia 1911.*

Commonwealth of Australia (1919). *Commonwelath of Australia Gazette*. No. 61, 23 May 1919, Canberra: Government Printer.

Dolling S (1999). Information about his grandfather, Senator Edward Mattner, provided in Adelaide (SA), 21 October 1999.

Evans R (1987). *Loyalty and Disloyalty: Social Conflict on the Queensland Homefront 1914–18.* Sydney: Allen & Unwin.

Evans R (1988). The Pen And The Sword: Anti-Germanism in Queensland during the Great War, and the Worker. In M Jurgensen & A Corkhill (Eds), *The German Presence in Queensland.* St Lucia: University of Queensland Press.

Ferguson N (1998). *The Pity of War: Explaining World War One.* New York: Basic Books.

Fischer G (1989). *Enemy Aliens: Internment and the Homefront Experience in Australia, 1914–20.* St Lucia: University of Queensland Press.

Frew C & Frew R (1988). *Sons to the Empire's Cause: Tumbarumba in World War I.* Tumbarumba: C & R Frew.

Fribourg A (1918). La 'carte de guerre' économique. *L'illustration,* 20 July 1918.

Fuchs KH (1936). Das Deutschtum in Australien: Eindrücke von einem Kreuzerbesuch. In Verband Deutsche Vereine im Ausland e.V. (Ed), *Wir Deutsche in der Welt.* Berlin: Stollberg, Otto, in Komm.

Gammage B (1974). *The Broken Years: Australian Soldiers in the Great War.* Canberra: Australian National University Press.

Gibbs P (1923). *The Hope of Europe.* London: Heinemann.

Graves R (1929). *Good-bye to All That.* London: Anchor.

Haggard HR (1885). *King Solomon's Mines.* London: Cassel.

Haggard HR (1887). *She.* London: Longmans.

Holloway EJ (1966). *The Australian Victory over Conscription in 1916–17.* Melbourne: Anti-Conscription Jubilee Committee.

Jose AW (1935). *The Official History of Australia in the War of 1914–18, Vol. IX, The Royal Australian Navy 1914–18.* Sydney: Angus & Robertson.

Jurgensen M & Corkhill A (Eds) (1988). *The German Presence in Queensland.* St Lucia: University of Queensland Press.

Knibbs GH (Ed) (1914). *Official Year Book of the Commonwealth of Australia Containing Authoritative Statistics for the Period 1901–13*. Melbourne: Commonwealth Bureau of Statistics.

Knight B (née Falkenberg) (1999). Information about her uncle Syd Falkenberg provided in Connellys Marsh (TAS), 6 April 1999.

Lake M (1975). *A Divided Society: Tasmania During World War I*. Melbourne: Melbourne University Press.

Libcom Group (2006). 'Steven' of Libcom Group, *1917: The Etaples Mutiny* [Online]. Available: www.libcom.org/history/1917-the-etaples-mutiny.

McKernan M (1980). *Australians in Wartime: Commentary and Documents*. Melbourne: Nelson.

Minister for Public Instruction (1912). *Technical Gazette of New South Wales*. Vol. 2, part 1, February 1912, Sydney: Minister for Public Instruction.

Musgrave S (1999). Information about her brother Max Johann Gerlach provided in Adelaide (SA), 13 November 1999.

Preston P (1983). From Rebel to Caudillo. *History Today*, 33(11): 4–10.

Robson LL (1970). *The First A.I.F.: A Study of its Recruitment 1914–18*. Melbourne: Melbourne University Press.

Rost A (2000). A German in the AIF. *Queensland Family Historian*, 21(2), May 2000.

Rule EJ (1933). *Jacka's Mob*. Sydney: Angus & Robertson.

Sainsbury P (2000). Information about her distant relative Leopold Novak Augstein / Leo Austen provided in Canberra (ACT), 9 June 2000.

Serle G (1982). *John Monash: A Biography*. Melbourne: Melbourne University Press.

Verhey JT (1992). *The Spirit of 1914: The Myth of Enthusiasm and the Rhetoric of Unity in World War 1 Germany*. PhD thesis, University of California, Berkeley. Published as a book in 2000, CUP.

von Bose T(1930). *Schlachten des Weltkrieges: Die Katastrophe des 8. August 1918*. Vol. 36, Berlin: Gerhard Stalling.

White R (1986). Motives for Joining Up: Self-Sacrifice, Self-interest and Social Class, 1914–18. *Journal of the Australian War Memorial*, 9: 3–16.

Williams JF (1995). *Quarantined Culture: Australian Reactions to Modernism 1913–39*. New York: Cambridge University Press.

Williams JF (2003). *German Anzacs and the First World War*. Sydney: UNSW Press.

1915 (1982). Miniseries (5x77min), screenplay by P Yeldham, directed by D Drew & C Thomson.

7
Land Ownership, Indenture and a "Migration-prone" Personality: Aspects of the Emigration from the Duchy of Nassau to Australia in the 19th century[1]

Kathrine M. Reynolds

Indenture[2], land ownership and a "migration-prone"[3] personality can be viewed as three possible determinants in stimulating migration from the Duchy of Nassau in the 19th century to Australia. The following discussion of the migration of a relatively large group from this area is based on a corpus of hitherto unpublished letters – referred to as the Frauenstein Letters (1855–83) – originating in the village of Frauen-stein (near Wiesbaden). Supporting primary data were collected from

---

1 This paper is based on work undertaken for a PhD project (Reynolds 2008) in the Department of Germanic Studies, University of Sydney. This was subsequently published (Reynolds 2009).
2 Indenture, whereby "an apprentice was bound to a master" for a certain length of time, giving his labour in return for wages, has existed since the 15th century (Little, Fowler & Coulson 1968: 988). The British government also used this form of contract to supply labour to its overseas colonies, and in Australia in the 19th century, thousands of European migrants were brought out to develop the wine and pastoral industries when Britain could not find sufficient labour among its own citizens (Reynolds 2009: 20–32).
3 Lüthke and Cropley conducted interviews with migrants and non-migrants in 20th-century Germany. They found that migrants were more able than non-migrants to tolerate a separation from familiar people and objects, and more self-reliant with a "high degree of personal independence". They suggested these migrants had a "migration-prone" personality (Lüthke & Cropley 1990: 153), and their definition has been used as the basis for this work.

state archives[4] and church records[5] in Germany, as well as from the unpublished diaries both of German citizens who did not emigrate, e.g. Anton Schneider from Frauenstein (1829–83) (Schneider 2005), and those who did, such as Johann Müller (Berry) (1872–1940), Johann Müller (Mudgee) (1855–66) and Peter Rheinberger (1871–1929). The letters are of two types: those to relatives in Australia, and those from migrants writing home to Nassau.

The unpublished personal accounts, when coupled with state archival material and other official documentation, provide a unique view of the migration process. Statements by the emigrants and their families about migration provide a source of qualitative data that can be usefully contrasted with quantitative data provided by the state. Often what was recorded by the state was not consistent with that provided by the individual and vice-versa, and for this reason, comparing the Frauenstein letters with the official information yields a unique view of migration and furthers our understanding of that process.

Since the male and female construct of history can be shown to be different (Glassberg 1996: 9–10, 22), the Frauenstein letters may also add to our understanding of migration and its role in our history, as a substantial number of the letters were written by women, thereby providing their view of the migration process.

The 19th century in central Europe was one of great turmoil, with far-reaching industrial changes. There were mass emigrations as well as a revolution in the notion of work,[6] public health (Porter 1997: 397–427), and politics.[7] Many factors have been posited as the causes of emigra-

4 Census data (Frauenstein *Census Data,* Hessisches Hauptstaatsarchiv Wiesbaden [HStAW] Abt. 246/406) and land titles (Frauenstein Stockbuch, Hessisches Hauptstaatsarchiv Wiesbaden [HStAW], Abt 362/33 Frauenstein A).
5 Births, deaths and marriages (Frauenstein Kirchenbuch, Film Nr. 146, 147, 148, 149, Limburg Bistumsarchiv).
6 Many areas of modern Germany rapidly changed from being agrarian to proto-industrial, and then became fully industrial, throwing millions of workers into chaos. These changes "reduced the ability of substantial segments of the population to earn their living where they lived, thus increasing their need to migrate to seek work" and encouraged "high rates of temporary mobility" (Hochstadt 1999: 178).
7 "In the 18th century, German Europe had been divided into 300 territories" but was reduced to 39 in 1817 after the congress of Vienna (Clark 2001: 41). After 1866, many small countries like "Hanover, the Electorate of Hesse, the Duchy of

tion from German-speaking Europe, such as restrictive marriage laws, war and conscription, floods and drought, religious persecution and poverty (lack of food, crop failure, crop disease) (Kamphoefner 1995: 19–33; Jackson & Moch 1996: 57; Bade 2003). However, land ownership and the problem of partible inheritance, which saw family holdings reduced to non-viable areas, has not always received significant attention in the scholarly literature. New lands, such as North and South America, and Australia, were opened up to immigrants, and people left the Old World of Europe and Great Britain in their millions, to venture to these new and exotic places. One of the many claims made is that migrants were attracted by land (Fogleman 1995: 16) and its availability in new countries, whereas in Europe and Britain there was little land available for poorer people,[8] and population growth had also put pressure on the supply of land (Baines 1985: 14).

Until the late 19th century, the reasons for these mass migrations were generally accepted as those posited by the emigrants themselves. As a result, these were subject to little analysis by scholars. More recently, migration has become the subject of investigation as governments and their administrators have wanted not only to better understand the causes and effects of these massive movements of people, but also to enable an "informed" selection of citizens, choosing those who would become productive members of society (Zolberg 2006: 1). Ever since Ravenstein[9] first proposed his theory of migration, scholars have been debating the reasons for these large movements of people, and most scholars[10] perceive that emigrants were "pushed" out of their country of

Nassau, Schleswig and Holstein, and the Free and Imperial City of Frankfurt am Main" were subsumed under the control of the Prussian Empire (Breuilly 2001: 149).
8 When Ravenstein presented his definition of migration, using census data, to members of the Royal Society in 1889, one member commented that where "a population treads upon each other's toes, there was a disposition to seek more open spaces" (Ravenstein 1889: 303) and this idea has achieved currency.
9 In essence, Ravenstein's "theory of migration" was totally economically and labour-based. He suggested that people moved because there were improved means of movement such as railroads from "spots where they were not wanted to fields where their labour was in demand" (Ravenstein 1885: 167).
10 Most scholars concur that labour is the basis for migration: however, even at the presentation of Ravenstein's second paper on migration in 1889, a member of the audience dissented and suggested that "the spirit of adventure had quite as much to do

origin where socioeconomic circumstances were poor, and "pulled" to a new country, attracted by a better environment than the one they left. The term "push-pull" has since been used.[11]

However, this "push-pull" theory does not explain all the facts. In Ravenstein's work, which compares census data over a ten-year period from 1871 to 1881, only 3 per cent of the entire population moved, although discrete pockets showed greater movement (Ravenstein 1885: 170). Nevertheless, in many instances, it was the entire population that suffered, albeit to varying degrees, the same environmental effects such as war, religious persecution, and even poor economic circumstances (Ravenstein 1885, 1887; Morawska 1996: 196–97; Massey et al. 2005: 7; Tampke 2006: 20).

The acceptance of this "push-pull" theory of migration has seen many 20th-century scholars aggregate a variety of forms of migration (with the exception of refugee migration) into one, usually delineated by country of origin (e.g. German or Italian emigration), contending that its cause was underpinned by factors enunciated in this theory (Tampke 2006: 20). Few scholars[12] have looked at data from both the country of origin and the country of settlement, possibly because the country of emigration often has scant interest in those who leave, and for the country of settlement, there is often the problem of a foreign language to contend with for scholars to gain access to migration information. As a result, migration research has been deeply rooted in the ideology of the country of settlement.

Much of the Australian debate about the origins of the German migration of the 19th century has centred on either religious[13] or po-

with the migration as the mere desire for more bread and butter" (Ravenstein 1889: 304), suggesting a psychological component to migration. Since then, other scholars (Cropley et al. 1986; Cropley 1986; Lüthke 1989; Lüthke & Cropley 1990; Cropley 2005) have investigated a psychological component of migration and have convincing evidence to support their contention that the psychology of the individual plays a large part in stimulating emigration.

11 This term "push-pull" has been used to denote all economic labour migrations, and any migration predicated on the individual moving from what they believe to be poor socioeconomic environments to those they perceive to be better are so termed.

12 Exceptions are Bade 2003; Lubinski 1995; Reich 1995.

13 The emigration of Pastor Kavel from Klemzig in 1838 with less than 200 people

litical persecution (which affected a small minority) or poor economic circumstances, which in the case of the Frauenstein emigrants (and perhaps other similar German migrations to Australia at the same time) can be shown to not necessarily be true.[14]

Another factor, seldom discussed, is the individual's psyche. Some scholars working with emigration in the 20th century in Hamburg found that people would tell an interviewer (or family, neighbours and friends) what they perceived these people wished to hear, even though the reasons underpinning their behaviour (in this case emigration) may in fact have been quite different (Cropley 1986; Cropley, Becker, Lüthke & Lüthke 1986; Lüthke 1989; Lüthke & Cropley 1990; Cropley 2005). In other words, it was possible that despite the fact that people said they had to leave their homeland because conditions were dreadful, this was not necessarily the case. On the basis of their data, Cropley, Becker and Lüthke identified several personality types, with a range from "migration-prone" to "stay-at-home", and found that, depending on a person's predisposition to emigrate, they were likely to either emigrate, or remain at home, quite independently of the reasons they gave for their migration. This predisposition to emigrate could explain why only such a small number of citizens from the same community take the momentous step to emigrate, even though all may suffer the same environmental factors.

Some authors (Kopittke et al. 1999–2005) have studied passenger lists of ships leaving Hamburg for Australia, and even though some Swiss and Scandinavian nationals appear in these lists, there were approximately 35,[15]747 emigrants from Hamburg to Australia from 1850–78,

---

who called themselves religious refugees to South Australia has underpinned the historical narrative of German emigration to Australia, even though the numbers were comparatively small (Schubert 1997). One could make a case that the Kavel migrants were also assisted emigrants, as Pastor Kavel spent two years in England before the migration, finding the money to move his people with the help of George Fife Angus (Schubert 1997: 76).

14 Although the 19th-century German emigration to Queensland and South Australia had some political overtones, the religious migrations are the ones the Australian populace is aware of when considering German settlement in Australia (Harmsdorf 2001; Corkhill 2001).

15 A Nassau *Morgen* at the time was a unit of area and 2500 m² or 0.25 hectares.

the majority of whom were German-speaking and came from the myriad of German states (in 1850, there were approximately 39 states) in existence at that time, such as Bavaria, Württemberg, Nassau, Saxony, Prussia. This large number of German emigrants from Hamburg was further increased by German-speakers who left European ports such as Le Havre, Bremen, Antwerp, and also by those leaving English ports like Plymouth, but who were deemed to be English, as their last port was an English port (Williams 2003: 18). In all, at least 54,000 German-speaking people left Europe (Groth 1932: 276) for Australia. The bulk of these were assisted migrants and their families, whom the colonial authorities in Australia desperately needed to help with critical labour shortages in the pastoral and wine industries.

Much information lies buried in diverse archives in Germany. These, together with archives in the country of arrival, contain information that could enable scholars to present a more complete and realistic picture of the migration process and its factors.

My study investigates the emigration in the mid-1850s from the Duchy of Nassau to Australia in general, and from the village of Frauenstein to Australia in particular, and can demonstrate that this latter migration was not a simple process explained by the "push-pull" theory. Three points raised by my work which can now throw light on this migration are: an investigation of land ownership, the facility of indenture and the psychological predisposition of the person to migration.

In the 1850s, many of the citizens in the Duchy of Nassau[16] (including the villagers from Frauenstein) owned land, giving them an income and food. Many worked simultaneously in trades such as printing or bricklaying, or as domestic servants (Reynolds 2009). It was believed that 10–15 *Morgen* of land were needed to raise a family of six, although no qualification was given about the type of land and its ability to produce (Jäger 1993: 262).

This region was a wine-growing area and for this reason was targeted by migration agents hoping to find people willing to migrate to

---

Many states had different sizes for measurement www.sizes.com/units/morgen.htm
16 The Duchy of Nassau was enclosed by the River Rhine on its southern and western boundaries, and by the Lahn River to the north. The western boundary with the French shifted as wars occurred, as did all of the Nassau boundaries.

Australia as vinedressers. The mechanism of indenture saw migration agents select the recruits and organise their passage. One agent was Wilhelm Kirchner, a former merchant from Frankfurt who advertised in local German newspapers, and after the successful arrival of four boats in 1849–50,[17] asked settlers to write a story about their experience. He added their ecstatic accounts to the second edition of a book he published to encourage people to emigrate, called *Australia and its Advantages for Emigrants* (Kirchner 1850).

At least 1,416 people (Struck 1966: 131) plus their families migrated to Australia from the Duchy of Nassau. From the village of Frauenstein, approximately 142[18] people came to Australia between 1852–54, of whom 29 were indentured males. Under the indenture program, these males – with their wives and children – had their fares paid by the colonial government in Australia. On arrival they were contracted to work for two years and were given homes, as well as rations and a small wage of approximately £20 per annum. Assisted German immigrants were forced to repay a proportion of their travel costs, whereas British immigrants were not (e.g. from an annual wage of £20, Jacob Müller of Frauenstein had to repay £13 [Berry Papers 1855: 25]).

Despite the somewhat onerous repayments of travel costs, this method of recruiting using indenture took the risk out of migrating, as the emigrants had employment, homes and food for at least the first two years in Australia. At no other time[19] in the history of Frauenstein

---

17 The four boats that left from Britain were the *Beulah* (187 people), the *Harmony* (31 people), the *Parland* (168 people) and the *Balmoral* (27 people) (NSW State Records, Immigrant Index 1844–59).

18 This number is an approximation. People were forced to advertise their intention to emigrate in the local newspaper, the *Herzogliches Nassauisches allgemeines Intelligenzblatt*, so that debtors could call in their debts. One German author (Struck 1966: 192) identified 28 adults from Frauenstein who advertised their intention to emigrate. A local villager, Anton Schneider (Schneider 2005), however, recorded 142 who emigrated, as Struck's tally did not include families and instead only those who advertised. These were, in general, the breadwinners. Some people came to Australia but were not on any of the "formal" lists, some died, and others were born en route.

19 This migration from Frauenstein was recorded beside entries of births and marriages in the church record books in Limburg, revealing that this phenomenon was restricted to 1852–54. While the Frauenstein emigrants left during this two-year

did so many people emigrate *en masse*, and the effect of indenture and its concomitant assistance with travel costs together with the help to settle into the new country[20] would appear to have acted as a far greater stimulus than has hitherto been accepted.

The migration from Nassau was not uniform, either with respect to the time at which it occurred, or the area from which people came. The two major years that accounted for most of the emigration to Australia were 1854–55. Similarly, the districts from which the emigrants came were also different. The Australian emigration from Nassau was predominantly from three districts: Eltville (43.5 per cent), Rüdesheim (25.8 per cent) and Wiesbaden (12.8 per cent).

In recent research, some of the English emigrants to Australia in the 19th century have been shown to be self-selecting since they chose to emigrate. They were not indigent misfits, but were in fact better educated and with more money than those who remained at home (Haines 1997: 23). Similarly, it can be demonstrated that those who emigrated from Frauenstein were not destitute, impoverished people, but rather, literate artisans with some assets (i.e. they owned assets such as land), who were prepared, with economic and physical assistance, to migrate to Australia.

Vogel's data from 1843 for the entire Duchy of Nassau, showed that there were 806 villages within the 28 districts of the Duchy of Nassau at that time and that the mean amount of land available per person over the entire Duchy was 4.6 ($\pm$1.4)[21] *Morgen* (Vogel 1843).[22] An analysis of the amount of land (*Morgen* per person) was computed for the various villages which lost emigrants to Australia, compared with those which did not, and those which lost relatively few persons (Reynolds 2008: 56). The mean amount of land per person was reduced to 3.9 ($\pm$1.3) *Morgen* in villages from which more than 10 persons emigrated to Aus-

---

period, the majority of the emigrants to Australia from the Duchy of Nassau left between 1854–55.

20 Many indentured people were also provided with rations and accommodation as part of their indenture contract (Alexander Berry Papers, Mitchell Library [MLMSS 315/72]).

21 '$\pm$' refers to the standard error of the mean.

22 Vogel presents individual data for each of the 806 villages within the Duchy and these computations have been derived from his data (Vogel 1843).

tralia, and increased to 6.0 ($\pm$ 3.4) *Morgen* per person for those villages with less than ten emigrants.

While these three categories are different in absolute terms,[23] there is no statistical difference in the amount of land held by villagers in those villages which lost many emigrants, compared to those which lost none, signifying that the amount of land owned was not a driving force in the decision to emigrate.

All families of emigrants from Frauenstein to Australia[24] owned some land, indicating that they were not landless paupers. However, six of the indentured men had no land themselves, although one of these had a father with a large amount of land, namely 22 *Morgen*. The majority had small parcels of land, ranging from one to ten *Morgen*. Nevertheless, when letters from villagers are studied, the local working life is described in some detail, suggesting that people lived, worked and survived quite adequately on small plots of land (Reynolds 2009).

One local female who did not emigrate, Eva Leitz, refers to her husband working in the forest preparing wood as well as carting fruit to Wiesbaden to sell (Letter 14, Frauenstein 1865, Eva Leitz to Jacob Müller, Anna Maria Müller and children). She and her husband owned one and a half *Morgen* of land. Nevertheless, over the course of the letters they still managed to buy two houses:

> We sold our house to Kasper Kirchner for 480 *Gulden* and bought another from George Schlimm for 970 *Gulden*[25] (Reynolds, 2009: 153).

Other residents, the Schmitt sisters, earned their living by sewing and being in service. On the death of their brother, Christina Schmitt complained that her brother and his wife, Klara, could have lived well:

> If only our Johan was still alive, they could have had quite a nice existence. Klara has a few good fields, and they also had

---

23 3.9 ($\pm$1.3) appear to be numerically different to 6.0 ($\pm$ 3.4) but statistically these numbers are the same: there is no difference between them and hence no effect.
24 These data were recorded from the *Stockbuch* for Frauenstein, which lists all land transactions, mortgages, taxes on land, type of land (e.g. house or quality rural) from 1830–1900 and is held in the Wiesbaden archive (Frauenstein Land Titles, Hessisches Hauptstaatsarchiv Wiesbaden [HStAW], Abt 362/33 Frauenstein A).
25 Translated by Emilie Kolb, Kathrine Reynolds and Irene Reuter.

a few from us, although they did not need to pay us anything for them in return. Of course, they had to pay 25 *Gulden* interest and tax and then another 10 *Gulden* in rent to Kleppers because we had planted our cherry trees on their land.[26] (Reynolds 2009: 157)

Thus, land was a commodity, used for rental and also for growing produce. Despite these land holdings, many of the Frauenstein people who emigrated to Australia made their decision to emigrate quite quickly, selling land they had acquired only months previously. One Frauenstein resident who emigrated, Jacob Müller (Eva Leitz' brother), began buying land in April 1845 at the age of 23 when he purchased some fields.[27] He continued buying and by 1851 had 2.1 *Morgen*. By the time he emigrated in 1854, Jacob Müller and his wife, Anna Maria, had purchased 4 *Morgen* of land, including a house in Frauenstein. This house, which was only purchased in April 1853, was described as consisting of a house (22' long and 27' high) with a barn (16.5' x 11'), a courtyard and a garden. Jacob Müller sold all his property on 28 August 1854, only two months before emigrating, as did many other Frauenstein villagers. Thus, the purchase of his home only 12 months before emigration suggests that he was not a person driven out by poverty, even though his holding was not immense. Jacob Müller would appear to have made his decision to emigrate rather rapidly – there is otherwise no explanation for his slow acquisition of land and property from 1845 to 1853 and then his sudden sale of everything in August 1854, prior to leaving in October 1854.

Other Frauenstein emigrants display a similar pattern to Jacob Müller. Most had some land, but an analysis of the data shows that many were still purchasing land up to a year before they emigrated. One local diarist, Anton Schneider, wrote that the migration "spirit" had first struck in spring 1852, and that it resurfaced again in 1854, following the glowing reports coming back to the town of the successful migration experiences of those who first emigrated (Schneider 2005: 41–42). He emphasises the precipitousness of the emigration, and the

---

26 Translated by Emilie Kolb, Kathrine Reynolds and Irene Reuter.
27 Frauenstein Land Titles, Hessisches Hauptstaatsarchiv Wiesbaden (HStAW), Abt 362/33 Frauenstein A.

excitement that seized the local people, as well as the effect of letters from earlier emigrants containing positive information about the migration experience.

The Frauenstein people who migrated to Australia were predominantly families, some with large numbers of children. Some paid their own fare, such as the mayor, Nicholas Horn, his wife and his seven children. Yet the majority of the working males who emigrated from Frauenstein did so with assistance from the colonial government in Australia, reinforcing the notion that indenture[28] played a big part in their decision to emigrate. Their spirit of adventure possibly stimulated those who were "migration-prone" into leaving their homes, whereas others, living under the same conditions, chose not to avail themselves of the opportunity. This theory of personality-type with people being "migration-prone" or "stay-at-home" (Cropley 1986; Cropley, Becker, Lüthke & Lüthke 1986; Lüthke 1989; Lüthke & Cropley 1990; Cropley 2005) goes some way to explaining the facts (viz. that only a small proportion of any population ever migrate) which underpin much of the emigration of the 19th century, in general, and the emigration from Frauenstein, in particular. Indenture and a "migration-prone" personality were possibly the major factors underpinning the emigration from Frauenstein from 1852–54.

The prospect of land ownership was not mentioned by diarists or letterwriters from Frauenstein. In Australia, land was not free and its availability changed from time to time, as successive administrators and the British government changed their minds about who should own and control land. Initially land was given to almost anyone,[29] but by 1842 the government restricted land sales and raised the price from 5/-

---

28 Indenture provided a mechanism to facilitate emigration, but few of the Frauenstein people, in absolute terms, accepted this offer (29 out of 169 adult males) (census data – Hessisches Hauptstaatsarchiv Wiesbaden [HStAW], Abt 246/406). However, those who did accept were not necessarily leaving worse conditions behind to go to better ones in Australia, the majority owning land and surviving nicely.

29 From 1788 to 1831, land was generally granted by the governor, but from 1831 to 1850 land was sold or leased under conditions which varied from one colony to another (Clark 1973: 217). Between 1850 and 1860, there was much agitation about the previous methods of selling government land, which concentrated land

per acre to £1 per acre in the Nineteen Counties in an effort to ensure there were sufficient workers in the colony (Clark 1973: 239). As 40 acres were deemed to be necessary to support a family, £40 was needed to buy a farm from 1861 onwards, when the *Robertson Land Act* was introduced, although settlers could squat on land for three years before it was surveyed and before they had to pay for it (Evans 2005: 28).

Many of the Frauensteiners no doubt hoped to buy land again, but this did not happen to all of the emigrant generation. Some Frauenstein emigrants, such as the Fuchs brothers in Armidale, bought 40-acre blocks in the town. Others, like Jacob Müller and his wife and their 11 children, remained with their original employer, becoming tenant farmers for the rest of their lives. Jacob Müller's son, Johann, finally bought land at Meroo Meadow on the break-up of the old *Coolangatta* estate after the death of Alexander Berry's heir in 1893 (Müller 1872–1940).

Thus, although land and its ownership has often been posited as a reason many German-speaking emigrants left Europe, in the case of the Frauenstein emigration to Australia in 1852–54, it would seem that land ownership did not play a part in their decision to emigrate. Instead, it is likely that other factors stimulated this emigration, not the least of which was indenture. This mechanism to transport people must have appealed to the Frauensteiners, as so many (19 per cent of the adult male villagers) made up their minds quickly and emigrated. Migration only appealed to a proportion of the population and was not universal within families. It is possible that the people from Frauenstein were adventurers like those identified by Cropley (2005) in his study, having "migration-prone" personalities. Never again in Frauenstein did this phenomenon occur, even though several citizens and siblings of the emigrants suggested in their letters that they wanted to emigrate (Reynolds 2009). There was no mechanism for them to do so, and for those left behind, the opportunity had come and gone. They did not have the money, the ability, or the motivation (without indenture) to transport themselves so far away, although many moved to nearby towns such as Wiesbaden or Mainz for work. It would seem that in the case of the

---

in the hands of the squatters, denying land to the majority of settlers. The *Robertson Land Act* grew out of this agitation (Clark 1971: 93–174).

Frauenstein emigration of 1852–54 to Australia, a "migration-prone" personality, combined with the facility of indenture, were the likely stimuli to emigration.

Bibliography

Bade K (2003). *Migration in European History*. A Brown (Trans.). Oxford: Blackwell Publishing.

Baines D (1985). *Migration in a Mature Economy*. Cambridge: Cambridge University Press.

Berry Papers (1855). Alexander Berry Papers, Mitchell Library, no. MLMSS 315/72.

Breuilly J (2001). Revolution to Unification. In J Breuilly (Ed), *19th Century Germany: Politics, Culture and Society 1780–1918*. London: Arnold, 138–61.

Clark CMH (1971). *Select Documents in Australian History 1851–1900*. Sydney: Angus and Robertson.

Clark CMH (1973). *Select Documents in Australian History 1788–1850*. Sydney: Angus and Robertson.

Clark C (2001). Germany 1815–48: Restoration or Pre-March. In J Breuilly (Ed), *19th Century Germany: Politics, Culture and Society 1780–1918*. London: Arnold, 40–65.

Corkhill A (2001). German Settlement in Queensland 1838–1939. In J Jupp (Ed), *The Australian People: An Encyclopaedia of the Nation, Its People and Their Origins*. Cambridge: Cambridge University Press, 369–70.

Cropley A (1986). Migration and Environment: Some Psychological Considerations. *Environments* 18(3): 6–20.

Cropley A, Becker K, Lüthke K & Lüthke F (1986). Forming the Decision to Emigrate to Australia: Some Recent German Experience. *Australian Journal of Politics and History*, 32: 52–62.

Cropley A (2005). Psychological Factors in the Satisfaction of Post-World War Two German Migrants with Life in Australia. Paper presented at the conference "The German Presence in South Australia." University of Adelaide, 30 September–1 October 2005.

Evans R (2005). *Sail and Steam on the Shoalhaven*. Nowra: Shoalhaven Historical Society.

Fogleman AS (1995). Immigration, German immigration and 18th century America. In E Reichmann, LJ Rippley & J Nagler (Eds), *Emigration and Settlement Patterns of German Communities in North America*. Indianapolis: Max Kade German-American Center, Indiana University-Purdue University, 3–22.

Frauenstein Census Data (1854), Hessisches Hauptstaatsarchiv Wiesbaden [HStAW], Abt 246/406.

Frauenstein Land Titles, Hessisches Hauptstaatsarchiv Wiesbaden [HStAW], Abt 362/33 Frauenstein A.

Glassberg D (1996). Public History and the Study of Memory. *The Public Historian*, 18(2), 7–23.

Grothe H (1932). *Die deutschen in Übersee*. Berlin: Zentralverlag.

Harmsdorf I (2001). German Settlement in South Australia until 1914. In J Jupp (Ed), *The Australian People: An Encyclopaedia of the Nation, Its People and Their Origins*. Cambridge: Cambridge University Press, 360–65.

Hochstadt S (1999). *Mobility and Modernity: Migration in Germany 1820-1989*. Ann Arbor: The University of Michigan Press.

Jackson J & Moch LP (1996). Migration and the Social History of Modern Europe. In D Hoerder & L Page Moch (Eds), *European Migrants: Global and Local Perspectives*. Boston: Northeastern University Press, 52–69.

Kamphoefner W (1995). German Emigration Research, North, South, and East: Findings, Methods and Open Questions. In D Hoerder & J Nagler (Eds), *People in Transit: German Migrations in Comparative Perspective 1820-1930*. England: Cambridge University Press, 19–33.

Kirchner W (1850). *Australien und seine Vortheile für Auswanderer*. 2nd ed, Frankfurt am Main: H.E. Brönner.

Little W, Fowler HW & Coulson J (Eds) (1968). *The Shorter Oxford English Dictionary on Historical Principles, Vol. 1, A-M.* 3rd ed., Oxford: Oxford University Press.

Lubinski A (1995). Overseas Emigration from Mecklenburg-Strelitz: The Geographic and Social Contexts. In D Hoerder & J Nagler (Eds), *People in Transit: German Migrations in Comparative Perspective 1820–1930.* England: Cambridge University Press, 19–33.

Lüthke F (1989). *Psychologie der Auswanderung.* Weinheim: Deutscher Studien Verlag.

Lüthke MF & Cropley A (1990). Decision Making and Adjustment Difficulties: A Counselling Strategy for Working with Migrants. *Australian Psychologist*, 25(2): 147–64.

Massey DS, Arango J, Hugo G, Kouaouci A, Pelegrino A & Taylor JE (2005). *Worlds in Motion: Understanding International Migration at the End of the Millennium.* Oxford: Clarendon Press.

Morawska E (1996). Labor Migrations of Poles in the Atlantic World Economy, 1880–1914. In D Hoerder & LP Moch (Eds), *European Migrants: Global and Local Perspectives.* Boston: Northeastern University Press.

Müller J, *Diary 1872–1940*, Berry (unpublished).

Müller J, *Diary vol. 1 21/3/1855–1866.* R-M Jansohn (Trans.), Mudgee Historical Society, 1973 (unpublished).

NSW State Records, Immigrant Index (1844–59) [online]. Available: http://www.records.nsw.gov.au?ASP/index4459.asp, (Accessed 20 November 2003).

Porter R (1997). *The Greatest Benefit to Mankind: A Medical History of Humanity from Antiquity to the Present.* London: Harper Collins.

Ravenstein EG (1885). The Laws of Migration. *Journal of the Royal Statistical Society*, 48(2): 167–235.

Ravenstein EG (1889). The Laws of Migration. *Journal of the Royal Statistical Society*, 52(2): 241–305.

Reichmann E, Rippley LJ & Nagler J (Eds) (1995). *Emigration and Settlement Patterns of German Communities in North America.* Indianapolis: Max Kade German-America Center, Indiana University-Purdue University.

Reich U (1995). Emigration from Regierungsbezirk Frankfurt/Oder, 1815–93. In D Hoerder & J Nagler (Eds), *People in Transit: German Migrations in Comparative Perspective 1820–1930.* England: Cambridge University Press, 19–33.

Rheinberger P, Diary 1871–1929, (unpublished).

Reynolds KM (2008). The Frauenstein Letters: Aspects of the Nineteenth Century Emigration from the Duchy of Nassau to Australia. PhD thesis: University of Sydney.

Reynolds KM (2009). *The Frauenstein Letters: Aspects of the Nineteenth Century Emigration from the Duchy of Nassau to Australia.* Bern: Peter Lang.

Schneider A, *Diary 1829–83* [online]. Available: http:home.t-oline.de/home/michel-walluf/schnfrau.htm (Accessed 26 January 2005).

Schubert D (1997). *Kavel's People.* Adelaide: Open Books Press.

Struck W-H (1996). *Die Auswanderung aus dem Herzogtum Nassau (1806–66).* Wiesbaden: Franz Steiner Verlag.

Tampke J (2006). *The Germans in Australia.* Port Melbourne, Vic.: Cambridge University Press.

Vogel CD (1843). *Beschreibung des Herzogthums Nassau.* Wiesbaden: Bayerla.

Williams JF (2003). *German Anzacs and the First World War.* Sydney: UNSW Press.

Zolberg AR (2006). *A Nation by Design: Immigration Policy in the Fashioning of America.* New York: Russell Sage Foundation.

8
The German Accounts of Cook's Voyages[1]

Fredericka van der Lubbe

Up to now many people have treated the subject matter of James Cook and his voyages, but there is room for another treatment of the Cook material. In this paper I plan to survey the German accounts of the Cook voyages and say a little bit about the background to some of the accounts.

I am not the first to look at the German view of the Cook voyages. Leslie Bodi, in two essays (1959, 1983 [2002]) in particular, writes on the treatment of James Cook in German literature and of course goes quite deeply into how the names Cook and Forster (that is Johann Reinhold Forster and his son, Georg Forster) cannot really be separated. In particular, Bodi surveys the essays on Cook by Georg Christoph Lichtenberg and Georg Forster. Bodi also discusses two other narratives of the Cook story, the children's biographies by Pabst and Campe. In his biography of Johann Reinhold Forster (1976), Michael Hoare also treats the works which the Forsters wrote in some detail but does not bring out much to do with the task of translation, in which Georg Forster was intimately involved, while Klaus-Georg Popp (1976) writes an extremely detailed essay on Forster's and Lichtenberg's roles as communicators of the Cook message, and the background to their contributions. In addition, an essay by Noel Macainsh (1979) looks at Heinrich Zimmermann and his unauthorised Cook story.

1 I am grateful to Basser Library, the Australian Academy of Science, Canberra, for their financial assistance under the Moran Fellowship, to investigate Hoare's earliest work on the Forsters, and particularly his treatment of their contribution to the literature on Cook's second voyage. I would particularly like to thank Ms Rosanne Walker, Librarian, for her kind assistance.

My approach to the subject is slightly different from those of Bodi, Hoare and Popp in that it is chiefly that of analytical bibliography: I focus on translators' forewords, introductions by publishers, letters to do with publishing and similar material. The literature falls into several categories:

- three official translations into German of the Cook voyages, authorised by the British Admiralty, all published by Haude & Spener;
- an unauthorised German account, by Zimmermann, which was suppressed at the request of the British Admiralty, but which popped up later in French and Dutch;
- numerous accounts without permission of the British Admiralty which were translated into German; some are more authoritative than others;
- "pirate" reprints; I have omitted their names for reasons of space, but they also do not usually offer anything in terms of translators' or publishers' forewords; they are usually just the official edition, reprinted;
- also a striking number of Cook biographies; Kippis, translated from the English, was the official version, but there are numerous others originally written in German. Of most note are probably the above-mentioned Lichtenberg essay and two essays by Forster, but there is also a subset which is children's literature.

This project is ongoing, and I intend to focus on the background to the three official editions and also examine the background to three pieces published in the wake of Cook's death. I would like to bring out the following ideas: that the direction of the flow of information took a decisive turn after 1780, that the Forsters were part of the German "ownership" of the Cook event, and that there was considerable jockeying for position in the Cook industry – the race for the press.

The First Voyage

There is little doubt that there were great expectations of the German translation of the first voyage, based on its sales performance in England. The official account of the first voyage, edited by Dr Hawkesworth, was published in London in 1773 and ran almost immediately into a second edition before it could be translated into any other languages. The Hawkesworth edition was translated into German by Johann Friedrich Schiller, the editor of the *New Review*, a review journal for foreign works, and a translator of English books of some importance (Fabian 1976: 132). The German translation was published in 1774 by Haude & Spener, the Berlin booksellers, who became the German publishers of the official translations, and also published a number of other volumes relating to the Cook voyages. If the names of the Forsters were inseparable from the Cook voyages, then Haude & Spener were *the* publishers of Cook material. Most significantly, Schiller's translation of the Hawkesworth edition was the first and only one of the works on Cook published by Haude & Spener for which they applied to and received Royal privileges from Friedrich, King of Prussia. This was the equivalent of copyright. For this, they expected that in every part of Prussia and its provinces there would be protection for some 20 years from reprinting or concurrent translation, as this would attract a penalty of 500 *Reichsthaler*. They for their part ensured the quality of the book, especially the etchings, which compared favourably with the French and the English editions, and were awaiting the support of the German public.

The extent to which this type of venture was fraught with risk is pointed out by Georg Forster in a letter to Sir Joseph Banks dated 20 June 1781;[1] his great fear regarding the *third* voyage was

> [I mean] the pitch to which the fraud of reprinting piratical Editions of books, is risen in Germany. The honest bookseller is now obliged to take every precaution in order to prevent the pirate from reprinting a book, which has a run among the publick; and there are but two ways of securing his property; the one to come out with the book unexpectedly, so that his Edition may go off before the other bookseller can get his re-impression forward; the other to make paper & print as bad as possible, by which means the enemy has no great profits to expect, because he cannot give his Edition cheaper than the Original.

---

1 National Library of Australia Digital Collections, Manuscripts, MS 9 Series 3, Item 77d–77f; here, Part 1.

Unfortunately there was no general copyright protection in the 18th century in Germany (Fabian 1976: 135). Saxony had one of the earliest laws against reprinting, enacted in 1773, but Württemberg continued to deem reprints legal, and in south-west Germany, reprinting therefore flourished as a trade. Treaties between England and Prussia, and England and Hanover were not signed until the 1840s, so that throughout the 18th century, English authors had no avenue for protecting their work from translation or reprinting in Germany.

Spener in fact was, as we later find out through Georg Forster,

> considerably injured by the translation of Hawkesworth's Voyages, where he was tricked by those piratical fellows, who care for no privilege, because they live under the protection of some petty German prince or another.[2]

The Second Voyage

Schiller's name was never associated with the Cook voyages again. In the meantime, the much more colourful Forsters had entered the scene, and their involvement in the second voyage was to permanently affect the flow of information on the Cook voyages. Most important of all for the history of the translations of the Cook voyages is the bitter dispute between the Forsters and the British Admiralty, headed by the Earl of Sandwich. While Hoare treats the dispute in his biography of J.R. Forster, his treatment neglects the effect that Georg Forster's *Letter to the Earl of Sandwich* had on the progress of the Continental translations.[3] This document is crucial for understanding the true situation of the Forsters in England, for understanding exactly why and when the Forsters published their *Reise um die Welt* [*Voyage Around the World*], and subsequent work done by the Forsters and their acquaintances. The *Letter to the Earl of Sandwich* (1778) is a detailed, 25-page account of the grievances that the Forsters had against the British Admiralty, followed by affidavits sworn by both men.

---

2 National Library of Australia Digital Collections, Manuscripts, MS 9 Series 3, Item 77d–77f, Part 3 (Part 4) (Cassel, 20 June 20 1781).

3 In his earliest work, Hoare also makes some brief mention of the Forsters' contribution to the Continental translation of Georg Forster's *Voyage round the world* (Hoare 1966: 8).

At the outset of their relationship with the British Admiralty, the understanding on which the Forsters proceeded was that Cook did not see himself in a position to write a treatise on the voyages. This had also been the case for the English account of the first voyage. Under a verbal agreement, the Forsters were hired by the British Admiralty to work as naturalists aboard Cook's second voyage on the Resolution, and to produce an official account of the voyage. It was crucial to them to have the right to an official account for reasons of legitimacy. In spite of their subsequent disagreement, every time the Forsters wrote an account they acknowledged that they travelled at the expense of the British government or that the voyages were undertaken at the behest of George III. The legitimacy conferred by the Admiralty's recognition that this was the official account would confirm the Forsters' authority and the accuracy of detail, which would in turn make their work more saleable; it would bolster their status not only in England, but also on the Continent. George III was still a Hanoverian king, and his word had status on the Continent as well. The Admiralty's recognition was also crucial for reasons of support. As officially acknowledged translators the Forsters would also be entitled to support from the Admiralty, which might be financial or may allow privileged access to certain documents, information or images, as we will soon see.

Unfortunately, in the Forsters' view, the British reneged on their promise. They were willing to accept an account by the elder Forster, but not one written as a unified narrative. Their work was to be written as discrete entries functioning as an adjunct to Cook's diaries. The naturalist Daines Barrington was appointed to cut down Forster's work, but Forster absolutely refused to allow this. As for Cook's part in this, although Cook had not originally intended to write up his own diaries as an account, as the Forsters saw it, Cook subsequently realised that there was money to be made from the venture and committed himself to the writing, again edging out the Forsters, with his friend Sandwich's approval. Moreover, the Forsters saw an additional reason for their misfortune, which was also documented in the *Letter to the Earl of Sandwich*: Sandwich's mistress Martha Ray saw and wanted some tropical birds which the Forsters had brought back with them as live exhibits. However, they had already been promised to the Queen, so that when Miss Ray saw the Forsters, there was resultant ill humour on Miss Ray's side and embarrassment on the part of the Forsters. They saw this as contributing to the disfavour they felt they received. All this was recorded in a public document by Georg Forster in defence of his father, which Michael Hoare (1976: 179–81) views as a last-ditch attempt to save at least some of the privileges to which they thought themselves entitled.

The Forsters did publish their own English account, *A Voyage Around the World*, in 1778, and managed to publish it some six weeks before Cook's account could come out, so as to try to capture a good share of the market. Forster senior had been forbidden by the Admiralty from publishing anything before the official accounts came out, but this did not apply to his son Georg.

Georg Forster writes:

> my Lord, if you did not choose to keep conditions which you or your plenipotentiaries had granted, and others which you had signed, or if you were resolved not to reward us; was it necessary that you should inhumanly destroy our other means of getting an honest livelihood? You gave orders to the publishers of Capt. Cook's voyage to sell that book at the same price as mine, though a work with 63 elegant copper plates engraved by the first artists, instead of being sold for two guineas, would without your Lordship's interference have been sold for four guineas, agreeably to the customary price of such publications. Thus you enticed the purchasers to prefer the Captain's book to mine, for this plain reason, that with it they received 63 plates into the bargain. In order that Capt. Cook's profit might not be lessened through your generosity to the public, you made him a present of the expences [sic] of paper and print, over and above the gift of all the plates. By thus lavishing the public money, you were enabled to retail the books below prime cost: like that charitable shoe-maker who used to steal the leather, and to give away for nothing the shoes which he made of it. The contrivance has the desired success; and I am a loser by two thirds of what I must otherwise have earned (Forster 1778: 18–19).

More importantly for the Continental accounts, however, is the revelation that the Forsters felt themselves disadvantaged in their ability to publish translations as well, as Georg writes in the same letter:

There is another article, my Lord, in the agreement of the 13th of April, 1776, which has been arbitrarily infringed, to our prejudice. It was expressly stipulated in the agreement, that my father should receive the sheets of Capt. Cook's narrative, as fast as each was printed off, and proofs of the plates as soon as any were engraved, for the purpose of giving him an advantage in point of time, to make translations of the work into the French and German languages. Capt. Cook left England long before his manuscript was put to the press; and appointed certain agents to manage the publication of the work in concert with my father. These persons refused to furnish my father with sheets and with proof-impressions of the plates. He instantly applied to your Lordship for redress; but you were pleased to refer him back to the very persons of whom he complained. He hath your letters on the subject. I believe no man ever heard of a more flagrant violation of common equity. Capt. Cook's agents seeing they were not controuled, persisted to refuse the fulfilling of the agreement, and deprived my father of an advantage, which at the very lowest would have been worth to him £1000 (Forster 1778: 19).

This disadvantage did in fact culminate in financial disadvantage to the Forsters, who were in dire straits at the time of writing. Georg further calculates what this deprivation of privileges was worth to them:

If what the world reports of your Lordship, be consonant to truth, our demands upon you are trifling in comparison to those of the public, and ought to be answered, because your agent had promised much more. I shall leave to your own determination to fix the amount of our *annual* provision; but with regard to my father's profits of the publication, they are as follows. Had his work been printed with Capt. Cook's, the whole together would have formed *three* volumes in Quarto, which according to the common price of books of prints, must have been sold at six guineas, but I will only put them down at three, conformably to the price of Capt. Cook's account of the voyage, which was fixed so low by your Lordship, in order to injure the sale of mine. Three thousand copies have been sold of Capt. Cook's work, and as many would have been sold of the joint publication. The *nett produce* of this last, after deducting certain expences, would have been at the very lowest, *six thousand* pounds. One half of this sum is my father's due, by the written agreement of the 13th of April 1776. If he had been furnished as it was stipulated in the agreement, with proof-sheets and proof-impressions of the plates, he would have cleared £500 by the French translation, and as much by the German. He therefore demands £4000 upon the strength of an agreement signed by your Lordship, even though he should waive the advantage, which the conditions agreed to by the Hon. Mr Barrington secured to him. I repeat, my Lord, that if there is any thing like equity in this world, you cannot refuse to pay my father *four thousand* pounds, which will not yet make him amends for what he has suffered whilst it hath been unjustly withheld. For the present I must entirely leave it to your love of justice, whether you will pay, or not pay my father. But do not, my Lord, persevere in oppressive acts, for no other reason, but because there is *now* no power to control you (Forster 1778: 24–25).

While this was a serious charge, it is also apparent that their estimate of the German share of the market was a small sum when compared with the overall sales from the English version – about a twelfth. Nevertheless, it was an eighth of their income at a time when they could ill-afford competitors.

Georg Forster did complete the translation of the account of the second voyage, and *Reise um die Welt*, first translated into German between the years 1778–80, ran into several editions, well into the 1780s.

The Death of Cook

Soon after, the death of Cook in February 1779 brought a flurry of publications as soon as the news became known. Interestingly, the direction of information flow changes about this time. Information about the Cook voyages now starts to come independently from German speakers; some of the information has its origins with the Forsters but there were also some other Germans aboard the voyages who wrote about Cook without exclusive reference to English information, such as Heinrich Zimmermann. Others digested English information in a journalistic fashion, such as Lichtenberg, Pabst, Campe and a number of anonymous writers. The Forsters' name comes up everywhere, even if only by assumed association. Although they did not entirely control the path of information to Germany, their name is one that dominates by virtue of their close pecuniary interest in the matter.

The very first published account in Europe of Cook's death was a German one, written by the Berlin geographer Anton Friedrich Büsching (1724–93). After the death of Cook in O-Why-He, the ship's log was dispatched overland from Kamchatka to the British envoy in St Petersburg by sledge, on 29 April 1779. Cook's log and a letter by his successor Clerke detailing their progress and Cook's demise reached the English envoy James Harris in St Petersburg on 10 January 1780. He then made the log and letter known to the German naturalist Peter Simon Pallas (1741–1811), with Pallas in turn informing the Englishman Thomas Pennant (1726–98), and Büsching, who published the news in his journal in two parts, on 10 January and 17 January 1780.[4] This second letter was, in the view of Popp (1976: 251f, n191) virtually a reproduction of Cook's and Clerke's reports, which Georg Forster then transmitted to Georg Christoph Lichtenberg on 19 January 1780.

There was also controversy regarding the publication of details of Cook's voyage and death; Büsching, in fact, managed to beat the English to the punch. Cook's death was reported in the *London Gazette* of 11 January 1780, a fact that was apparently not hailed by the English admiralty (Popp 1976: 251f, n191), who were already censoring the information that circulated about Cook's voyages by restricting the journals and logs of individuals who had been part of the voyages. Whether Büsching's account is the same as the one forwarded to Banks by Georg Forster in a letter of 20 January 1780[5] is not known, but Forster was here again responsible for acting as conduit between the English-speaking world and the German world.

Also a first to the press in Europe, the extremely rare *Nachrichten von dem Leben und den Seereisen des berühmten Captain Cook* [*News about*

---

4 Jg. 8, St 2 , 10. Januar 1780, St 3, 17. Januar 1780.
5 NLA Digital Collections MS 9 Ser 3 Item 74–74a, Part 1.

the Life and Voyages of the Famous Captain Cook] (1780, Reval & Leipzig) is, according to Cook's bibliographer Beddie, the first monograph anywhere on the death of Cook. The substance of the text is taken from a letter to the anonymous editor, written at Kensington, dated 4 February 1780, before news of Captain Cook's death had reached England, and before the third voyage had even ended. Beddie ascribes authorship to J.R. Forster (1970: 452). I suggest the informant is to be found in the publisher Albrecht and Compagnie's circle of acquaintances. The editor received the news from a friend in Kensington at the time when Georg Forster was living in Kassel, while his father had been in Halle since 1779. This effectively rules out both men as sources of the letter.

Another writer who responded very quickly to the death of Cook was Georg Christoph Lichtenberg, who together with Georg Forster produced a journal.[6] By good fortune, the journal was ready for publication quite close to the time of Cook's death, allowing Lichtenberg to strike while the iron was hot. His essay on Cook was published in the first volume of their journal, in March 1780 (Lichtenberg 1976). Although Lichtenberg had had the means to gather information on Cook personally from colleagues such as Banks, Solander and Hodges, he scarcely mentions Cook in his diaries or correspondence, other than to note a trip to Deptford,[7] where he saw the resolution. According to Georg Forster's letter to Sir Joseph Banks of 27 March 1780,[8] it is evident that the Forsters were the chief informants for Lichtenberg's life of Cook. It is fleshed out with information from Hawkesworth and Marra, who produced an unauthorised account of the second voyage in 1775. Lichtenberg, ever with an eye for the sensational, produced a warts-and-all account of Cook, which certainly portrays him as a great man, but also as mildly stingy, emphasises his peasant background (Lichtenberg 1976: 143), and brands him a hothead, indeed, his fatal flaw (ibid: 171f).

---

6 The *Göttingen Magazine of Sciences and Literature*.
7 With a Herrn v. Adams, on 30 November 1775 (Gumbert 1977: 207).
8 NLA Digital Collections MS 9 Ser 3 Item 75–75a, Part 2. See also Hoare (1976: 202).

The Third Voyage

The translation of the third voyage was also business for the Forsters, and although they had damaged their reputation in England, we have access to some of the behind-the-scenes manoeuvring that took place to ensure that Georg was able to have rights to the translation. In the first instance, Georg wrote to his friend Sir Joseph Banks (10 January 1781),[9] to see if he could influence the decision:

> I am now to solicit, Your Interest, my dear Sir, according to Yr Kind promise in Yr last, in order to obtain me the sheets & proofs of all the plates as early as possible, as I intend to give a compleat and exact translation in German of the new Voyage. I hope Ld. Sandwich will have no objection to my enjoyg the benefit of this preference, and if it might advance my interest in this respect, you may assure his Lordship, that the advantage will be wholly my own, & not devolve to my father. This is no time & no place to repeat, how much I lament that my father's temper made the breach so wide, and forced me to become an unwilling champion in his cause. Yet so much I must needs say, that I am sorry I marred my own success in England, if it is true, what I have oftentimes been told since, that Ld. Sandwich meant to have provided for me handsomely.

Banks proposed dropping Forster's name from the application to the Admiralty, to which suggestion, Forster readily agreed (letter 20 June 1781),[10] and instead proposed the name of his publishers Haude & Spener; Herr Spener was by now a good friend of Forster's and he correctly expected that any rights won by them would flow onto him as well.

Banks' preferences regarding the Continental translations were not able to proceed without question. In fact, Captain James King (1750–84), who had been one of the Captains aboard the third voyage, sent a letter to Lord Sandwich, dated 11 September 1783,[11] regarding the

---

9 NLA Digital Collections MS 9 Ser 3 Item 77b, Part 2.
10 NLA Digital Collections MS 9 Ser 3 Item 77d–77f, Part 1.
11 NLA Digital Collections MS 7218 Item 23.

publication of the English account of the third voyage and his concerns about how quickly Continental booksellers would publish their translations. King had a deeper interest in the work, as part of the English account was his. According to King, the editor of the English version, Dr John Douglas,[12] was in a bad humour as Banks had changed French booksellers. Douglas had then prevented Banks from sending off the sheets to the French bookseller as soon as they were printed, together with proofs of the prints, fearing that the French edition might come out within a very short time of the English account, if not before the English account, which was the very worst possible case. As in previous matters, it was important for the Admiralty to retain control over release of the information.

Lord Keppel[13] had evidently "agreed to Sir Joseph's proposal of sending two copies of the letter proofs & prints, as they were worked off, to the French and German booksellers."[14] King was told of this and conveyed the message to Banks regarding Lord Keppel's approval, but cautioned him also regarding Douglas' fears. He reminded Banks that the account of the last voyage was not given to Forster until a fortnight before publication of the English version. It seems the Forsters' narrative may have bitten the Admiralty harder than admitted.

While Banks took this on board, he gave an undertaking that they would not publish till a year after the English version. King was immediately on guard, and asked Lord Sandwich his opinion; seeing that Banks would have no way of preventing the French and German booksellers of publishing as soon as they pleased, he felt that Sandwich would have more influence with Banks:

> No one certainly can object to Sir Jos. giving a preference
> to any foreign bookseller he pleases, but to prejudice in the
> smallest degree the sale & circulation of the English Edition,
> on which the credit of the whole [business] will so much de-
> pend, I am sure your Lordship will think is what ought to be
> carefully avoided; I also wish your Lordship to understand

12 1721–1807, Canon of Windsor and St Paul's.
13 Augustus Keppel, 1725–86, 1st Viscount Keppel, First Lord of the Admiralty after Sandwich.
14 NLA Digital Collections, MS 7218, Item 23, Part 3.

that a preference in the usual course is the most that the French bookseller has any right to; Mr Webber[15] assures me, that the best price is paid for the paper he sends, and even an additional sum given to have the bad sheets picked out.[16]

The English edition of the third voyage was published in 1784, some four years after the return of the vessels to England. And completion of the German translation was still a long way off.

Wetzel

There was in fact fierce competition for the translation of the final voyage, which Georg Forster can only have been expecting, having no other means of protection other than to work swiftly, if he expected to maintain quality. Competition came from the Anspach councillor and librarian, Johann Ludwig Wetzel. Wetzel was fully aware that Haude & Spener had announced in their forthcoming translation by Georg Forster in mid-1784, and, as it had not yet been published by 1785, Wetzel was very willing to go head to head with them and compete for market share. He estimated that his translation would cost in all probability about half of what Georg Forster's Berlin edition would cost, an attractive proposition for buyers. Wetzel advertised for subscribers to his translation, to be published in five volumes (Wetzel 1785: 463–64). His intention was to have no more than 600 subscribers, which meant that he projected takings of over 9000 *Reichsthaler* for this project. He also gives us some idea of what the original English version cost: he says a few thousand copies, at five guineas a copy, sold out within three days. Copies sold later cost 8, 10, even 15 guineas a copy, and the octavo edition likewise sold out very quickly. He suggests that for this reason the German market would be able to support more than one translation of the third voyage, particularly in view of the small circulation projected. We have good records of how successful Wetzel was in his venture, as his translation carries the names of the subscribers to his volumes, and the number of copies to which they subscribed (Wetzel 1787: b1r).

---

15 John Webber, illustrator on Cook's third voyage (1776–80).
16 NLA Digital Collections, MS 7218, Item 23, Part 4.

Wetzel advertised that the first volume would be completed by Michaelmas (Wetzel 1787: a4^r), but it was only completed in April 1787. Although he had hoped to keep issuing volumes regularly and finish issuing all volumes by 1788, this was not to be the case. Volumes two and three came relatively soon, but the fourth volume was delayed by some four to five years, and was not published until April 1794. The series was not completed by Wetzel, who died in 1809. In September 1811 W.G. Gaßert of Anspach took over publication, even though it was covered by few subscribers, because he thought the work useful, and published the final volume.

Forster's edition of the third voyage, by contrast, was professionally executed, and published in only two volumes, in May 1787 and in 1788, even if the delay gave Wetzel moment. Of course, Wetzel's offer would have made Haude & Spener's marketing job that much harder: perhaps in response to Wetzel's pricing challenge, Haude & Spener advertised the costs for both volumes as a modest ten *Thaler*.

Bibliography

Anon (1780). *Nachrichten von dem Leben und den Seereisen des berühmten Capitain Cook [News of the life and the voyages of the famous Captain Cook]*. Reval & Leipzig: Albrecht & Compagnie.

Anon (1787). *Dritte und letzte Reise um die Welt des Leutenants J. Cook, Befehlshaber der königlichen Korvette die Resoluzion, in den Jahren 1776 bis 1778 [Third and last voyage around the world of Lieutenant J. Cook, commander of the Royal corvette the Resolution, in the years 1776 to 1778]*. Brünn [Brno]: Joseph Georg Trassler.

Anon (1797). *Cooks Leben [Life of Cook]*. Tübingen: I.G. Cottaschen Buchhandlung.

Beddie MK (1970). *Bibliography of Captain James Cook*. Sydney: The Library of New South Wales, 2nd edition.

Bodi L (2002a [1959]). Georg Forster: The "Pacific Expert" of Eighteenth-Century Germany. In L Bodi (Ed), *Literatur, Politik, Identität: Literature, Politics, Cultural Identity*. St Ingbert: Röhrig Universitätsverlag, 29–54.

Bodi L (2002b [1983]). James Cook in der deutschen Literatur [*James Cook in German literature*]. In L Bodi (Ed), *Literatur, Politik, Identität: Literature, Politics, Cultural Identity*. St Ingbert: Röhrig Universitätsverlag, 67–84.

Büsching AF (Ed) (1780). *Wöchentlichen Nachrichten von neuen Landkarten, geographischen, statistischen und historischen Büchern und Sachen* [*Weekly news of new maps, geographical, statistical and historical books and matters*]. Jg. 8, St 2, 10. Januar 1780, 9–12.

Campe JH (1786–90). *Sammlung interessanter und durchgängig zweckmässig abgefasster Reisebeschreibungen für die Jugend* [*Collection of interesting travelogues all written for children*], n.p. [8 Vols.].

Cook J & King J (1788). *Des Capitain Jacob Cooks dritte Entdeckungs-Reise … Aus den Tagebüchern des Capitain Cook und der übrigen nach seinem Ableben im Commando auf ihn gefolgten Befehlshaber Clerke, Gore und King imgleichen des Schiffswundarztes Herrn Anderson herausgegeben* [*Captain James Cook's Third Voyage of Discovery … Published from the Diaries of Captain Cook and the remaining Commanders Clerke, Gore and King as well as the Ship's Surgeon Mr Anderson after his Death*]. JGA Forster (Trans.). Zweyter Band. Berlin: Haude & Spener.

Cook J & King J (1787–1812). *Capitain Cooks dritte und letzte Reise; oder, Geschichte einer Entdeckungsreise nach dem Stillen Ocean …* [*Captain Cook's third and last voyage; or, history of a voyage of discovery to the Pacific Ocean …*] JL Wetzel (Trans) Anspach: JL Wetzel.

Cook J (1778–80). *Geschichte der See-Reisen und Entdeckungen im Süd-Meer welche auf Befehl Sr. Grosbrittannischen Majestät George des Dritten unternommen worden sind. Aus den Tagebüchern der Schiffs-Befehlshaber und den Handschriften der Gelehrten Herren J. Banks, Dr Solander, Dr J.R. Forster und Herrn G. Forster, welche diesen Reisen als Naturkündiger beygewohnt haben herausgegeben* [*History of the Sea-Voyages and Discoveries in the South Seas Undertaken by Order of His Majesty George III. Published from the Diaries of the Scientists Messrs J. Banks, Dr Solander, Dr J.R. Forster and Mr G. Forster who Accompanied these Voyages as Naturalists*], 2 Vols. JGA Forster (Trans.). Berlin: Haude & Spener.

Fabian B (1976). English Books and their Eighteenth-Century German Readers. In *The Widening Circle: Essays on the Circulation of Literature in*

Eighteenth-Century Europe. PJ Korshin (Ed). Philadelphia: University of Pennsylvania Press, 117–96.

Forster JGA (1778). *A Letter to the Right Honourable the Earl of Sandwich, First Lord Commissioner of the Board of Admiralty*. London: Printed for G. Robinson, in Pater-Noster-Row.

Forster JGA (1778–80). *Johann Reinhold Forsters ... Reise um die Welt während ... 1772 bis 1775 ... beschrieben und herausgegeben von dessen Sohn und Reisegefährten [Johann Reinhold Forster's ... Voyage Around the World From ... 1772 to 1775 ... Described and Published by his Son and Travelling Companion]*, 2 Vols. JGA Forster (Trans.). Berlin: Haude & Spener.

Forster G (1976 [1781]). Fragmente über Kapitän Cooks letze Reise und sein Ende [*Fragments about Captain Cook's last voyage and his death*]. In K-G Popp (Ed), *Cook der Entdecker. Schriften über James Cook von Georg Forster und Georg Christoph Lichtenberg [Cook the Discoverer. Writings on James Cook by Georg Forster and Georg Christoph Lichtenberg]*. Leipzig: Reclam, 175–200.

Forster G (1967a [1787]). Cook der Entdecker [Cook the Discoverer]. In K-G Popp (Ed), *Cook der Entdecker. Schriften über James Cook von Georg Forster und Georg Christoph Lichtenberg [Cook the Discoverer]*. In *Cook the Discoverer: Writings on James Cook by Georg Forster and Georg Christoph Lichtenberg*. Leipzig: Reclam, 5–137.

Gumbert HL (Ed) (1977). *Lichtenberg in England: Dokumente einer Begegnung. Bd I. Einleitung und Text [Lichtenberg in England: Documents of an Encounter. vol. I. Introduction and Text]*. Wiesbaden: Otto Harrassowitz.

Hawkesworth J (Ed) (1774). *Geschichte der See-Reisen und Entdeckungen im Süd-Meer welche auf Befehl Sr. Grosbrittannischen Majestät unternommen und von Commodore Byron, Capitain Wallis, Capitain Carteret und Capitain Cook, im Dolphin, der Swallow und dem Endeavour ... ausgeführt worden sind; aus den Tagebüchern der verschiedenen Befehlshaber und den Handschriften J. Banks ... [History of the Sea-Voyages and Discoveries in the South Seas Undertaken by Order of His Majesty of Great Britain and Carried out by Commodore Byron, Captain Wallis, Captain Carteret and Captain Cook, in the Dolphin, the Swallow and* the Endeavour ... from the Diaries of the Various Commanders and the Manuscript of J. Banks]. JF Schiller (Trans). 3 vols. Berlin: A Haude & JC Spener.

Hoare M (1966). The contributions of JR and G Forster to the literature of Cook's Second Voyage 1772–75. MA thesis, Monash University, Basser Library, Australian Academy of Science, MS 51 Box 1 Item 8.

Hoare M (1976). The Tactless Philosopher: Johann Reinhold Forster (1729–98). Melbourne: The Hawthorn Press.

Kippis A (1789). Leben des Capitain James Cook, von Andreas Kippis ... [Life of Captain James Cook, by Andrew Kippis ...] Hamburg: B.G. Hoffmann.

Lichtenberg GC (1976 [1780]). Einige Lebensumstände von Captain James Cook [Some life circumstances of Captain James Cook]. In K-G Popp (Ed), Cook der Entdecker. Schriften über James Cook von Georg Forster und Georg Christoph Lichtenberg [Cook the Discoverer: Writings on James Cook by Georg Forster and Georg Christoph Lichtenberg]. Leipzig: Reclam, 138–74.

Macainsh N (1979). A Plain Man's View of the Pacific: Some Notes on Heinrich Zimmermann and His Background with a Portrait. In W Veit (Ed), Captain James Cook: Image and Impact: South Seas Discoveries and the World of Letters, vol. 2. Melbourne: Hawthorn Press, 1972–79, 50–63.

Marra J (1775). Journal of the Resolution's Voyage ... London: F. Newbery.

Mautner FH (Ed) (1976). Georg Christoph Lichtenberg: Briefe 1766–99. 4. Band [Georg Christoph Lichtenberg: Letters 1766–99, Vol. 4]. Frankfurt / Main: Insel Verlag.

Pabst JGF (1783–84). Die Entdeckungen des fünften Welttheils; oder, Reisen um die Welt: Ein Lesebuch für die Jugend [The Discoveries of the Fifth Part of the World; or, Voyages Around the World. A Reader for Children], 4 Vols. in 2. Nürnberg: Felsseckerische Buchhandlung.

Pallas PS (1780). Des Herrn Doctors und Professors Pallas umständlicherer Bericht von des Cap. Cooks Entdeckungen und Tode [Professor and Dr Pallas' Longer Account of Capt. Cook's Discoveries and Death]. In AF Büsching (Ed), Wöchentlichen Nachrichten von neuen Landkarten, geographischen, statistischen und historischen Büchern und

Sachen [*Weekly News of New Maps, Geographical, Statistical and Historical Books and Matters*]. Jg. 8, St 3, 17. Januar 1780, 17–38.

Popp K-G (Ed) (1983). *Cook der Entdecker: Schriften über James Cook von Georg Forster und Georg Christoph Lichtenberg*. [*Cook the Discoverer: Writings on James Cook by Georg Forster and Georg Christoph Lichtenberg*]. Leipzig: Reclam.

Wetzel JL (1785). Ankündigungen [Announcements], *Journal von und für Deutschland* [*Journal of and for Germany*]. 2 Jg., 11 St., 463–64.

Zimmermann H (1781). *Reise um die Welt mit Capitain Cook* [*Voyage Around the World with Captain Cook*]. Mannheim: CF Schwan.

IV
Imaginations of Australia in German Literature

9
"Wen die Schande einmal gefaßt hat …": Therese Huber's *Abentheuer auf einer Reise nach Neu-Holland* and the Question of Guilt

Judith Wilson

Accused of a crime she did not commit, the female protagonist of Therese Huber's novel *Abentheuer auf einer Reise nach Neu-Holland* (1999:177), the convict Francis Belton, cries bitterly:

> "Wen die Schande einmal gefaßt hat, dem folgt sie, wie dein Körper der Schatten!" [Once it has touched you, shame follows you like the shadow follows your body!]

This could be said of both of the central characters of Huber's story who, caught in the maelstrom of the French Revolution, have chosen exile or been banished to the penal colony of New Holland, to atone for their guilt. Rudolph, the text's narrator, is a disillusioned revolutionary who has left Europe and embarked on a journey to New Holland to preserve what remains of his moral integrity and restore his sense of self-worth. Francis Belton is a convict who was found guilty of theft and condemned to transportation. Once happily married to a mutineer inspired by revolutionary ideals, her life was destroyed when her husband, now believed dead, was banished to Botany Bay, leaving her without support and without protection from the schemes of an unscrupulous mentor. On arrival in the penal colony, the future of both characters appears bleak – the convict inhabitants of New Holland lack any incentive to pursue a more virtuous life. Only those who have been pardoned or have served their sentence and been given the right to own property have regained their sense of honour (T. Huber 1999: 139).

Their prospects improve, however, with a shift to Norfolk Island, the home of the model emancipist couple, the Watsons. When past histories are disclosed, questions of guilt resolved and past connections restored, Norfolk Island becomes the site of a new model community in which the shadow of shame is dispelled and human dignity restored.

Huber's story, a combination of epistolary novel and fictional travelogue, family romance and social utopia, was written in 1793 and published in the magazine *Flora* (1793–94) by her erstwhile lover and later husband, Ludwig Huber.[1] It has thus far attracted little scholarly interest, and yet it is unusual in a number of respects – it is considered to be the first work of world literature to be set in the penal colony of Australia, it is one of the earliest German literary responses to the radicalisation of the French Revolution by a woman whose life was immediately affected by it, and it is one of the few so-called Frauenromane [women's novels] to consider the theme of revolution.[2]

Leslie Bodi was the first to recognise the significance of Huber's work for German-Australian comparative studies, and in 1966, he published an English translation and a detailed introduction to the text.[3] The second was Alan Corkhill, who in 1990 included a discussion of the text in his comprehensive outline of German literary perspectives on Australia, *Antipodean Encounters: Australia and the German Literary Imagination 1754–1918*. Both Bodi and Corkhill acknowledge the uniqueness of the text's setting (Bodi 2002: 59; Corkhill 1990: 24) and its interest as a fascinating document of its time (Bodi 2002: 65; Corkhill 1990: 33), but both dismiss it on the basis of its literary deficiencies, its inaccuracies and its failure to engage with its foreign location. For both, the setting is little more than a decorative backdrop chosen largely because it was far away and little known (Bodi 2002: 62; Corkhill 1990: 28). This view is challenged by Michaela Krug (1998) in a much more affirmative reading of the text that foregrounds the issues of gender and social exclusion. Krug, although clearly unaware of Corkhill's work, comes to a similar

---

1 *Flora* 4, 1793: 241–74; *Flora* 1, 1794: 7–43, 209–75.
2 For a discussion of women's novels that treat the revolution, see Henn (1989) and Meise (1989).
3 The article was republished unchanged in a representative selection of Bodi's writings in 2002. All references in this article are to the later edition.

conclusion about the central role of the female characters in Huber's text. In her interpretation, Norfolk Island provides Huber with an "as yet barely inscribed location" for a postrevolutionary social order, the kernel of which is the mother-centred middle-class family. The family is opposed to the "public sphere of male activism" and provides the stability and continuity necessary to overcome the trauma of the revolution (Krug 1998: 359–60).

The focus of this article is the thematic complex – revolution-guilt-regeneration. In relation to this complex, I want to examine three aspects of the text, which, in my view, warrant further investigation: the setting, the role of the family and Francis' story. Is the setting just an exotic location that is incidental to the themes of revolution and regeneration? Is the family presented as a private sanctuary and retreat from the public sphere of revolution, or does it perhaps also have a political function? What is Francis' role in the text? Is there any connection between her "sentimental" story and the political strand of the narrative? These are some of the questions I will consider in the main part of my discussion, but before I begin, I will briefly, by way of background, outline the political and personal circumstances in which Huber's text was written and which it clearly reflects.

Huber may well have identified with Francis Belton's heartfelt cry of despair. Huber's story was written at a time of great political turbulence and personal crisis. In 1792, the French Revolution crossed the German border, and Mainz, where Huber had moved with her family in 1788, was transformed into a republic. Huber's husband, the famous world traveller and writer, Georg Forster, joined the republican movement and became a leader of the Jacobins in Mainz. But the republic was short-lived. In 1793, the Prussians reclaimed it, and the German monarchs outlawed Forster and put a price on his head. Therese, who had fallen in love with their friend and boarder, the Saxon diplomat, Ludwig Huber, took advantage of the imminent Prussian invasion to escape the city, her unhappy marriage and their complicated ménage à trois, fleeing with her children to Strasbourg and from there to Neuchâtel, where Ludwig Huber later joined her. She too was now an outcast, vilified by Forster's friends as the destroyer of his personal happiness, vilified by his foes as the wife and collaborator of a traitor, rejected by family and friends, and an object of public outrage and derision. In an anonymous satire *Die Mainzer Klubbisten zu Königstein oder die Weiber decken einander die Schanden auf* [*The Mainz Club in Königstein or the Women Expose their Disgrace*] published in 1793 after Mainz was returned to German control, "die Forsterin" is represented as a faithless wife who inflamed the hapless Forster with her revolutionary fire, only to abandon him when her passion for democracy gave way to her passion for Huber. In the light of her personal history, it is perhaps not surprising that the central concern of Huber's text is the question of guilt.[4]

The question of guilt was not just a personal matter, but one central to the moral dilemmas posed by the bloody turn of the Revolution. The Reign of Terror and the possibility that the Revolution would engulf the German states led to heated debates about the legitimacy of revolution as a means of reform. As hope gave way to fear, hostility and rejection, supporters of the Revolution were confronted squarely with the question of their own moral responsibility and culpability and were forced to reconsider their position. Was violence a regrettable, but inevitable part of revolutionary change – or an immoral aberration? Was it possible to distinguish between the ideals of the Revolution and their consequences – or did support for the one necessarily entail moral responsibility for the other? What were the alternatives? What were the values that could sustain and renew society?[5]

In a letter written on 11 September 1792, Ludwig Huber, following the slaughter of prisoners in Paris jails, expressed his horror that the enthusiasm of the last years had given way to fanatical and cannibalistic atrocities. The most unfortunate, he says, are probably those who believed in the age of reason and acted accordingly, and who have now, in the dark confusion that has befallen them, lost direction, indeed lost everything (L. Huber 1806: 446). This is precisely the position of Huber's narrator, Rudolph, who, by Huber's own admission, was modelled on her husband, Georg Forster.[6] It is, moreover, the subject of one of the

---

4 For a detailed account of Huber's life, see Geiger (1901). Brief accounts in English are provided by Bodi (2002), Corkhill (1990) and Krug (1998).
5 For a succinct account of German responses to the Revolution, see Zantop (1992).
6 In the foreword to *Das einsame Todbett* [*The Lonely Deathbed*], (1804), the sequel to the *Abentheuer*, Huber clearly links Rudolph with Forster, and in a letter

most important scenes in the novel, a conversation between Rudolph and Henry Belton, Francis' husband, the banished mutineer, about the legitimacy of rebellion. Rudolph and Henry see New Holland initially not as the chance of a new beginning, but as "das weite Land ohne Leben und ohne Mord" [a huge land without life and without murder], an isle of the dead, its stillness doubly oppressive in the midst of such natural abundance (T. Huber 1999: 156). While this perception is clearly misguided, as far as the penal colony is concerned, it does raise one of the most controversial issues of the Revolution: the problem of violence. The horror and disillusionment that drove Rudolph into self-exile have so shaken Henry's conviction in the ideals that inspired him to lead the Welsh miners' rebellion, regardless of the cost to his family, that he looks to his older and more experienced counterpart to restore his sense of moral integrity. Rudolph's response is cautiously equivocal – on the one hand, he justifies Henry's action in terms of his legitimate inability to tolerate oppression and absolves him of guilt, on the other, he sanctions Henry's punishment as the necessary consequence of the rule of law and a demonstration of its strength. In conclusion, however, he condones any form of partisanship as an honourable error and inveighs against those who adopt a position of self-righteous neutrality (T. Huber 1999: 162–69). Where Rudolph's sympathies lie is evident in other parts of the text. Despite his feelings of guilt and disillusionment, he cannot suppress his admiration for the "foolish, goodhearted, half-naked people [he saw] raising themselves from their physical wretchedness in an overpowering desire to be free" (Bodi 1966: 23–24). He is deeply moved when two French ships are sighted flying the tricolour and Francis' daughter, Betty, responds by singing a line from the Marseillaise. His final letter ends with his desire to hear news of the fight, which, for the first time, made him feel what it meant to have a fatherland and the rights of a citizen (T. Huber 1999: 252).

The associations of the penal colony with guilt, exile and rehabilitation make it a perfect location for a reconsideration of the problem of moral responsibility raised by the Revolution. Had Huber wanted to advocate a return to a state of Rousseauian natural innocence as an antidote to

to Meyer written in 1804, she declares Rudolph is Forster as he appeared to her in his letters following their separation (Bodi 2002: 57).

revolutionary terror, as Bodi has suggested, Tahiti would have been a much more obvious location. Following French, British and German accounts of this South Sea arcadia, it had become a metaphor of natural abundance, a mirror of all that Europe was lacking and a fashionable focus for escapist fantasies and fictions (Brunner 1967: 120f). But Tahiti is represented in European accounts as paradise before the Fall and the characters in Huber's story belong to the realm of the Fallen. Rudolph notes with irony that, had it been known that he was a revolutionary, he may well have been transported to New Holland free of charge (T. Huber 1999: 89). Exiled from Europe, the revolutionaries share the fate of its banished delinquents and must, in a sense, also serve their sentence, or at least justify their actions.

Before the revolutionaries can begin a new life in a new world, their belief in their own and others' humanity must be restored. As both Krug and Corkhill have correctly observed, in Huber's text, it is the middle-class family that embodies the values essential to their reintegration and to the development of a new social order. On the way to New Holland, the ship stops at Cape Town where Rudolph made a stopover as a young man on a voyage of discovery. There he finds the same native family in the same idyllic setting. This scene makes him acutely aware of his own homelessness. The family, encapsulated in this image of loss and longing, becomes thereafter the point towards which both plot and characters gravitate. Rudolph compares himself with a bird in search of a new nest after his was destroyed by a storm or a group of malicious boys (Huber 1999: 208), and in a way, this is true of all of the main characters. The Beltons and the Watsons are – through fate, misfortune, their own or others' mistakes – torn from their nests and live their new lives with the painful memory of the family members from whom they have been separated and who they assume are dead. But fate and the novel conspire in their favour, and all are miraculously reunited on Norfolk Island. In a resolution reminiscent of the family tableau of sentimental drama, Francis is restored to her husband, Henry to his wife and daughter, and Mrs Watson, who has become for Henry a type of foster mother, discovers in Francis the daughter she had abandoned. In the re-formed family, the past can be overcome and humanity restored through love, empathy and trust – Francis' sense of self is restored on the journey by the concern of the ship's doctor, Sidney, for her welfare (T. Huber 1999: 197), and her honour is restored by her husband's faith in her virtue (T. Huber 1999: 177). Francis' and Henry's story returns to Rudolph the memory of his youth and his capacity to feel (T. Huber 1999: 240), and even the hardened Mrs Watson cannot resist the children's openness and need for love. One could almost conclude that the novel's primary concern is the celebration of the sentimental family.

Previously the family was often seen as typical of the restricted scope of the Frauenroman (Gokhale 1996: 11), but more recent studies have drawn attention to the central role of the family in 18th-century public debates and to the political dimension of domestic fiction (Hunt 1992; Kontje 1998; Landes, 2001; Zantop 1997). The family, which was the mainspring of middle-class identity and repository of middle-class values, was not simply a private sanctuary and refuge, but served as a model for redefining the relations between rulers and their subjects, for humanising the public sphere and initiating political and social reform. Its many-faceted public role is reflected in Huber's text where it is presented as an ideal model of governance and as a source of values that will be more enduring than the legacy of monarchs – Phillip is praised as a governor who rules over his subjects like a father (T. Huber 1999: 200), the Watsons are held up as an example of moral uprightness whose memory will surely outlive the monuments of princes (T. Huber 1999: 227). It is presented as an alternative to other family models based on money, duty or Christian charity, and as the model for and metaphor of a re-formed society in which Europe's banished might someday again find a place. In establishing an opposition between the public sphere of the revolutionaries and the private sphere of the family, Krug tends to understate its public role as a critical mirror of the society that gave rise to their activism. The family is also used as a means of exerting influence on the formation of political opinion in Germany by enlisting reader sympathy for the revolutionaries.

In the light of its history, the choice of Norfolk Island as the site of Huber's new model community may seem rather improbable. Under the harsh regimes of some of its more sadistic commandants, the island rapidly gained a reputation as a place of deprivation, brutality and despair. The first settlement on Norfolk Island was abandoned in 1814, but it was reinstated as a penal colony in 1825, this time with no view to reform. On the contrary, it was to be a punitive deterrent for repeat offenders and, as such, the ultimate in convict degradation. As a result, Norfolk Island has gone down in history not as an island paradise and site of social renewal, but as an island hell, the nightmare inversion of enlightened dreams of progress and social amelioration. Initially, however, both Botany Bay and Norfolk Island were seen as natural paradises with great potential for European settlement. This is how they were represented by James Cook, Joseph Banks and Georg Forster, Huber's first husband, who, as a young man, had accompanied Cook on his second voyage of discovery (1772–75) and was present when Cook took possession of Norfolk Island in 1774. The decision to establish penal settlements in Botany Bay and on Norfolk Island was, in part, based on their positive reports.[7]

Georg Forster retained an interest in the South Seas, and with his father, Johann Reinhold Forster, became Germany's main mediator of information on new developments in the Pacific region (Bodi 2002: 59). In 1787, one year before the penal colony was established, Forster published an essay entitled "Neuholland und die brittische Colonie in Botany-Bay" [New Holland and the British colony in Botany Bay] (Forster 1985: 161–83) in which he predicted that New Holland would follow the example of America and become "the future home of a new civilized society" (Bodi 2002: 62). The convicts, he claimed, would become law-abiding and productive colonists on regaining their full human rights and becoming proprietors and cultivators of land (Forster 1985: 163). Forster's conviction is repeated almost verbatim in Huber's text (T. Huber 1999: 139) and is affirmed by the transformation of Francis Belton's errant parents, the Watsons, from self-seeking and irresponsible speculators into model colonists. Despite the harsh reality with which he was confronted, Arthur Phillip, the first governor of the colony, seems to have shared Forster's optimism. While acknowledging the difficulties that beset the main settlement in New Holland, Phillip, on the basis of the favourable reports he had been sent by an island commandant eager to please and keen for promotion, extolled the natu-

---

7 Norfolk Island's history is examined in detail in Hoare (1982), Hughes (1988) and Nobbs (1988).

ral attributes of Norfolk Island and painted such a positive picture of the settlement's prospects, that Grenville, the Secretary of the Home Office, even briefly considered making it the main settlement and jeopardised its future by recommending that more convicts be sent there (Hoare 1982: 14–15).

If one compares the following excerpts, it is immediately obvious that the depiction of Norfolk Island in Huber's text is based on the description of the island in the account based on Phillip's reports, *The Voyage of Governor Phillip to Botany Bay* (1789) which was published in Germany in 1790:

> We went towards the centre of this small island where at the foot of a round hill a crystal-clear river rushes forth, dividing further up into several arms … The sight of these great flax fields is one of the loveliest I beheld. The slender stalks, of the most beautiful green and reaching far above a man's head, bent in the gentle breeze that blew from the sea … The top of the hill and the whole of the south and east sides are covered with enormous pines whose dark green is enhanced by a pleasant foreground of cabbage palms and banana trees, and I also observed a low bush among them the fruit of which resembles our red currants (Bodi 1966: 50).

> At, or near Mount Pitt, rises a strong and copious stream, which flowing through a very fine valley, divides itself into several branches … Of plants that afford vegetables for the table, the chief are cabbage palm, the wild plantain, the fern tree, a kind of wild spinage, and a tree which produces a diminutive fruit, bearing some resemblance to a currant … But the productions which give the greatest importance to Norfolk Island are the pines and the flax plant, the former rising to a size and perfection unknown in other places … the latter … growing in great plenty, and with such luxuriance as to attain the height of eight feet (Auchmuty 1970: 47–48).

Corkhill uses this passage to demonstrate the implausibility of Huber's island idyll (Corkhill 1990: 28–29), but it is, in fact, not far removed from Phillip's description, which displays a similar tendency towards the picturesque.[8] It is true that Huber ignores "the seamier side of penal servitude" in her novel (Corkhill 1990: 31), but if her image of the island is fanciful, it owes much to the persistence of fancy in accounts normally considered to be more realistic and objective. Huber's depiction of the island corresponds with Phillip's reports and accords with Forster's Enlightenment vision of its future. The appeal of Norfolk Island as the location of a new social order lay undoubtedly in its promise as the site of a real experiment in social regeneration whose outcome was still uncertain when Huber wrote her story.

The island setting, moreover, inscribes Huber's text in a tradition of island utopias or, perhaps more correctly, Robinsonades to which her story represents a contribution and possibly a critical alternative.[9] In the wake of Defoe's *Robinson Crusoe* (1719), the island had become a topos of middle-class self-discovery and self-assertion (Großklaus 1993: 21), but Crusoe's island is exclusively male.[10] One of its most popular fictional reincarnations in Germany was Schnabel's *Die Insel Felsenburg* (1731–43), which Huber read as a child (Geiger 1896: 16). Schnabel's island community is not exclusively male, but resolutely patriarchal. State and family orders correspond – the community is governed by its founding father, Albert Julius, and the figure of authority in the island families is the father (Vosskamp 1983: 100). This is a topic that clearly needs further investigation, but it could be argued that Huber's island community is an attempt to develop an alternative to the male-centred models of the male coloniser and the patriarchal family on which many Enlightenment thinkers based their vision of and hopes for a new society.

As Krug has noted, the figure of integration in the re-formed family in Huber's text is Francis Belton (Krug 1998: 358) who becomes the mother of the new community (Krug 1998: 359). The question of guilt is also central to her story and used to sustain the dramatic tension of the narrative and engage reader interest. On the journey, Francis attracts

---

8 The typical elements of the picturesque landscape are described by Coetzee 1988: 48.
9 Glaser gives an overview of islands in utopian literature, Brunner an account of islands and their representation in German literature.
10 Phillips (1997) includes a chapter on Robinson Crusoe and its British reincarnations in his examination of adventure stories and their impact on the construction of race, gender, religion and language.

the interest and attention of Rudolph and Sidney by the contradiction between her appearance and behaviour, and her conviction as a criminal. Is it possible that a woman who appears to be the embodiment of propriety and femininity and is so different from the other women convicts can be as guilty as they are (T. Huber 1999: 95)? The mystery of Francis' guilt or innocence is not solved until she is reunited with her husband and encouraged by his love and trust to reveal her story. When Henry was banished, she was ostracised by family and friends and forced to fend for herself and her child. She found employment, but when she resisted the unwanted advances of her unscrupulous employer, he threatened to expose her as a thief. When he then resorted to force, she stabbed him. On his confession, she was exonerated of murder, but he died before clearing her of the accusation of theft that resulted in her transportation.

Francis' story is in many respects a typical sentimental story of virtue in distress, and she is a typical sentimental heroine. Modest, selfless, caring and blameless, she is cast in the mould of the new ideal of femininity that was propagated by writers like Rousseau[11] and popularised in sentimental novels, which helped anchor it in the collective imagination of their largely female readership. In the text she is the primary object of desire – the object of the narrator's curiosity and sympathy and the object of her husband's, Sidney's and her children's love. Rudolph, in fact, becomes so absorbed by Francis' story that it almost usurps his own and takes over the narrative (Krug 1998: 354). The full title of the magazine in which Huber published her novel, *Flora: Teutschlands Töchtern geweiht von Freunden und Freundinnen des schönen Geschlechts*, indicates that the magazine was directed primarily at the female reading public, and this is underlined in a foreword to Huber's story, which thus far has not been republished. In the foreword, the alleged editor admits the improbability of Francis' story, but claims for it a truth that overrides its implausibility and suggestively encourages the identification of the reader with its female protagonist who is clearly meant to be seen as a model.[12]

---

11 In her discussion of the genesis of the middle-class conception of womanhood, Ehrich-Haefeli shows just how influential Rousseau was in Germany (1993: 96f).
12 *Flora* 4, 1793: 241–42.

But although in most respects exemplary, Francis fails to internalise two significant requirements of her role – woman's natural passivity and submissiveness, and her dependence on the judgments of others (Rousseau 1974: 333, 346). In the sentimental novel the emotional potency of virtue peaks when it is violated. Richardson's Clarissa is raped, as are a number of sentimental heroines cast in the Richardson mould (Todd 1986: 69). But unlike her counterparts, Francis does not submit to her fate. Instead, she puts a quick end to the advances of her would-be rapist with a kitchen knife, which she plunges with remarkable strength through his neck into his chest (T. Huber 1999: 190). She never expresses concern or remorse about the propriety of her action, and her right to resist violation with violence is never questioned. In her case, the text seems to condone a much more radical response to the problem of oppression than it does in the case of the text's revolutionaries. Despite her desperation and distress, Francis, moreover, refuses to be cowed by her condemnation and public dishonour, declaring that she has always made a distinction between laws and opinions and her own convictions (T. Huber 1999: 121). Seen from a gender perspective, Francis' characterisation is an example of the way in which Huber reproduces and affirms the parameters of conventional gender roles but, at the same time, displaces them by translating them in and on her own terms. She thereby expands the space in which behaviours normally proscribed by the discourse of femininity can be articulated and accommodated.[13] This is in keeping with the text's promotion of a model of community in which women play a more significant role. Could there, however, be a more direct connection between Francis' story and the theme of revolution?

In the text Rudolph's guilt remains strangely abstract – we never discover what his role in the Revolution was, but subtle links are established between his destiny and Francis', suggesting that her story might in some way mirror his. In a scene reminiscent of the meeting of kindred souls in Goethe's *Die Leiden des jungen Werthers* (1774), an unspoken bond is established between them when a French ship is sighted, stirring their memories of the cause of freedom. The story of Francis

13 Cf. Hook-Demarle's concept of *élargissement d'espace* [expansion of space], quoted in Meise 1989: 69.

and her husband reminds Rudolph of his own youth and recalls the pain of parting from his friends. The scene in which Henry seeks and receives Rudolph's absolution has a direct parallel in the confessional scene in which Francis' honour is restored by Henry's faith in her virtue. The rape of Lucretia to which Rudolph refers in his disquisition on violent rebellion also has its counterpart in Francis' story, but here it has quite a different outcome.[14] Helmut Peitsch, Helga Meise and Marianne Henn have all drawn attention to the connection between private family morality and revolutionary politics in Huber's better-known novel, *Die Familie Seldorf*, which was written a short time after the *Abentheuer*. While the connection in the *Abentheuer* is less explicit, the links between the two strands of the narrative suggest that Francis' story could be read as a sentimental parallel to the story of Rudolph, the revolutionary, one which gives the author greater freedom to adopt a more radical position on the questions of guilt, oppression and violence.

In both revolutionary and anti-revolutionary rhetoric, the Revolution was often associated with female transgression and domestic disorder (Stephan & Weigel 1989: 5). Those who threatened the foundation of Enlightened natural and moral order were commonly represented as rapacious furies, sexually indeterminate monsters, dangerous dissimulators, or prostitutes (Henn 1996: 1–2; Hunt 1992: 89f). Francis' fate reflects almost exactly the gendered barbs of which women were often both the literal and metaphorical objects. She is initially accused of murder, ultimately condemned for theft, sentenced to transportation with a shipload of prostitutes and suspected of dissimulation by those most sympathetic to her plight. If this connection is more than a coincidence, Francis' inner defiance, ultimate absolution and reinstatement as the good mother of the community could be interpreted as a direct challenge to the rhetoric of denigration and exclusion of which Huber herself was a victim.

In the re-formed family on Norfolk Island, Huber's characters are freed from the stigma of shame and their honour is restored. But Ru-

---

14 The story of Lucretia and its reincarnations is discussed in Donaldson (1982). It was used in revolutionary rhetoric to justify the overthrow of the feudal order, but is used by Rudolph to demonstrate the need to contain excess on both sides of the political spectrum.

dolph continues his journey, taking Sidney, who has fallen hopelessly in love with Francis, with him. The text's open end underlines the fact that the island community is an ideal still to be realised, perhaps unrealisable, and establishes it as a site of longing for the reader. In her letters, Huber often referred to herself as "der umgetriebene Sohn der Erde" [the wandering son of this earth] (Hahn 1993: 7) and may, in this instance, have identified more with the perspective of the text's displaced wanderer. She remained in exile till 1798, and although she became a successful author and publisher, the shadow of shame followed her beyond her own lifetime and long coloured her image in German literature and the reception of her works. This has changed particularly since the Olms publishing company began republishing her novels, stories and correspondence in 1989. My article is a contribution to the ongoing process of rehabilitation and aims to stimulate further critical interest in a work that is still relatively unknown. In imagining the penal colony as the site of a new, more humane society and linking it with the cause of freedom, it could be claimed that Huber gave the image of Australia a much more positive start in German literature than has been previously assumed.

Bibliography

Auchmuty JJ (Ed) (1970). *The Voyage of Governor Phillip to Botany Bay with Contributions by Other Officers of the First Fleet and Observations on Affairs of the Time by Lord Auckland.* Sydney: Angus and Robertson.

Berghahn KL & Seeber U (Eds) (1983). *Literarische Utopien von Morus bis zur Gegenwart.* Königstein/Ts.: Athenäum.

Anon (1907). Die Mainzer Klubbisten zu Königstein oder die Weiber decken einander die Schanden auf. In F Blei (Ed), *Deutsche Literatur-Pasquille.* Leipzig: Julius Zeitler, 5–39.

Bodi L (2002). Adventures on a Journey to New Holland and the Lonely Deathbed: Two Novels of Therese Huber as Documents of Their Time. In L Bodi, *Literatur, Politik, Identität: Literature, Politics, Cultural Identity. Österreichische und internationale Literaturprozeße,* vol. 18. St Ingbert: Röhrig Universitätsverlag, 55–67.

Brunner H (1967). *Die poetische Insel: Inseln und Inselvorstellungen in der deutschen Literatur.* Stuttgart: Metzler.

Christadler M (Ed) (1990). *Freiheit, Gleichheit, Weiblichkeit: Aufklärung, Revolution und die Frauen in Europa.* Opladen: Leske & Budrich GmbH.

Coetzee JM (1988). *White Writing: On the Culture of Letters in South Africa.* New Haven, London: Yale University Press.

Corkhill A (1990). *Antipodean Encounters: Australia and the German Literary Imagination 1754–1918.* Bern, Frankfurt a. M., New York, Paris: Peter Lang.

Donaldson I (1982). *The Rapes of Lucretia: A Myth and its Transformations.* Oxford: Clarendon Press.

Ehrich-Haefeli V (1993). Zur Genese der bürgerlichen Konzeption der Frau: der psychohistorische Stellenwert von Rousseaus Sophie. In *Freiburger literaturpsychologische Gespräche* 12: 89–135.

Forster G (1985). Neuholland und die brittische Colonie in Botany-Bay. In Akademie der Wissenschaften der DDR (Ed) *Georg Forsters Werke: Sämtliche Schriften, Tagebücher, Briefe 5.* Berlin: Akademie-Verlag, 161–83.

Geiger L (1896). *Dichter und Frauen: Vorträge und Abhandlungen.* Berlin: Verlag von Gebrüder Paetel.

Geiger L (1901). *Therese Huber 1764 bis 1829. Leben und Briefe einer deutschen Frau.* Stuttgart: Cotta Nachfolger.

Glaser HA (1996). *Utopische Inseln.* Frankfurt, Berlin, Bern, New York, Paris, Vienna: Peter Lang.

Gokhale VB (1996). *Walking the Tightrope: A Feminist Reading of Therese Huber's Stories.* Columbia: Camden House.

Haas R (1990). Therese Huber: Teilemanzipation und Schriftsterinnenkarriere durch die Französische Revolution. In M Christadler (Ed), *Freiheit, Gleichheit, Weiblichkeit: Aufklärung, Revolution und die Frauen in Europa.* Opladen: Leske & Budrich GmbH, 75–93.

Hahn A & Fischer B (Eds) (1993). *"Alles … von mir!" Therese Huber (1764–1829): Schriftstellerin und Redakteurin.* Marbach: Deutsche Schillergesellschaft.

Heffernan JAW (Ed) (1992). *Representing the French Revolution: Literature, Historiography, and Art.* Hanover and London: University Press of New England.

Henn M (1989). The Other Voice: the Reaction of German Women Writers to the French Revolution. *Occasional Papers in German Studies* 8: 1–23. Frankfurt: Jonas Verlag und Historisches Museum Frankfurt, 143–58.

Heuser M (Ed) (1991). *Romane und Erzählungen 7.* Hildesheim, Zurich, New York: Olms.

Hoare M (1982). *Norfolk Island: An Outline of its History 1774–1981.* 3rd ed. St Lucia, London, New York: University of Queensland Press.

Huber L (Ed) (1793). *Flora. Teutschlands Töchtern geweiht von Freundinnen und Freunden des schönen Geschlechts 1.* Tübingen: Cotta, 241–42.

Huber T (Ed) (1806). *L.F. Hubers Sämtliche Werke seit dem Jahre 1802 nebst seiner Biographie.* Tübingen: I.G. Cottasche Buchhandlung.

Huber T (1966). *Adventures on a Journey to New Holland and the lonely deathbed.* Leslie Bodi (Ed). Rodney Livingstone (Trans). Melbourne: Lansdowne Press.

Huber T (1999). Abentheuer auf einer Reise nach Neu-Holland. In M Heuser (Ed), *Romane und Erzählungen 7.* Hildesheim, Zurich, New York: Olms, 84–253.

Hughes R (1988). *The Fatal Shore.* London: Pan.

Hunt L (1992). *The Family Romance of the French Revolution.* Berkeley and Los Angeles: University of California Press.

Krug M (1998). 'A Huge Land Without Life and Without Murder': Australia in Therese Forster-Huber's Adventures on a Journey to New Holland. In P Monteath & FS Zuckerman (Eds), *Modern Europe: Histories and Identities.* Adelaide: Australian Humanities Press, 353–63.

Kontje T (1998). *Women, the Novel, and the German Nation 1771–1871: Domestic Fiction in the Fatherland.* Cambridge: Cambridge University Press.

Landes JB (2001). *Visualizing the Nation: Gender, Representation, and Revolution in Eighteenth-Century France*. Ithaca: Cornell University Press.

Meise H (1989). Politisierung der Weiblichkeit oder Revolution des Frauenromans? In I Stephan & S Weigel (Eds), *Die Marseillaise der Weiber: Frauen, die Französische Revolution und ihre Rezeption*. Hamburg: Argument, 55–74.

Monteath P & Zuckerman FS (Eds) (1998). *Modern Europe: Histories and Identities*. Adelaide: Australian Humanities Press.

Nobbs R (Ed) (1988). *Norfolk Island and its First Settlement 1788–1814*. Sydney: Library of Australian History.

Peitsch H (1984). Die Revolution im Familienroman. *Jahrbuch der deutschen Schillergesellschaft* 28: 248–70.

Phillips R (1997). *Mapping Men and Empire: A Geography of Adventure*. London and New York: Routledge.

Rousseau JJ (1974). *Jean-Jacques, Émile*. B Foxley (Trans). London, Melbourne: Dent.

Stephan I & Weigel S (Eds) (1989). *Die Marseillaise der Weiber: Frauen, die Französische Revolution und ihre Rezeption*. Hamburg: Argument.

Todd J (1986). *Sensibility: an Introduction*. London, New York: Methuen.

Vosskamp W (1983). 'Ein irdisches Paradies': Johann Gottfried Schnabel's Insel Felsenburg (1731–43). In KL Berghahn & U Seeber (Eds), *Literarische Utopien von Morus bis zur Gegenwart*. Königstein/Ts.: Athenäum, 95–105.

Zantop S (1992). Crossing the Border: the French Revolution in the German Literary Imagination. In JAW Heffernan (Ed), *Representing the French Revolution: Literature, Historiography, and Art*. Hanover and London: University Press of New England, 213–37.

Zantop S (1997). *Colonial Fantasies: Conquest, Family, and Nation in Precolonial Germany, 1770–1870*. Durham, London: Duke University Press.

10
Europe's Utopia or Paradise Lost? The Depiction of Australia in Urs Widmer's *Liebesbrief für Mary [Love Letter for Mary]*

Birte Giesler

German-Australian Encounters in Literature and on TV

Without doubt, there is great interest in Australia in the German-speaking world today. Television stations are abuzz with documentaries and reports on Australia, the "red continent Down Under". Most of these programs report on visitors travelling across the virtually endless and sparsely populated vastness of the Australian Outback and the Red Centre. Although Australian capital cities may be mentioned and shown as beautiful, sun-kissed places, these documentaries and reports hardly ever feature Australian urban life or actual Australian society as central topics.[1] Against the backdrop of such an "outback" image of Australia it is hardly surprising that German translations of books such as Bruce Chatwin's *Songlines* or Marlo Morgan's *Mutant Message Down Under* be-

---

1 In 2006, a new genre of TV program emerged in the German-speaking media scene. *Goodbye Deutschland! Die Auswanderer* is a "doku-soap" produced and broadcasted by the German television network VOX that looks at the lives of German emigrants and expatriates. Whilst not exclusively focusing on German emigrants/expatriates in Australia, this "doku-soap" features former expatriates who have returned to Germany. With a narrative voice that wavers between awe and schadenfreude, current and past expatriates as well as expatriates-to-be are accompanied by the camera crew during preparations for their departure, their arrival in the new country and upon their return to Germany, respectively. For general information on the program see: de.wikipedia.org/wiki/Goodbye_ Deutschland!_Die_Auswanderer, accessed 15 December 2008.

came bestsellers in Germany. Hence, Bruce Chatwin's *Traumpfade*[2] was included in the series *50 Great Novels of the 20th Century* that the major German newspaper *Süddeutsche Zeitung* compiled in 2004 and 2005. As Michael Schönhuth and Rebecca Freßmann have stated, in 2002, Marlo Morgan's *Traumfänger*[3] was owned by about every 15th German household (Schönhuth/Freßmann 2002: 2). At the same time, however, 50 per cent of German households do not possess any more than 50 books in total (Schröder 2006). So, one can assume that the German "archive of cultural knowledge" catalogues a solitary, very specific image of the contemporary world Down Under. In regard to contemporary German feature films on Australia, Alison Lewis states:

> the German interest in the Antipodes is much narrower than is commonly thought. Apart from the familiar icons of Australia, the kangaroos and koalas, the Olympic Games in Sydney, the outback and beaches, Germans as a whole seem distinctly uninterested in aspects of our culture that deviate from these easily recognisable features of the Australian way of life. Once the exotic patina is stripped away the charm of Australian culture quickly seems to fade. Germans seem distinctly uncomfortable with an image of Australia that does not celebrate the curious, the exotic or the uncanny (Lewis 1995: 257).[4]

Urs Widmer's Liebesbrief für Mary

Written by the well-known contemporary Swiss writer, Urs Widmer, the novella *Liebesbrief für Mary* [*Love Letter for Mary*] was first published in 1993. Although most parts of the narration play out in Switzerland and Italy, Australia looms large in the tale. At first glance, *Liebesbrief für Mary* seems to take part in the trend that perceives Australia to be an "innocent" untouched Aboriginal country. When referring to Australia,

---

2 Chatwin's *Songlines* has been translated into German as *Traumpfade*, literally "dream paths".
3 Morgan's *Mutant Message Down Under* has been translated as *Traumfänger*, which literally means "dream catcher".
4 On images of Australia in German literature see Corkhill (1990) and Jurgensen (1992).

Widmer's text is emphatically politically incorrect and uses traditional metaphors and images of colonial literature in an ironic and exaggerated way. This paper will analyse whether the novella merely redesigns the stereotypical image of Australia as an Aboriginal country that is "untouched and close to nature", or whether it plays on this image in order to point at the significance of the image itself. This paper argues that rather than being part of the trend that describes Australia as a place close to nature, far away from Western civilisation, *Liebesbrief für Mary* is highly ironic, mocking this perception of contemporary Australia.

Liebesbrief für Mary narrates the story of the young Irish-born Mary Hope and her two admirers in Zurich, Switzerland, who are rivals for her affection. Loving the same woman is not the only commonality between the lachrymose Helmut and the second jilted lover whose name the reader never comes to know. The two men are close; they live in shared accommodation with others and have been friends since kindergarten. The two rivals are competitors not only in matters of love, but also in matters of literature and language. Both are authors – and each accuses the other of being a really bad poet. Mary, however, escapes the two rivals by quietly "doing a runner" to Australia. Mary ends up living in the Australian desert with her new Aboriginal lover, so that this initial Irish-Swiss love triangle expands into an Indigenous-Australian-Irish-Swiss love quadrilateral. However, the beloved Mary leaves an emotional disaster behind her in Zurich. Helmut pines over Mary. Both antagonists travel, one after the other, from Switzerland to Australia in order to search for Mary and to convince her to return to Switzerland. Both of them make their journey in vain. Helmut turns on his heels (turns tail) when he actually sees Mary from afar in the "eternal desert" (LfM 13).[5] Back in Europe, he writes a love letter to Mary because "writing is easier than speaking. Speaking is easier than acting" (LfM 16). Indeed, his hesitation is such that it is quite doubtful whether Helmut really wants to send off his letter at all. However, his impudent kindergarten friend and competitor firmly believes that Mary would actually prefer to be his penfriend (LfM 9, 60). He steals the letter in a grotesque and literally bloody tussle and then travels to

---

5 The abbreviation "LfM" refers to the paperback edition of *Liebesbrief für Mary* specified in the bibliography to this article: Widmer 1995b.

Australia himself. Although he manages to deliver Helmut's letter, after having read Helmut's confessions, Mary nevertheless prefers to stay in the Australian desert where she is running a takeaway shop and petrol station, together with her new Aboriginal partner.

Back in Europe, the two equally rejected homecomers continue living their writer's lives, in their shared house, until the day when this thoroughly ironic and tragicomic story takes a sudden swing towards its grotesque ending. One day, the unnamed rival suddenly bursts into tears during dinner, screaming loudly for Mary (LfM 92). When Helmut tries to comfort his devastated friend, the two eventually fall down the staircase together and Helmut breaks his neck. All the flatmates move out immediately after the fatal accident, so that Mary's unnamed ex-lover stands literally alone at the end of the novella. However, if one takes a closer look, it becomes apparent that this unnamed rival has stood alone from the outset. At the beginning of the novella, Mary is already living in central Australia and Helmut is already dead. Helmut's anonymous rival is both the commentator on Helmut's letter and the frame narrator of the whole story. As narrator, he conceives the love letter to be Helmut's legacy that the latter wants to present to the reader. The reproduction of the letter takes the form of a frame narrative; it is preceded by a brief preface and rounded off with a short epilogue. Prefacing his presentation of Helmut's letter is the account of how both the narrator and Helmut came to know Mary.

After finishing his presentation of Helmut's love letter, the narrator recounts a day where he by chance browsed through to a TV program showing a desert. In the middle of this desert, he saw a petrol station and around the petrol station, he observed several men wearing white astronaut's suits gauging the soil with long rods. The equipment hanging from the men's belts was blinking and beeping. There were helicopters all around. He also saw two helpless people next to the petrol station, a small man and a blond woman, standing in front of a small hut resembling a takeaway outlet. He could see that they were the only people in the vicinity not wearing protective clothing. The narrator states that he could not discern whether the woman was crying or not, but that both the man and the woman were quickly ushered into a car that immediately left the area (LfM 99).

From the similarity of this televised scene with the settings and details of Mary's new life in Australia, the reader understandably develops a hunch that the narrator has indeed observed Mary and her partner being rescued from a radioactively contaminated central Australia. At this point, the otherwise rather amusing plot of *Liebesbrief für Mary* turns to a serious factual issue: Australia has been associated with nuclear destruction and radioactive pollution since the beginnings of military and public use of nuclear materials: 1) In the past: between 1953 and 1965, the Outback ranges of South Australia were used as a test area for atomic bombs by British military forces with tremendous environmental and health impacts, particularly for the Indigenous inhabitants of the area.[6] 2) At present, the idea of making central Australia the global nuclear waste dump has been a topic of ongoing political discussion.[7] 3) With regard to the future, works of science fiction anticipate the nuclear devastation of Australia. An early and famous example is Nevil Shute's novel *On the Beach*. First published at the peak of the Cold War and during the time when atomic bomb trials were being undertaken in the Australian desert, the novel narrates a post-apocalyptic end-of-the-world story set in 1963: the effects of radioactive waste from a nuclear war have wiped out the entire northern hemisphere, with only Australia and New Zealand surviving the disaster. However, anticipating that the after-effects will reach the southern hemisphere at any moment, Australians review their lives, establish new relationships and prepare for their tragic demise. Shute's

---

6 On British bomb tests in Australia, see: Arnold 1987; Cross 2001. Film clips of the bombings can be watched online at: www.sonicbomb.com/modules.php?name =Content&pa=showpage&pid=111, accessed 28 January 2009. For information on the lack of concern in regard to the health-related consequences upon Aboriginal populations living in the test area (for the most part scarcely clothed and barefoot), as well as on recently unearthed documents revealing that Australian army personnel and civilians were deliberately used as human guinea pigs, in that they were not provided with sufficient protective clothing in order to study the effects of radiation, see the Australian Nuclear Veterans Association's website at: users.bigpond.net.au/anva/index.html, accessed 27 January 2009.

7 For more information on "scientific" arguments why Australia would geologically be the "perfect" ultimate disposal location for nuclear waste, see the website of the Anti-Nuclear Alliance of Western Australia at: www.anawa.org.au/ waste/pangea.html, accessed 27 January 2009.

novel was translated and published in German in 1958 as *Das letzte Ufer* [*The Final Shore*]. A perceptive reader may interpret the name of Widmer's female protagonist – Mary Hope – as a character reference to Shute's main female character, whose name is Mary Holmes and is in denial about the impending nuclear disaster (Shute 1957).

Linguistic Migrations in Liebesbrief für Mary

The most notable element of Widmer's *Liebesbrief für Mary* is its linguistic shape. Almost half of the text is Helmut's love letter, which is written in English, or rather, German-Pidgin-Australian-English, a really bad "high-school English". As a result, some parts of this "English" text are probably almost incomprehensible for non-German-speaking readers and are arguably virtually untranslatable into genuine English. The opening of Helmut's letter reads:

> Dear Mary. – I write to you in English, although, as you know better than anybody else, my English is horrible, a terrible stammer, a catastrophy [!], a constant search for the right word, a search which ends always the same way, I mean, I find the wrong word and open the door to a new misunderstanding. Probably only a German speaking reader might understand this letter. But, you agree, dear Mary dear, if I spoke German with you, the misunderstanding would be even greater … you mix up just everything, even Liebe [love] and Leid [suffering]. Schmerz [pain] and Herz [heart] (LfM 12).

However, this anonymous narrator not only presents Helmut's letter, but also comments on it by means of seven footnotes inserted into the letter itself. In fact, these footnotes make up a slightly larger volume of the novella than the letter itself. Thus, the novella consists of two first-person narrators delivering two versions of the same story (Mohr 1993: 37). In his book review in the Berlin newspaper *Tagesspiegel*, Bruno Preisendörfer points out that the narrator's notes do not simply comment on Helmut's letter, but actually disassemble it (Preisendörfer 1993: VII). Hence, the whole text is effectively the report of a rivalry between two speeches. Due to the fact that half of the text is written in a foreign language, while the fictitious author reflects on the obstacle of writing and reading a foreign language, the whole novella can and should be read against the backdrop of a poetological statement made by Urs Widmer in his Graz lectures on poetics: "All contemporary literature is built on the awareness that one's own language is in fact *not* one's own" (Widmer 1995a: 40).[8]

Mocking the German-speaking Swiss-Australian culture clash

The ambivalence between that which is one's own and that which is not one's own or rather, between the Self and the (Foreign) Other, pervades Urs Widmer's oeuvre. In *Liebesbrief für Mary* the poetological and thematic significance of the ambivalence between the Self and the Other becomes especially relevant, particularly if one looks at the ironic depiction of Australia as the foreign country per se. Indeed, what happens to Widmer's three Europeans when they come to Australia seems as strange as it is funny, especially since the convoluted and contradictory narrative perspective makes use of the comic tools of repetition, intensification and exaggeration. According to the unnamed narrator, Helmut found out that Mary took a plane from Zurich to Sydney where she moved into a bed-and-breakfast and worked as a German teacher at the Berlitz school. Wandering around while learning the next lesson for *Basic German* by heart and consequently not watching her step, Mary had accidentally stepped on an Aboriginal songline:

> she came upon one of those dream paths that no one can see and no one can leave once they're on it. She walked and walked, and at the end of the path, 2500 miles south-west, stood Mr Smith with wide open arms, Mr Smith who had always known that one day an inattentive woman would be caught in his trap. He watched how she, dusty and exhausted approached between the cacti and the boulders, and he thanked fate, which could also have given him a bulky fat woman (Widmer/Stoehr 1994: 181).[9]

---

8 All translations Birte Giesler and Maria Veber unless otherwise indicated. The original reads: "Alle zeitgenössische Literatur baut denn auch auf der Erkenntnis auf, daß die eigene Sprache *nicht* die eigene ist." Original emphasis.
9 The original reads: "geriet sie auf einen jener Traumpfade, die niemand sieht

As the reader learns shortly before this point, John Smith is an "Aborigine who looks as though he had fallen into an ash can. Grey" (Widmer/Stoehr 1994: 179).[10] The reader also learns that his Aboriginal name is Akwerkepenty, "which apparently means 'Child that travels far'" (Widmer/Stoehr 1994: 179).[11] He runs a petrol station at "Nosucks, Australia, a place consisting of two or three houses, in the middle of the Warburton desert" (Widmer/Stoehr 1994: 179)[12] (The plausibility of the purported "facts" relating to Mary's Australian living conditions will be discussed later in this paper). Via Helmut's letter the reader learns that Helmut had rushed to the airport and had taken the next flight to Sydney as well, as soon as he had heard about Mary's flight to Sydney. While taking English lessons at the Sydney Berlitz school, he heard about a former German teacher named Mary Hope who vanished on her way through a little park (LfM 18). He searched for Mary's path, eventually finding it:

> I followed you and was taken prisoner of the songline and remained its slave and saw finally at the end of an interminable desert a cabin, far away, and I walked and walked, singing in my head this one devilish melody to which you have access when you walk on a songline … I saw just nobody when I reached the place which is named Nosucks, as I learned with the help of a rusty inscription … Finally a cloud of dust emerged far away, between the hills where I came from, and I sat down behind a rock and looked at it. And out of the cloud came a dusty Toyota with a man and a woman inside, and the woman was you. Your man looked like, well, he looked

---

und niemand verlassen kann, wenn er einmal drauf ist. Ging und ging, und am Ende des Pfads, zweitausendfünfhundert Meilen südwestlicher, stand mit offenen Armen Mr Smith, der immer gewußt hatte, daß einmal eine Unbedachte in seine Falle tappen würde. Er sah ihr zu, wie sie staubig und erschöpft zwischen den Kakteen und Felsbrocken näherkam, und dankte dem Schicksal, das ihm ja auch eine Fette, Ungeschlachte hätte spendieren können" (LfM 8f).

10 The original reads: " Aborigine, der aussieht, als sei er in einen Aschenkübel gefallen. Grau" (LfM 5).

11 The original reads: "was 'Weit reisendes Kind' bedeuten soll" (LfM 5).

12 The original reads: "Nosucks, Australien, einem aus zwei, drei Häusern bestehenden Ort mitten in der Warburton-Wüste" (LfM 5).

strange. You know, I am not a racist, he just looked so strange to somebody like me. So grey, so small, moving like an ape … When the sun started to disappear behind the mountains, your man came to the veranda and took your hand, and you followed him inside the house, and I listened and listened and didn't hear anything. This was too much for me, and I got up and walked the same way back, with the same melody in my head. I reached Sydney after another uncountable number of days or months and took the next plane … to Zurich, where I arrived covered with red dust (LfM 18f).

Via the narrator's commentary on Helmut's letter, the reader learns that the narrator, too, took a plane to Sydney, after he had stolen the letter from Helmut and saw Mary's address on the envelope. Reading the letter during the flight, and hence knowing how both Mary and Helmut got to Nosucks, the narrator hires a car from the Avis desk at Sydney airport immediately upon his arrival. As he cannot find a place called Nosucks on the map, the Avis officer refers him to an Aboriginal man working in a cleaning crew at the airport, who, although unable to read the map, is able to tell the anonymous narrator the direction in which he has to head in order to get to Akwerkepenty's place. This man also sings the melody of the songline that leads to Akwerkepenty. The unnamed narrator continues the story by depicting a hilariously grotesque situation where he had immense difficulties trying to filter out the songline in the midst of Sydney's traffic noise and the difficulties he had to overcome while navigating his way over rugged terrain to Nosucks and back to Sydney in a small Japanese car.

However, that there should be something magical about Nosucks is not surprising at all. Nosucks is located in the "Warburton desert". But if one looks at a map of Australia, it becomes apparent that there is no desert with this name on the entire southern continent. While the 19th-century explorer Peter Warburton did name the Great Sandy Desert in Western Australia, there is no desert specifically named after him. "Nosucks" can most certainly be construed to be Utopia – literally, the perfect place: "No-sucks" is the place where there are no negative elements, no things that "suck". The loaded name of the small town can be considered a mocking and pert English translation of the

French "Sanssouci" – "without cares" – the name that the Prussian King Frederick the Great coined for his famous and splendid castle in Potsdam. If one takes a closer look at Mary's new address, it becomes even clearer that masculine endeavour and desire both aim and answer to a place that is not part of this world:

> "Mrs. Mary Hope, Akwerkepenty-Pu, AUS 78777 Nosucks, Australia" (LfM 60).

Already at first glance, it is blatantly obvious to an Australian reader that a place declaring "AUS" to be the state or territorial abbreviation, followed by a five digit combination of numbers as the postal code, cannot possibly represent a real place or valid address in Australia. Instead, it not only accentuates the incredibility of the claim that this place is genuinely a location in Australia, but moreover hints that it is a magical site. The fantastical postcode consists of four sevens and one eight: the number seven stands as the divine number in Occidental and various other cultural histories (Lurker 1991: 679) and the number eight, through its linear continuity, explicitly portrays infinity, balance and happy new beginnings (Lurker 1991: 4). However phantasmagorical the address may be, the "supernatural" aspects discussed above become even more evident if one takes a closer look at the addressee's name: Mary Hope is a very allusive name in itself. It connotes purity, virginity, aspiration and optimism. Taking this name as encompassing such factors seems to be especially appropriate, since the narrator himself explicitly reflects – tongue-in-cheek – on the literary style of playing with meaning-loaded names (LfM 82). Hence, in the marvellous Australian "mailing address", the inaccessible loved one and the distant, magical place merge together. Australia becomes the unadulterated, wholesome virgin and the upholder of mankind's hope. In this way, the strange desert continent acquires a female connotation.

Affiliating unexplored continents and the desert with the female body recalls a notorious image in Western culture and ideology, since Sigmund Freud explicitly perceived of female sexuality as psychology's "dark continent" (Freud 1948: 241).[13] Apart from playing on this cultural

---

13 "Vom Geschlechtsleben des kleinen Mädchens wissen wir weniger als von dem des Knaben. Wir brauchen uns dieser Differenz nicht zu schämen; ist doch auch das Geschlechtsleben des erwachsenen Weibes ein *dark continent* für die

metaphor, *Liebesbrief für Mary* also plays with a variety of literary and cultural patterns concerning travel, discovery and anthropology, such as the siren song, the image of the noble savage, or the idea of utopia as the idyllic dream of something entirely different. Of course, Urs Widmer uses these traditional images and stereotypes in quite a deconstructive and comically mocking manner. In his Graz lectures on poetics, he points out that today a writer of travel literature in the traditional sense would be a ridiculous person. This is because travel and traditional travel writing had very much to do with the idea of utopia, the search for an unknown and completely different place. Widmer however argues that in this current era of globalisation and mass tourism, there will eventually be no unknown space left on earth for the locating, and thus location, of any such utopia (Widmer 1995: 44–47). In *Liebesbrief für Mary*, utopia reveals its classical double function as both an anticipation of the future, and a memory of the loss of something that once had been.[14] On the one hand, flicking into the TV program, the narrator anticipates central Australia's future as the nuclear dump of Western civilisation. In this sense, Utopian Mary-Australia turns out to be the u-topos, the "place apart" and "anti-place" per se. On the other hand, Helmut pines for his lost lover. At the novella's turning point, according to his own statement, the unnamed narrator bursts into tears after he heard himself screaming: "I cannot be without Mary!" (LfM 92) He describes the grotesque scene when he became shaken by waves of tears coming from an inner core of which he was not previously aware (LfM 93f). Thus, Mary-Australia turns out to be not only a projection on the part of both rivals. The frame-narrator even seems to be totally dependent on her. In fact, Mary-Australia can be interpreted as a suppressed part of the preposterous, arrogant, European male's Self being projected outwards.

Psychologie." [We know less of the sexual life of the young girl than that of the boy. We do not need to be embarrassed about this difference, since of course even the sexual life of the grown woman is a *dark continent* for psychology]. Original emphasis. See also *Expeditionen in den dunklen Kontinent*, a feminist reading of the psychoanalytic discourse by Rohde-Dachser (1997).

14 On the role of the concept of utopia in some other texts written by Urs Widmer, see Jaumann 1997: 210.

Conclusion

In conclusion, Urs Widmer's *Liebesbrief für Mary* can be considered a highly ironic piece of intercultural literature. Toying with language problems and colonial stereotypes whilst rejoicing in its political incorrectness, the text ironically points to the actual experience of culture-clash. The comically bilingual text is not only in part virtually incomprehensible for non-German-speaking readers, but also practically untranslatable into genuine, standard English. Because it talks about culture-clash by mocking a certain conventionalised perception of the fifth continent, the full effect of the novella is furthermore arguably inaccessible for those readers who know little or nothing about the actual heterogeneity of Australian culture, sticking instead to the harmonious cliché of a simplified, exotic place and people.

Bibliography

Anti-Nuclear Alliance of Western Australia. [Online]. Available at: www.anawa.org.au/waste/pangea.html (accessed 27 January 2009).

Arnold L (1987). *A Very Special Relationship. British Atomic Weapon Trials in Australia.* London: Her Majesty's Stationary Office.

Australian Nuclear Veterans Association. [Online]. Available at: users.bigpond.net.au/anva/index.html (accessed 27 January 2009).

Corkhill A (1990). *Antipodean Encounters: Australia and German Literary Imagination 1754–1918.* Bern, Frankfurt a. M., New York, Paris: Peter Lang.

Cross R (2001). *Hedley Marston and the British Bomb Tests in Australia.* Kent Town: Wakefield Press.

Freud S (1948), Die Frage der Laienanalyse. Unterredungen mit einem Unparteiischen. In Gesammelte Werke. *Chronologisch geordnet,* vol. 14. Werke aus den Jahren 1925–1931. Frankfurt a. M.: Fischer, 207–96.

Goodbye Deutschland! Die Auswanderer. [Online.] Available at: de.wikipedia.org/wiki/Goodbye_Deutschland!_Die_Auswanderer (accessed 15/12/2008).

Jaumann P (1997), Dunkle Kontinente. Das Fremde im Eigenen. Zur Prosa Urs Widmers. In Ingo Breuer & Arpad A. Sölter (Eds), *Der fremde Blick: Perspektiven interkultureller Kommunikation und Hermeneutik*. Wien: Studienverlag, 207–27.

Jurgensen M (1992). *Eagle and Emu: German-Australian Writing 1930–1990*. Brisbane: University of Queensland Press.

Lewis A (1995). Dreamtime in Germany: Images of Australia and Indigenous People in New German Cinema. In Manfred Jurgensen (Ed), *German-Australian Cultural Relations Since 1945*. Proceedings of the conference held at the University of Queensland, Brisbane, from September 20–23, 1994. Bern, Berlin, Frankfurt a. M., New York, Paris, Wien: Peter Lang, 257–72.

Lurker M (Ed) (1991). *Wörterbuch der Symbolik*. Stuttgart: Alfred Kröner.

Mohr D (1993). Das harte Los trifft beide Verehrer: Urs Widmers gewitzter 'Liebesbrief für Mary'. *Berliner Zeitung*, 2 December 1993, Nr. 282, 37.

Preisendörfer B (1993). "Verwirrung um einen Liebesbrief. Urs Widmers literarischer Schabernack: Mary und ihre glücklich-unglücklichen Freunde." *Der Tagesspiegel*, 10 October1993, VII.

Rohde-Dachser C (1997). *Expeditionen in den dunklen Kontinent: Weiblichkeit im Diskurs der Psychoanalyse*. Frankfurt a. M.: Fischer Taschenbuch.

Schönhuth M & Freßmann R (2002). Mutant Message Down Under. Popularizing Anthropology or lie?- Eine kritische Materialsammlung zu Marlo Morgans Buch: Der Traumfänger. [Online] Available at: www.uni-trier.de/index.php?id=14013: 2 (accessed 28/1/2009).

Schröder A (2006). *ebooks und Bücher: Empirische Untersuchung zum Leseverhalten*. Saarbrücken: VDM.

Shute N (1957). *On the Beach*. London, Melbourne, Toronto: Heinemann.

Sonicbomb.com [online] Available at: www.sonicbomb.com/modules.php ?name=Content&pa=showpage&pid=111 (accessed 28/1/2009).

Widmer U (1995). *Die sechste Puppe im Bauch der fünften Puppe im Bauch der vierten und andere Überlegungen zur Literatur*. Grazer Poetikvorlesungen. Zurich: Diogenes.

Widmer U (1995b). *Liebesbrief für Mary*. Erzählung. Zurich: Diogenes.

Widmer U & Stoehr (1994), *Liebesbrief für Mary*: Auszug. *Love letter for Mary*: excerpt. Ingo Stoehr (Trans.) *Dimension*[2] 1.1: 178–87.

www.ingramcontent.com/pod-product-compliance
Lightning Source LLC
Chambersburg PA
CBHW041130280326
41928CB00059B/3312